T0350546

Survive and Thrive in Building:

Fundamentals of Business Management

Survive and Thrive in Building:
Fundamentals of Business Management

NAHB | National Association of Home Builders

Survive and Thrive in Building: Fundamentals of Business Management

BuilderBooks, a Service of the National Association of Home Builders

Elizabeth M. Rich	Director, Book Publishing
Natalie C. Holmes	Book Editor
Circle Graphics	Cover Design
BMWW	Composition
Sheridan Books Inc.	Printing
Gerald M. Howard	NAHB Chief Executive Officer
Mark Pursell	NAHB Senior Vice President, Expositions, Marketing & Sales
Lakisha Campbell, CAE	NAHB Vice President, Publishing & Affinity Programs

Disclaimer

This publication provides accurate information on the subject matter covered. The publisher is selling it with the understanding that the publisher is not providing legal, accounting, or other professional service. If you need legal advice or other expert assistance, obtain the services of a qualified professional experienced in the subject matter involved. Reference herein to any specific commercial products, process, or service by trade name, trademark, manufacturer, or otherwise does not necessarily constitute or imply its endorsement, recommendation, or favored status by the National Association of Home Builders. The views and opinions of the author expressed in this publication do not necessarily state or reflect those of the National Association of Home Builders, and they shall not be used to advertise or endorse a product.

© 2012 by NAHB. All rights reserved. No part of this book may be reproduced or utilized in any form or by any means, electronic or mechanical, including photocopying and recording or by any information storage and retrieval system without permission in writing from the publisher.

Printed in the United States of America

15 14 13 12   1 2 3 4 5

Library of Congress Cataloging-in-Publication Data

Survive and thrive in building : fundamentals of business management.
   p. cm.
ISBN 978-0-86718-677-2 (alk. paper)
   1. Construction industry—United States—Management.   2. Building trades—United States—Management.   3. House construction—United States.   I. National Association of Home Builders (U.S.)
HD9715.U52P76 2011
690ʾ.80684—dc23

2011023259

For further information, please contact:

National Association of Home Builders
1201 15th Street, NW
Washington, DC 20005-2800
800-223-2665
http://www.BuilderBooks.com.

Contents

8   New Home Sales Management   87

9   Estimating   99

Acknowledgments

NAHB's Single Family Small Volume Builders and Business Management and Information Technology committees thank the following people for contributing to this book: Bill Allen, John Barrows, Mike Benshoof, Michael Bosgraaf, David Bossart, Fred Dallenbach, Dennis Dixon, Rob Dietz, Carol M. Flammer, Martin Freedland, Bruce Frost, Michelle Hamecs, Alan Hanbury Jr., Timothy J. Hassett, Dan Levitan, Steve Linville, Meredith Oliver, Vince Napolitano, Randy Noel, Richard Pagotto, Ron Robichaud, Robert Ross, Charles (CJ) Schoenwetter, Carol Smith, Brandon Tedder, Felicia Watson, Bob Whitten.

Introduction

Starting up a new business as a home builder is both a thrilling and a frightening experience—even for those who are old-hand entrepreneurs. Here is the thrilling part: Entrepreneurship offers you a great opportunity to earn a living using your skills while giving you the freedom to make your own decisions. But what might be daunting to many fledgling business owners is the personal risk. Some builders have even likened their businesses to gambling. Why? Home building can convey both high profits and devastating losses—sometimes both within a short period.

Being unprepared and ill-informed, having little or no tactical planning, and making reactive rather than proactive decisions can lead to business failure, even if times are good. However, business ownership does not have to be a stomach-churning roller coaster ride. By preparing yourself with the vision, managerial competence, knowledge about the business, and strategic planning, you will be able to maintain your equilibrium during inevitable ups and downs in the housing market.

Survive and Thrive in Building: Fundamentals of Business Management will serve as a guide for helping you to better understand the challenges and responsibilities that accompany home building business ownership. It is written for those who have been thinking about starting a construction company "one day." And it is for the current owners who like to keep their business skills honed and up-to-date. *Survive and Thrive in Building* draws on the wisdom of industry experts by sharing their experiences in crucial areas of the home building business such as finance, marketing, law, the work force, and quality management. It will show you how to construct a foundation for your business start-up that is as strong as those on which you build your homes. Then your company will be able to withstand the natural ups and downs of the housing cycle and be positioned for growth when you are ready.

A viable business requires a plan for identifying, serving, and selling to a sustainable market of housing consumers. You then organize your business to best serve those customers while strategically minimizing your risk and maximizing your profits. Be prepared: starting up and growing a home building company may require you to shed some of the roles and duties many builders enjoy, like "working in the trenches." Instead, you will spend much of your time seeking new business opportunities, developing proposals for financing, monitoring financial reports, finding and recruiting trade contractors, training employees, working with customers, and ensuring that your legal and regulatory house is in order.

In addition to those broad areas, *Survive and Thrive in Building* will help you to become informed about the details of marketing, estimating, contracts, purchasing, and *accounting*, which are as important to the potential success of your business as knowing your construction guidelines. Attending to these details will help you to build a positive reputation in your community—and having a solid reputation is everything in the home building industry.

And just before you make the commitment to start up a company, check out your mental attitude: You must approach each project in building your business as an opportunity, and not just as a means for keeping your business going for the next week, month, or year—you are in this for the long haul.

Survive and Thrive in Building helps you understand the knowledge, skills, and strategies you can apply to foster lasting success in the home building industry. At the back of the book are a glossary and a list of resources to refer to when you are ready to take the leap into start-up business ownership or move to the next step: positioning your home building company for growth.

1

Thriving as a Small-Volume Builder

If you are like many small-volume builders, you may have thought at one time or another of starting your own construction business. Working your way up to business ownership can be an appealing thought after spending years working in the trenches, honing your craft, and taking pride in your workmanship. But it is only after opening their doors as a small business that many fledgling entrepreneurs realize that attending to the details of foundations, framing, and finish carpentry are very different skills from having the vision and management acumen to run a profitable enterprise. If you want to thrive long term in the industry, you must invest similar time, effort, and discipline in acquiring the knowledge to conceive, manage, and grow a profitable business as you did in learning your particular construction trade.

Small-Volume Home Builder Defined

What is a small-volume builder? According to the National Association of Home Builders (NAHB), a small-volume builder constructs 25 or fewer homes a year. These builders comprise most (about 70%) of NAHB's builder members, and two-thirds of them build fewer than 10 homes a year. Like other entrepreneurs—perhaps you—these builders decided to open up shop to have more independence, be their own bosses, and make more money. Perhaps they worked for another builder and decided they could do it better. Or they may have simply scanned the housing market and determined that conditions were favorable for a start-up home-building business.

Many small-volume builders say they are competitive, energetic, and driven—all desirable qualities for an individual who must have stamina to build a company from the ground up. Unfortunately, the so-called "A" personality traits that may accompany the desirable characteristics can lead to impatience and stubbornness, and impede planning, organization, and progress. Learning whether you have the right temperament will be essential for determining whether you can make it in the business world.

Success Strategies for Small-Volume Builders

What makes a small-volume builder successful? In addition to having the temperament to withstand the cyclical nature of home building, small-volume builders who have found long-term success in the industry understand the following fundamentals of running a profitable business:

- **You must have a strategic plan.** This plan is not just compatible with your personal goals; it is designed, written, executed, and monitored to ensure that you achieve them. Successful builders run their businesses; they don't let their companies run them.

- **You must have a business plan.** This plan provides a direction for your business, laying the groundwork for all other functions. It will help you answer the following questions:
  - What do you want your company to achieve?
  - What actions will help you (and your company) attain these goals?
  - Who must perform these actions, when, and in what order?

- **You must have a marketing plan.** Before breaking ground on anything, you must decide who your customers will be, where to find them, and know what they want. Profitable builders market in lean as well as flush periods. Recognize that marketing is a long-term investment that pays off in years, rather than in weeks or months.

- **You must be systems oriented.** Everything in your home building company—from how telephone calls are handled to how you measure financial performance—is organized with written procedures and tied together in a systematic whole. Although you cannot anticipate out-of-the-ordinary events, you still can plan for the unexpected.

- **You must sell relationships and service, not just price.** Competing on price alone is a race to the bottom. Providing excellent service that fosters good relationships with customers is the best marketing investment you will make. It encourages referrals and no-bid contracts because clients know they can trust your company to deliver a quality product.

- **You must practice good financial management.** Understanding the difference between owner's compensation and profit, and between margin and markup, are the first steps toward a viable company. But you also must understand the nuances of each build, and their financial consequences, in order to create the mix of projects that will earn enough profit to help you achieve the goals you set in your strategic plan.

- **You must delegate.** Despite its significant challenges, the beauty of company ownership is that you are in charge, so you must behave like a business owner. Don't just be your company's highest paid worker, use your work time wisely to steer the ship. Then surround yourself with strong, competent, and talented people you can trust to help you with the daily work of running your systems and projects.

Managing Resources Effectively

A successful manager-owner accomplishes objectives by efficiently and effectively using the resources available. As a builder, your resources are:

Human. The employees and trade contractors who work for and with a home building company represent a wealth of education, experiences, training, intelligence, and insight. People are a builder's most valuable resource—and often the most difficult one to manage.

Financial. Successful builders use capital wisely. They earn enough profit to meet obligations to investors and creditors, grow the business, and take home a salary.

Physical. These are the easiest resources to control and acquire. Builders may either directly furnish the materials, tools, and equipment to construct a home or hire trade contractors to do this.

Informational. To stay competitive to position your company for growth, you must collect, analyze, and disseminate information—about company performance, about what competitors are doing, and about your target customer. The most effective way to get useful information is by building a network with other builders and with people outside of the industry.

Developing a Functional System

Your success depends largely on how well you plan, organize, lead, and control your company. These functions work together to form a comprehensive management system.

Planning with Data

The logical way to prepare for future business activities and growth is to set attainable goals based on robust information and then create, in advance, specific step-by-step plans to enable your business to achieve those goals. Following are a few examples of how you can use information strategically to achieve goals:

- Read company financial reports to understand your business's current position.
- Develop pro forma budgets to assess the viability of proposed projects and staffing needs.
- Use market research to undergird effective, affordable, marketing plans.
- Assess market conditions and sales velocity of comparable projects in setting sales goals.
- Ensure that you have current labor and materials pricing for accurate estimates.
- Know the details of schedules so you can meet project deadlines.

Decide what information you need to run your business effectively and efficiently, and then choose or create reports and reporting systems that provide and organize that information.

10 Best Management Reports

Too many builders interpret control to mean "do." That is, they do everything, rather than delegating some responsibilities. To grow your business or at least have a life outside of your business, you must think differently. You must exert control at a higher level. Use management reports to monitor your company's performance and inform decisions. Home building industry consultant Bob Whitten recommends using these 10 management reports:

1. **Gross Profit or Job Analysis.** The *gross profit* report should be produced monthly to analyze the *profitability* of closed jobs. It can be sorted by model type, by project, or by geographic market location. In less stable conditions, this report should be updated and analyzed weekly for all jobs under construction. When one unit is more profitable than another, you can analyze why and correct problems before constructing additional units.

2. **Nine-Column Format Income Statement.** The nine columns include three each (actual, budget, *variance*) expressed in dollar amounts for the month and year, as well as the same three expressed in percentages for the year to

date. These *income statements* should be produced monthly, except for the very smallest volume builders. By comparing actual results with the operational budget, builders can monitor and manage by exception or variance. (Sales revenue changes will impact monthly numbers as a percentage of revenue, so monthly numbers should be compared only with their own specific budget areas. Year-to-date numbers are best compared with sales revenue benchmarks.)

3. **Comparative Balance Sheet and Ratio Analysis.** This monthly report shows cash balances, what your company owes, and what is owed to your business. Movement within each period as well as from month to month allows you to spot trends in your business. The cash coverage ratio is the amount owed as a proportion of cash on hand and will help you with your *draw* schedules. Other ratios to track include: debt to equity, current ratio, and *inventory* turn ratio.

4. **Cash-Flow Forecast Report.** The production/closing schedule feeds this report, revealing when the company will receive loan draws by phase of construction and by unit. This report allows time to plan for lines of credit when cash flow is negative or for investing available cash. The report is updated weekly or for each pay date and at the end of the month.

5. **Traffic, Sales, Starts, and Closing Report.** For moderate-to-large builders, this may be the most frequently used report. It compares sales, starts, and closings for the week, month, and year-to-date against established budgets. The report helps assess advertising efficiency.

6. **Weekly Job-Cost Variance under Construction Report.** This labor-intensive report may not be necessary once your job cost variances are somewhat controlled and consistent. In the end, the most meaningful percentage to track is that of variances to final job cost budget (not sales or revenue). Sales price changes will not impact your variances, which are job cost matters, not a function of sales price.

7. **Job-Cost Variance Report on Closed Jobs.** This report, for senior managers, should be updated monthly. The averages can be graphed easily and measured against a benchmark (a target of 1.5% variance costs as a percentage of budget) to provide a two-minute look at job cost control for the company as a whole. Remember, each variance costs the company more than the amount of additional materials or labor shown on a *variance purchase order*. This report can show you whether your variances are costing you more or less over time as a percentage of total costs.

8. **Cost-Per-Square-Foot Pricing Analysis Report.** Using computerized spreadsheets enables you to calculate the cost per square foot for each item on

your job cost breakout. The figures can help you compare costs within projects or divisions and within model types to formulate budgets and base plan pricing. Doing so will help you achieve your targeted gross profit. It is the foundation of estimating for all builders.

9. **Customer Service and Warranty Report.** This report will help you identify trade contractors with more outstanding service requests than are acceptable and keep them from undermining your success. It summarizes the number of warranty requests, those outstanding, and the average number of days they are open.

10. **Customer Satisfaction Trend Report.** The goal is 95% customer satisfaction or better. To determine how you are doing, plot your customer satisfaction survey results (from your database or a Microsoft® Excel spreadsheet) on a graph and measure them monthly.

Organizing

Even if you are a sole proprietor or co-own your company with a partner, your organization includes trade contractors, suppliers, lenders, and business advisers such as lawyers and accountants, to help you daily and over the long haul. You can work more effectively with these individuals if you are organized. Organizing includes

- assembling the human, physical, and informational resources required to ensure the organization reaches its goals;
- identifying specific tasks that collectively will lead to achievement of the goals;
- allocating responsibility for completing those tasks; and
- coordinating the work of various individuals and units.

Leading

You must communicate company goals effectively. Post your goals in a conspicuous location in your office and make your mission statement part of your proposal template. Get buy-in to numeric goals and post progress updates often. Measure and track material waste, adherence to schedules, overall cycle time, actual versus estimated expenditures, and other factors that contribute to profits and losses. Delegate work and accountability for results as appropriate, communicating your expectations clearly up front and providing praise and tangible rewards for a job well done. Constantly reinforce how workers' performance impacts the company's business plan.

Learning Management Skills

To plan, organize, lead, and control effectively, builders must develop and use their technical, interpersonal, and decision-making skills. At the same time, they must have conceptual skills that allow them to see the "big picture" even as they go about the daily work of running a business.

Technical skills. You need a working knowledge of estimating, scheduling, accounting, financial management, customer service, and office management.

Interpersonal skills. The typical builder spends approximately 80% of every working day interacting with a broad range of people in a variety of settings. "People" skills—knowing how to communicate with others and understand their needs—allow you to work effectively with individuals inside and outside the company. These skills determine how well you execute every other management function.

Decision-making skills. A builder must make decisions quickly, usually with incomplete information but with serious consequences for making the wrong decision. Using a board of directors of noncompeting companies in your local home builders association (HBA), joining an NAHB 20 Club of similar firms from outside your service area, and cultivating other networks of business professionals, including online networks through social media, can help you make more informed decisions.

Conceptual skills. You must be able to analyze a situation, develop a plan of action, and take the steps necessary to implement a plan.

Managing Your Time

Your time has monetary value in your business so manage it just as you manage other resources. If you believe you are too busy to spend time reviewing financials, improving purchasing and estimating, and recruiting and developing better workers, your company will never achieve its full potential and you will struggle to fulfill your personal goals.

To learn time-management skills, consider taking a class through your local community college or an online training provider. You will learn to prioritize what is really important to you and to your business. Then you can structure your daily and weekly routines around your priorities, rather than letting others set your "to do" list for you. You will achieve business success and personal satisfaction.

Although many builders work 60 to 80 hours per week, some never "catch up." If you are constantly working late, taking work home, or rushing to meet deadlines, you need to develop time management skills. If you do, your productivity will increase, you will like your job more, you will be less anxious and tense, and you will be healthier.

- **Set specific short- and long-term goals.** Write goals that are measurable, action oriented, realistic, and time bound. Short-term goals are goals to be achieved in less than 1 year. Depending on economic forecasts, long-term goals might be for only 1–3 years. Some long-term goals, such as selling or transferring a business, could have targets of 20 or more years, but such a long period will be the exception rather than the rule.

- **Make daily "to do" lists.** Prioritize and organize tasks to minimize travel and get maximum productivity from your time.

- **Prioritize tasks.** Spend 30 minutes each day, either at the beginning of the day or at the end, making a "to do" list that will help you achieve your goals. Prioritize items on the list. You can perform some tasks and delegate others. Your list will change each day as you accomplish tasks.

- **Set reasonable expectations and deadlines for yourself and others.** This will keep everyone on task and moving toward the goal. Negotiating these deadlines ahead of time is one strategy for getting buy-in and ensuring accountability.

- **Learn to say "no."** If you are a good parent, you know how to say "no." The same applies to being a good employer. Being disciplined and assertive is a sign of strength, not weakness. Maintaining focus on and movement toward achieving long-term goals often means having to say "no."

- **Delegate tasks.** You have to let go to grow. Armed with specific expectations and accountability for their work, other people can manage and perform some tasks more efficiently than you can. Delegating will allow you to focus on the big picture.

- **Finish what you start and keep your promises.** This will help you protect your reputation and your brand, attract business, keep good employees, and maintain strong relationships with trade contractors.

- **Embrace technology.** Use the Internet, e-mail, and a smartphone to communicate quickly or in real time with customers, vendors, and staff. These tools allow you to send and receive information while in the field. Also, create templates on your word processor or spreadsheet, and learn how to create *macros* to eliminate repetitive typing.

Competing in Your Market

Although production builders generally enjoy the advantages that come with larger size, including economies of scale, capital, land holdings, name recognition, and the potential for greater efficiency in construction, there are still opportunities for small-volume builders to compete effectively. Even custom home builders, who may be resigned to long construction cycle times because of their unique product, can improve cycle time by using different approaches to working with trade contractors. For example, you can hold trades accountable for meeting your schedule by imposing predetermined monetary penalties for missed deadlines.

Small-volume builders enjoy certain advantages, including agility. With fewer projects, a small-volume builder can adjust product size, location, and other features quickly compared with a production builder occupying a large portion of a subdivision or an entire development. Even during the great housing recession, entrepreneurial small-volume builders were competing in niche markets such as the following:

- Multigenerational housing construction
- Remodeling
- Small rental project development
- Adaptive reuse of closed commercial properties
- Buying, rehabilitating, and selling foreclosure properties

To compete effectively, small-volume builders must understand how their strengths and weaknesses compare with those of their larger counterparts.

Advantages of Small-Volume Builders

Small-volume builders often have greater flexibility, more personal contact with customers, and, possibly, lower *overhead* than their larger competitors.

Greater flexibility. Larger builders generally have established bureaucracies that can slow decision-making and make their customer service susceptible to rigid policies. Small-volume builders often can move faster to take advantage of a special opportunity or changing market situation.

Lower overhead. Larger builders generally must support larger staffs, sometimes including several layers of management. These costs must be included in the home price and may even offset the discounts on materials that larger builders can negotiate. Small-volume builders generally enjoy lower overhead costs and can promote this to their customers.

More personalized customer relationships. Small-volume builders often develop closer, more personal relationships with their customers, leading to more repeat and referral business. Small-volume builders also are more likely to develop personal relationships with trade contractors, suppliers, and other members of their professional teams. These relationships often can increase the team's ability to work together toward common goals.

Managing a Family Business

Many building companies are family-run businesses controlled by one or more members of a family, and in which other family members may play active roles.

Family businesses often are successful because the family members find great satisfaction in working together. However, the intimate nature of family relationships can make these businesses susceptible to tensions and conflicts that, if not resolved, can prevent the business from achieving its goals.

As with any business structure, family businesses have both advantages and disadvantages.

The strength of a family's relationships often bolsters the business. Family members are more likely to stick with the business during tough times or to forego, at least temporarily, large salaries or dividends if the business needs capital. This sense of ownership can be a strong, positive motivator when building a business. In addition, some family businesses use the family theme to differentiate themselves from competitors. And many consumers perceive a family business as being more customer friendly.

On the other hand, in a business setting the relationships between family members can be more prone to emotion than those between unrelated employees. Sparks can fly when business and personal lives are intertwined or when issues of control and authority arise among family members. For example, if you discipline a son or daughter for a business-related issue, it can cause tension that persists when the family sits down together at the dinner table. Disagreements over business policies or direction may incite power struggles between partners or along generational lines.

Friction also can arise if family members with little or no experience are put in positions of authority over long-time, loyal nonfamily employees. These employees may feel passed over or that they are being treated unfairly. It is your responsibility to assess the skills and abilities of family members and other employees and base decisions on sound business judgment.

Finally, when family members compete with each other, nonfamily employees can be caught in the crossfire, which can destroy company morale. Follow these three common-sense principles in a family business:

1. Evaluate the abilities of family members honestly. Don't place family members in positions for which they lack the skills, experience, or training. That is not healthy for the business or for the family.

2. Apply uniform performance standards to family members and other employees.

3. Establish well-defined policies and procedures regarding family members' responsibilities and authority.

Adhering to these principles does not mean you must shy away from supporting your family's involvement in the business. It simply means that you, your business partners, or board must anticipate and prepare both family and nonfamily participants for the tasks and roles they will have to assume.

Bringing In Family Members

Many builders plan to pass the family business on to their children. If you are thinking about bringing children or other family members into an existing business, ask yourself the following questions:

- Does the family member want to join the business? It is a mistake to assume that a son, daughter, or other family member will share the same interest that you have in the business. Even if family members show some interest in home building, they may not thrive in a family-run business if the company structure does not allow sufficient opportunity for personal and professional growth.

- When should the family member join the business? In some families, a child's interest in the industry may compete with a desire to test and prove their abilities outside the family business. You, your company, and your child may benefit if you let your son or daughter develop their business experience elsewhere before joining the family business.

- Does the family member have skills, knowledge, and the temperament that will benefit the business? A founder-owner may have started the company based on a particular construction-related skill or a keen interest in operating a home building company. Other family members may possess neither the skills nor the mind-set to take over and run a business. You can damage your business if you give a family member an active role in it just because the opportunity exists.

- What education or training will be most helpful in preparing the family member to work in the business? Strategic planning and investment in training and education can help family members become valuable and respected additions to the company. Don't just "plug holes" by assigning roles to family members they may not be suited for. Instead, groom an incoming family member for a role that suits his or her personality and professional goals.

Managing Growth

Many small-volume builders consider growth a priority. Trying to take advantage of strong market demand without planning for growth, however, can place impossible demands on a small-volume builder's limited resources. As the company grows, you may need more expertise in marketing, finance, advertising, and human resources management. If you are unable or unwilling to delegate some responsibility, you will stunt your business's growth.

When you delegate responsibility, you must establish controls to monitor the employee's performance, identify problems or mistakes early on, and ensure that the employee completes his or her assigned tasks. Delegating responsibilities is a three-step process: (1) Assign specific duties. Explain clearly what you are delegating, the results you expect, and deadlines. (2) Grant the employee the authority to take the actions necessary to perform the delegated duties. (3) Impress upon the employee his or her obligation to perform the assigned duties.

The employee should understand clearly how far he or she may go without approval. Everyone who may be affected by this authority needs to know who is in charge.

The following guidelines will help you delegate authority and tasks appropriately:

- Work together with subordinates to identify activities that may be delegated.
- Establish mutually agreed upon performance standards.
- Provide employees with the resources they require to complete their tasks.
- Give employees access to all the information they need.
- Provide training when necessary.
- Provide timely and constructive feedback to employees concerning their performance.
- Communicate to employees how their assigned tasks relate to the "big picture" of the company's goals and objectives.
- Whenever possible, specify only the result to be achieved, and let your employees determine how to reach the goal. Allow employees the freedom to accomplish activities in their own way.

2

Determining Your Company Type

One of the first decisions a builder must make is how to organize a company legally. You can choose one of several types of legal organization, from *sole proprietorship* to incorporation. The one you select will significantly impact the following aspects of your business:

- Ownership distribution
- Owners' liability for the company's obligations
- Start-up costs
- Contingencies for owner death or retirement
- Owner's ability to transfer interest in the company to another party
- Company's ability to raise capital
- Senior management roles
- Taxation of profits and losses
- How profits and losses are taxed (i.e., individual vs. corporate rates, alternate minimum tax [AMT])

There are four legal forms of organization: sole proprietorship, *partnership*, *corporation*, and *limited liability company (LLC)*. Be sure you understand thoroughly the legal and tax implications of each type of organizational structure before you start your business. First, consult with an attorney about the advantages and disadvantages of each type of organization. Next, consider your personal financial situation while consulting with an accountant on the tax implications of each option. If you choose to create a partnership or an LLC, ensure that the other partners' personal and financial goals are compatible with yours. Finally, consider *liability*, duration of the business, availability of capital, and reporting requirements. You may want to create a separate legal entity for each project.

Sole Proprietorship

As the name indicates, a single individual owns a sole proprietorship. This is the simplest and least costly way to officially organize a business. In a sole proprietorship, all company *assets* belong to the owner, who can operate the business free of interference from partners, directors, or shareholders.

A sole proprietorship and its owner are a single entity in the eyes of the Internal Revenue Service (IRS). The proprietor receives all profits and assumes all losses, which are reported on proprietor's personal income tax return (typically Schedule C of the IRS 1040 income tax return).

Legally, a sole proprietorship ceases to exist when the owner dies, retires, or sells the business to another individual. If the owner ceases to do business, the sole proprietorship is effectively terminated, does not report income or deductions, and is not required to file an income tax return. There is nothing to pass on; the value is mostly in the name. Unless it can be successfully negotiated to another entity, it is worthless.

Partnership

When two or more people come together to own a business, they typically will form a partnership. Like a sole proprietorship, a partnership is generally easy and inexpensive to create. It is based on an agreement between or among its owners; no governmental approval is required. The main advantage of a partnership over a sole proprietorship is the partnership's ability to draw from a larger pool of talent and resources—its partners.

General

The most common form of partnership is the general partnership. As with sole proprietorships, a general partnership's income tax liability for profits and losses passes through to the partners. They must report profits or losses on their personal income tax returns. Although the partnership itself does not pay income taxes, it must file an informational return annually showing the partnership's profit or loss and each partner's share of these. Each partner then pays income taxes on his or her respective shares, whether the profits are distributed or left in the business. If the partnership suffers a loss, the partners may, subject to federal and state restrictions, deduct their shares of the loss from their personal income. If they have no current taxable income, they may claim a loss against prior year taxes (going back for no more than two tax years) or carry the loss forward to use as a deduction against future taxable years (for up to 20 years as needed).

If one of the partners dies, the partnership legally dies. Provisions for restructuring and continuing the business in the event of a partner's death often are included in the partnership agreement. The law limits transferring ownership to another party. In a general partnership, the remaining partners often have the right to refuse a transfer of interest. A surviving spouse could be denied a partnership stake even if otherwise qualified to participate. Some partnerships would prefer the number of partners to decrease so the remaining partners have more ownership in the future.

Like sole proprietors, the principals in a general partnership have unlimited liability. All partners may be held responsible not only for the partnership's obligations but also for the obligations of the individual partners, even for debts that may have been incurred outside of the business. For this reason, general partnerships are the least popular legal form of organization. A partner's divorce decree can force assets to be sold, or an accident involving a company car, even if it happens after hours, can bankrupt a business.

Limited Partnership

A limited partnership is an alternative to the general partnership, as it offers limited liability to at least some of the partners. A limited partnership has at least one general partner, with one or more limited partners. General partners manage day-to-day operations and assume full liability for the business's obligations. Limited partners' liability is confined to their investment in the business. In general, if limited partners become active in business operations, they forfeit their limited liability status.

For a company that includes many enterprises (construction, real estate, land development), a better alternative than a 50/50 partnership is to place one of the partners in an ownership position for some enterprises, and the other person in an ownership position for the others. You should

- assess the risk of spouse and children as owners;
- avoid exposing family members to personal guaranties; and
- consider creating a new company when transferring a business to the next generation.

Writing Partnership Agreements

Although a written agreement is not required, it is the safest way to protect the interests of the parties involved. The partnership agreement should include the following information:

- Date the partnership was formed
- Names and addresses of all partners

- Purpose of the business
- Amount invested by each partner
- Distribution of profits and losses
- Partners' rights and responsibilities
- Distribution of assets if the partnership is dissolved
- Surviving partners' rights to buy out the interest of a partner who quits or dies
- Extent to which partners may engage in outside businesses
- Procedures for settling partnership disputes

Incorporation

A corporation is a legal entity that is separate from the individuals who own and manage it. The corporation can sue and be sued; buy, hold, and sell property; engage in business operations; and commit crimes and be tried and punished for them.

A corporation is owned by its stockholders. Except in the case of an *S corporation*, there is no limit to the number of stockholders. Generally, shareholders do not have a legal right to act for the corporation or participate in its management. However, stockholders usually have other rights, such as the right to vote at stockholder meetings, the right to dividends, and the right to sell or transfer shares of stock. A change of stock ownership in a small corporation may have significant implications for its continued operation.

A major advantage of a corporate structure over a sole proprietorship or partnership is that it protects the owners' personal assets. Their liability is limited to the amount they have invested in the company. However, newly formed corporations or small *closely held corporations* often are unable to take full advantage of this benefit because individuals or organizations that contract with or loan money to such corporations often require the corporation's owners to provide *personal guaranties* for corporate obligations.

Another factor that distinguishes a corporation from a partnership is that if a stockholder dies or sells his or her shares, the corporation continues to exist.

Corporate Taxes

As a legal entity separate from its owners, a corporation pays corporate income tax on its profits. If dividends are declared and paid to stockholders, the money used to pay them will have been taxed at the corporate level. Stockholders who receive dividends report them as personal income and pay personal income tax on them. Thus, stockholder dividends are subject to *double taxation*. C corp tax rates are much lower than personal income tax rates that an S corporation would incur on profits. A C corp that does not pay dividends can invest the *retained earnings* in future growth, additional perks, increased pay, or as reserves to weather housing downturns. They are an inexpensive source of capital in tough times.

S Corporations

An S corporation offers most of the advantages of a corporation, without the disadvantage of double taxation. The S corporation passes taxable income or losses to its shareholders, who report their portion of the income on their personal income tax returns. Although it is a corporation, this type of company is taxed as a sole proprietorship or partnership. Like a partnership, an S corporation files an annual informational tax return that reports each shareholder's portion of the corporate income.

Among the requirements a business must meet to qualify as an S corporation are the following:

- A maximum of 100 shareholders
- Limit stock ownership to individuals, estates, and certain trusts
- Exclude nonresident aliens as shareholders
- Only one class of voting stock may be outstanding

The last requirement limits the ability to pass ownership of the entity to employees or other interested parties and still maintain voting control of the corporation with a second class of stock.

Corporate Requirements

Corporations must operate according to the rules and regulations established by the state in which they are incorporated. These requirements vary. Corporations must follow requirements on record keeping, reporting, annual stockholder meetings, and election of officers. Adhering to these requirements provides owners and managers with limited liability because they are operating under the protection of the so-called *corporate veil*. If the corporation fails to fulfill these requirements, the veil is lifted, and the individuals involved lose the protections and benefits afforded by the corporation.

Lawyers who want to sue the corporation, its owners, or managers, will look for inconsistencies in management in hopes of piercing the corporate veil. If the strategy works, they may be able to seek damages from the personal property of owners or managers. Builders who choose to organize their companies as corporations must adhere to all rules and regulations to avoid putting themselves and their businesses at risk.

Limited Liability Company

The limited liability company (LLC) combines the advantages of a partnership with the limited liability of a corporation. The LLC does not require any of its partners to assume unlimited liability, and partners do not have to forfeit limited liability if they take an active role in the business.

The LLC also has fewer restrictions than the S corporation. The LLC can have an unlimited number of partners, can own more than 80 percent of the corporation's stock, and its shares also may be held by corporations, partnerships, nonresident aliens, trusts, pension plans, and charitable organizations.

Although the LLC's tax pass-through feature to the personal tax filings of owners is similar to that of an S corporation (income and deductions pass through to its owners' individual income tax returns), LLC owners typically have greater flexibility in allocating profits and losses. Unlike an S corporation, in which profits are allocated in proportion to stock ownership, LLC members may allocate profits and losses as they desire, regardless of how ownership is divided.

Individuals who wish to set up an LLC must file articles of organization with their state government. They also must file an operating agreement that specifies the internal arrangements among members. The operating agreement should address these issues:

- The investment of each member
- When and how to make distributions
- How to allocate profits and losses
- What happens to the LLC when a member withdraws
- How to manage the LLC
- How to transfer interest in the LLC

Your company's legal organization impacts the range of options you will have in important areas, including start-up funding, ongoing financing, *risk management*, growth potential, earnings, taxes, transfer, and overall control. Therefore, make sure you understand the benefits and ramifications of each option before choosing the one that best fits your vision for your future as an owner.

3

Earning a Profit

Profit is the reward your company receives for successfully executing a sound and well-developed business plan. You earn this money for assuming the risk in running your company. Do not confuse profit with compensation. Your salary and benefits (compensation) are the short-term reward for your day-to-day work. Profit is a return over and above the wages you pay yourself. Some builders work for wages without thinking strategically about their company's profitability. This shortsighted approach ignores your financial risk. If you plan with profit in mind, you have a better chance of staying in business for the long term.

When you keep profit in the company, it becomes part of your stake in the business—your *owner's equity*. Profit kept in the business increases equity and builds reserves you can access in down cycles. It also increases the long-term value of your company. Depending on your corporate structure, you also can pay out the returns on your investment and lend them back to the company as needed. Some builders favor the latter approach as a risk-management strategy.

Planning for Profit

When developing a budget, consider profit first. In other words, don't let your profit margin become a residual, or afterthought, of your home building operation. The margin will vary by project. In determining your target profit margin, consider three broad areas:

1. How much you will earn considering overhead, not just materials and labor
2. Specifics of the jobsite such as its size, location, conditions
3. Status of the housing market

If you are building a large custom home, the amount of money you will earn by building the project may justify accepting a smaller profit margin, but only you can determine that margin based on your own experience. If you are building speculative inventory, you will determine a reasonable sales price based on comparisons with similar homes selling in the area. Develop your budget for the home by deducting profit, then overhead, and then land cost. The balance is the amount of money you have left to build the house.

Overhead includes the following costs, which are not confined to a particular home:

- Salaries and *other expenses* of running your office
- Sales and marketing, including commissions
- Project management (in the office and in the field supervising construction superintendents)
- Workers' compensation, vehicle, and general liability insurance
- Vehicles and cell phones
- Warranty (a variable potential future liability)

If you cannot construct a home within a budget that includes all of the so-called "hard costs" to build, plus overhead and profit, you must rethink your plan.

Home building industry consultant Charles C. Shinn Jr. offers the following strategy for developing budgets for *direct construction costs*: From the anticipated sales price, deduct profit first, and then land cost, operating expenses, warranty, and historical slippage. What is left is the amount you have to build a home. Next, determine the percentage that each of your *cost codes* represents in the sales price of the home. Then, design, specify, estimate, and build toward those targets. The budgeted amount for each cost code and the bid or estimate should be equal. Moreover, because you included warranty and historical slippage costs in direct construction, you protect your profit margin from being consumed by these costs.[1]

Measuring Profit

You can track your profitability using monthly, quarterly, and annual income statements. These financial management tools are discussed in Chapter 13. Once you understand your financial position, you can compare your performance to similar builders using NAHB's biennial *Cost of Doing Business Study.*[2]

---

[1] *The Cost of Doing Business Study, 2010 Edition*, NAHB Business Management and Information Technology Committee. Washington, DC: BuilderBooks.com, 2010.
[2] *The Cost of Doing Business Study, 2012 Edition*, NAHB Business Management and Information Technology Committee. Washington, DC: BuilderBooks.com, 2012.

What *net profit* should you aim for? Average builder performance (before the boom and bust cycle of the early twenty-first century) was a pretax profit of 3%–5% of revenue. Excellent performance generated 8%–12% of pretax profit. More than 12% is considered superior performance. A handful of builders make more than 15% net profit before taxes. These well-established companies have applied sound management principles consistently and some hold a unique market advantage.

If currently you are not at least achieving average performance in your *net profit margin*, aim for incremental improvements to your bottom line. For example, if your company earned 4.6% net profit last year, aim for 5% this year.

Increasing Profit

There are three ways to increase profit:

1. Increase volume
2. Decrease costs
3. Boost profit margin

Each of these options has benefits and drawbacks as follows:

Increasing Volume

By increasing sales volume, your company can benefit from economies of scale. You will have more buying power with suppliers, which may mean lower costs for materials. In addition, more construction projects may increase your name recognition in your market and attract more clients. Your income (but not necessarily profit margin) will increase.

However, many builders have grown themselves out of business by losing sight of the ultimate goal: increasing profit. Therefore, understand that more construction volume will increase your management challenges, overhead, and liability. If you lose control while growing your business, your profit margin will suffer.

Decreasing Costs

When you decrease costs, your savings will fall directly to the bottom line so you can lower your selling price without sacrificing profit margin. Decreasing costs requires investing time to work more closely with trades and suppliers, perhaps an investment of money for market research and new plans, and relentless oversight of estimating, purchasing, and warranty work. If you seek to cut costs by using cheaper grades of materials and the lowest-bid contractors, product quality will suffer, and you actually may lose market share and sacrifice profit.

To control costs effectively, you must keep detailed records of expenditures, compare them with budgets and estimates to find the sources of variances, and look for opportunities to reduce what you spend. Experienced builders have been able to reduce costs by changing designs, improving purchasing systems, controlling inventory, and managing risk.

Among the cost-cutting tips industry consultant Charles Shinn Jr. offers builders are the following:

- Improve working drawings by soliciting input from your trades and superintendent, if you have one. Use the information to develop a scope of work for your architect(s).
- Eliminate home *features* that buyers don't value and that are unnecessary to compete in your market. Instead, sell options and upgrades.
- Value-engineer plans, taking advantage of new cost-saving materials and opportunities to reduce construction waste.
- Only pay on purchase orders and use variance purchase orders to track unbudgeted costs. Aim for variances of less than 1% of direct construction costs.
- Break up turnkey trades. Instead, purchase materials and labor separately.
- Do not begin construction without a complete start package, including all customer selections. If a customer wants a change, and you can accommodate it, be sure your change order includes an adequate profit margin.

Improving Designs

Consider costs during the design process—doing so often results in significant savings. Too often, builders perceive the potential to reduce costs through design as applicable only to production builders or small-volume builders of low-cost housing. However, semi-custom and even custom home builders can achieve design-related cost reductions.

Improving Purchasing

Purchasing involves much more than picking up the phone and ordering materials from the local supplier. You must identify, select, order, and receive materials and services. A well-designed purchasing system is essential to executing all phases of purchasing efficiently.

Tips for design-based cost reduction

- Don't overengineer or overbuild.
- Design for standard sizes and lumber lengths.
- Work with the architect or draftsperson during the design process to ensure he or she understands your construction methods.
- Conduct basic market research to determine what your customers want and will accept. Do not waste money adding features they don't value.
- Simplify designs. Eliminate corners and offsets; reduce the number of rooflines.
- Minimize the linear footage of exterior walls.
- Use no-cost design services such as those truss manufacturers, or cabinet or window suppliers provide.
- Determine the optimal size for each design. Often, you can increase the square footage of a plan without increasing high-ticket items such as plumbing, *HVAC*, kitchens, and baths, thereby reducing the overall cost per square foot.

Monitoring Production and Materials

Controlling inventory is one of the most efficient ways to reduce costs. Use schedules to plan and maintain production and to order only the materials you need to complete the job. Prepare accurate *take-offs* and avoid wasting time and materials. Monitor employees and trade contractors to ensure they are caring for materials properly and using them efficiently.

Checklist for improved purchasing management

☐ Identify materials that offer the best value for customers.

☐ Periodically compare materials currently being used with other available materials.

☐ Stay informed about new cost-effective building materials and techniques.

☐ Keep abreast of changes in technology, availability, price, and customer preferences.

☐ For each type of material or trade contract, cultivate strong relationships with one or two suppliers or trade contractors. Partner with these suppliers and trade contractors to identify ways to control costs.

☐ Allow sufficient time for material deliveries. This step is especially crucial for special-order materials.

- [ ] Use purchase orders. Builders who use purchase orders plan their purchases by identifying the necessary materials and services for each construction activity in advance. Purchase orders also serve as an excellent mechanism to ensure that the quantities and prices of materials and services received are as ordered.
- [ ] Always consider total costs, including freight, installation, training, inspections, and warranty implications when making purchasing decisions.
- [ ] Take advantage of quantity discounts when appropriate. When deciding whether to buy in quantity, consider the interest that will be lost on the money invested in the materials and other costs associated with storage, handling, and damage.

Material storage and handling. Schedule materials for delivery as close to the time they are needed as possible. Materials delivered too far in advance can be an obstacle on the jobsite, be damaged by weather, or stolen. Plan where to store materials on the jobsite so they won't have to be moved before they are needed. A crew that spends 30 minutes moving a stack of plywood subflooring to get to the floor joist below is adding to your costs.

Waste reduction. Do not assume the framer uses materials the same way you estimated them. Provide a sheathing layout. Show the framer where to start and how to use the cut-offs, so you are not ordering extra materials at the last minute.

Increase Margin

Obviously, if you increase your profit margin with all other factors remaining stable, including the number of homes you build, you will earn more profit. You also could choose to build fewer homes with higher margins to yield the same overall profit. Finally, you could increase the number of homes you build and increase profit margin, which will yield even more profit.

Increasing profit margin carries risks as well as rewards, though. Although you don't want to price yourself out of a target market, you should position your company to benefit from the upside of the home building cycle. Consider raising margins if your research suggests the market will accept higher prices.

Table 3.1 illustrates the financial impact of a builder's planned shift away from building speculative inventory and toward more custom home building and remodeling work to increase profit margin. The builder tried, but failed, to maintain the same level of overhead. Overhead increased because insurance rates and sales and marketing costs rose along with revenue.

Table 3.1 A Builder's Multiyear Plan for Increasing Profit Margin

	Current YR	% Total Revenue	YR 2	% Total Revenue	YR 3	% Total Revenue	YR 4	% Total Revenue
Target Gross Profit (GP)			**15%**		**18%**		**20%**	
Revenue								
New Homes—Spec								
Lot 1	$250,000.00							
Lot 9	$265,000.00							
Total Spec	$515,000.00	31%	$520,000.00	29.8%	$550,000.00	30%	$350,000.00	17.9%
Custom Home								
Jones	$500,000.00							
Wilson	$375,000.00							
Total Custom	$875,000.00	53%	$900,000.00	51.6%	$950,000.00	51%	$1,200,000.00	61.5%
Remodel								
Harris Addition	$175,000.00							
Johnson Kitchen	$95,000.00							
Total Remodel	$270,000.00	16%	$325,000.00	18.6%	$350,000.00	19%	$400,000.00	20.5%
Total Revenue	**$1,660,000.00**	**100%**	**$1,745,000.00**	**100%**	**$1,850,000.00**	**100%**	**$1,950,000.00**	**100%**
Cost of Goods Sold (COGS)								
New Homes—Spec								
Land	$166,250.00							
Materials	$118,750.00							
Trade Contractors	$118,750.00							
Labor	$57,000.00							
Other	$14,250.00							
Total	$475,000.00	29%	$475,000.00	27%	$490,000.00	26%	$310,000.00	16%

(Continued on next page)

Table 3.1   (continued)

		Current YR	% Total Revenue	YR 2	% Total Revenue	YR 3	% Total Revenue	YR 4	% Total Revenue
Custom	Land	$-							
	Materials	$370,000.00							
	Trade Contractors	$259,000.00							
	Labor	$88,800.00							
	Other	$22,200.00							
	Total	$740,000.00	45%	$758,000.00	43%	$750,000.00	79%	$950,000.00	79%
Remodel	Materials	$77,000.00							
	Trade Contractors	$77,000.00							
	Labor	$55,000.00							
	Other	$11,000.00							
	Total	$220,000.00	13%	$258,000.00	15%	$270,000.00	15%	$300,000.00	75%
Total COGS		$1,435,000.00	86%	$1,491,000.00	85%	$1,510,000.00	82%	$1,560,000.00	80%
Gross Profit		**$225,000.00**	14%	**$254,000.00**	15%	**$340,000.00**	18%	**$390,000.00**	20%
Gross Margin		**14%**		**15%**		**18%**		**20%**	
	GP/New Homes	$40,000.00	8%	$45,000.00	9%	$60,000.00	11%	$40,000.00	11%
	GP/Custom	$135,000.00	15%	$142,000.00	16%	$200,000.00	21%	$250,000.00	21%
	GP/Remodeling	$50,000.00	19%	$67,000.00	21%	$80,000.00	23%	$100,000.00	25%
Overhead									
Marketing and Sales		$16,600.00	1%	$17,450.00	1%	$18,500.00	1%	$19,500.00	1%
General Administration (GA) & Overhead		$182,600.00	11%	$185,000.00	11%	$190,000.00	10%	$200,000.00	10%
Total Sales/GA&O		$199,200.00	12%	$202,450.00	12%	$208,500.00	11%	$219,500.00	11%
Net Profit		**$25,800.00**	2%	**$51,550.00**	3%	**$131,500.00**	7%	**$170,500.00**	9%
Net Margin		**2%**		**3%**		**7%**		**9%**	

Source: John Barrows, Certified Graduate Builder (CGB), Graduate Master Builder (GMB), Certified Green Professional (CGP) J. Barrows Inc.

This builder made a conscious decision to spend more money on marketing to reach the goal of doing more custom and remodeling work and building fewer spec homes, which reduced financial risk. The table shows that the strategy of focusing on the costs of construction, or increasing gross profit and trying to hold overhead steady, paid off in increased net profit.

The builder used the current year's actual costs to project future costs of materials, trade contractors, and labor. You can use spreadsheets similarly to project the possible impact—in dollars, cents, and profit margin—of your business plan.

Profit and Change Orders

Managed properly, change orders can keep you from losing money and time when clients decide to split a master bathroom in half after it has been rough-plumbed or to make other midstream changes to what you have agreed contractually to build.

"As builders, we're missing out on a lot if we are doing changes on just a time-and-materials basis," says John Barrows, an experienced custom builder.

One builder learned how to manage change orders the hard way—following a job that ended with 130 change orders totaling more than $100,000 and resulting in a six-month extension of the construction schedule. Another custom builder handles proposed changes with a simple two-part, carbonless form that requires a client signature before the cost impact of any change will be investigated. He charges an administrative fee, plus an hourly fee for researching and estimating a change. The charges are payable whether or not a client ultimately gives the go-ahead for a change.

Barrows ensures that change orders don't negatively impact his profit margin by including the cost of research, processing, and overhead. Insurance and job supervision expenses are among those reflected in a daily fee for delays beyond the original completion date that change orders cause.

More than Math

Calculating profit margin for a particular home or project is a simple mathematical exercise. But meeting or exceeding profit expectations for your company year in and year out demands constant data gathering, analysis, and making your best forecast for the economy and your specific market. The first requirement for earning the profit you need to bring the vision for your company to fruition is to set a specific profit goal. Only then can you manage the resources within your control that continually will bring more dollars to your bottom line.

4

Managing Risk

Risk is the possibility the builder will experience a loss or injury. Each day, builders face risks associated with sales, profitability, job-related injuries, and material damage or loss. Your corporate structure, contracts, quality of estimates, finance strategies, management controls, safety practices, and financial management either can increase or reduce your level of risk. Know your business. Stay connected and engaged with it. To reduce risk, do not hand over responsibility to someone else.

Three Types of Risk

You face three types of risk as a home building company owner:

Speculative risk. The possibility of earning a profit is speculative risk. Most business decisions builders make, such as whether to build and market a house that is not presold (a spec house) involve speculative risk.

Most builders are comfortable with speculative risk, and many embrace it. It is the reason they are in business for themselves rather than working for someone else. For these entrepreneurs, the expectation of a gain more than offsets the fear of loss.

Pure risk. Pure risk involves only the possibility of loss, with no potential for gain. The possibilities of property damage, theft, and worker injury are pure risks because there is no real gain if they do not occur, but there will be losses if they do. Because you cannot eliminate pure risk—only attempt to reduce it—you must develop a plan to manage it. Following Occupational Safety and Health Administration (OSHA) safety training and accident prevention guidelines is one pure risk management strategy. Another is establishing jobsite controls to minimize, for example, injuries to visitors to the jobsite or materials thefts.

Financial risk. Financial risk is the threat of losing money. Do not underestimate it. Evaluate every business opportunity (building a house, growing your company, diversifying into remodeling, or commercial construction) in terms of financial risk. What is the worst-case scenario? If the project fails, can your company survive? Financial risk increases when inventory, payroll, and other accounting functions are not managed and controlled properly. The cost of control should not outweigh the benefit of the control procedures, however; it should be proportional. What are you trying to protect? The greater the value of the asset, the more controls should be implemented.

Every decision carries risk. Knowing this will help you make sound decisions. Because housing demand is cyclical, economic conditions fluctuate, and government regulation and customers can be unpredictable, you are likely to experience financial loss. It is a cost of doing business. Be ready for it, even as you expect most of your projects to be profitable. If you fail to recognize the reality of financial risk when evaluating business opportunities, what might have been a minor loss can escalate into a catastrophe.

Risk of Injury

Although all builders face risk, the successful ones make sure they understand where there is potential risk, so they can find ways to minimize it.

Injuries to employees. By law, employers must provide a safe work environment. They also must provide wage replacement and medical benefits to employees who suffer work-related injuries or health problems. Under state workers' compensation laws, an employee generally cannot sue his or her employer for negligence in conjunction with a work-related injury. There may be exceptions for violations of federal and state anti-discrimination laws, sexual harassment, or deliberate and willful intent to injure workers, but absent these exceptions, generally, state laws will govern a worker's remedies.

The requirements for carrying workers' compensation vary from state to state. Study the legal requirements in your particular jurisdiction. Regardless of whether you must carry the insurance, you are obliged to compensate injured employees.

Injuries to trade contractors or their employees. Under certain conditions, builders must assume liability for injuries to trade contractors or their employees. A builder may be held liable if an injured trade contractor or his or her employee can prove that the injury resulted because of the builder's negligence. In addition, if a trade contractor's employee suffers an injury on your jobsite and the trade contractor cannot meet the compensation requirements, you may have to compensate the injured worker. Many states require general contractors to be responsible for any trade contractors who work on the jobsite.

Injuries to visitors and passersby. Liability claims are not limited to workers. Customers, real estate agents, suppliers, building inspectors, passersby, and even trespassers may claim an injury for which the builder is held liable.

Injuries occurring in completed homes. The liability for injuries suffered by individuals after the customer takes possession and moves into the home may fall to the builder if the injury is caused by a defect that was known to the builder but not disclosed to the owner.

Injuries and damage from automobile accidents. A builder's liability may extend beyond the jobsite to include accidents involving the builder's vehicles. The liability also may extend to employees' vehicles if they are used for company business.

Balancing Costs

Risk management is evaluating risks and seeking ways to minimize the total costs associated with them. Builders must understand two types of costs: The first is the cost incurred if a potential loss becomes an actual loss, such as paying to repair an uninsured building damaged by fire. The second type is the cost to reduce the risk of incurring even greater costs. These could include the cost of purchasing insurance against loss by fire. To effectively manage, you must understand and balance both types of costs.

In short, builders must analyze fully their exposure to loss in order to protect their companies against loss from pure risk. An effective risk management program helps builders

- identify risks that could cause dollar losses;
- estimate the severity of the losses;
- estimate the costs associated with reducing the risks; and
- select the best ways to deal with each risk.

Identifying Risks

To identify risks, first analyze your company's resources. Determine the value of each resource and what could happen to destroy that value. Next, evaluate the risks associated with the firm's activities. Determine what injury or loss could result from each activity and the potential cost of injury or loss.

You can use the following information sources to identify risks:

- NAHB's Labor, Safety, and Health Department
- OSHA publications
- State labor agencies
- Insurance companies
- Your company's accident history

Reducing Risks

Although you cannot avoid risk completely, you can reduce it. Conduct a comprehensive analysis of operating procedures and decision making to identify areas where you can lessen risk. Following are some specific steps builders can take to reduce risk:

Choose jobs carefully. Avoid jobs that require unfamiliar equipment, materials, or activities. Ensure contracts are current and properly reflect the scope of the particular project.

Use accepted materials and methods. Use accepted materials and methods. Before incorporating new materials and techniques into a home, you should determine whether these new products, techniques, and materials are suitable for the particular project and thoroughly familiarize yourself with these items before using them. You also can reduce risk by not using products that contain or produce hazardous materials.

Establish financial controls. Establish financial controls to protect the company against potential losses due to pilfering or embezzlement. Controls are either preventive (they stop loss from occurring) or detective (they discover a loss before it is too late to recover it).

Consider implementing the following five controls:

1. Limiting access. Access controls govern procedures and limit access (to assets, materials, inventory, cash) to the appropriate person or people to reduce the risk of pilfering or theft. An employee's level of access should be commensurate with his or her job functions.
2. Safeguarding assets. This type of control is physical, rather than procedural—for example, holding cash and key documents in a safe that is not in a readily accessible area.

3. Segregation of duties designates individuals to control only specified parts of a larger process. For example, the bookkeeper does not have check-signing authority, does not open the bank statements, and does not balance the checkbook. Instead, the owner or his or her designee reviews all bank statements and signs all checks.

4. Recording financial information. Recording financial information means that the appropriate employee (accountant or bookkeeper) records the information in the proper amount, in the proper *account*, and in the proper time. Errors or omissions in any of these three areas can reveal anomalies.

5. Execution of transactions. Ensure that compliance documents and transactions (regulatory, legal, and tax documents, for example) are handled correctly. Hire experienced workers and adequately train employees to perform tasks. A clerk should not prepare a tax return.

Select the appropriate legal form of organization. Your company's legal structure (i.e., sole proprietorship, partnership, corporation, LLC) helps determine your degree of personal risk. As discussed in chapter 2, some types of organization can reduce your exposure to loss by segregating personal assets from company assets. Follow the requirements of the legal structure once it is set up to minimize personal liability. For example, when creating a corporation, LLC, or S corporation, do not commingle personal and business funds. This ensures personal assets remain just that—personal.

Follow manufacturer's instructions. Most products builders install in their homes come with a manufacturer's warranty and specific installation instructions. Many builders have learned the hard way that the surest way to void a manufacturer's warranty is to disregard the installation instructions. Ensure that your employees are trained in the proper way to install products. If possible, have the manufacturer provide training on the proper installation method to ensure manufacturer warranty coverage. When a manufacturer refuses to stand behind a product, frequently it is because the product was installed using methods not recommended by the manufacturer. As a result, the builder may have to assume responsibility for any defective conditions.

Develop a safety program. Every builder must develop a safety program. From the day they join the company, employees must understand that they must follow all safety and health rules and regulations as well as company safety policies and procedures. Establish and enforce policies and procedures to guide employee behavior. Provide safety equipment such as a hard hat, hearing protection, and safety glasses. The National Association of Home Builders (NAHB) has a safety program that provides a customizable template to help you develop a safety

Safety Tips

- Establish safety policies and procedures for the company's safety program.
- Evaluate the jobs your employees and trade contractors perform to identify potential hazards.
- Periodically inspect all equipment to ensure that guards and safety devices are in place and working properly.
- Ensure that employees are trained to use tools and equipment properly.
- Require that employees always wear proper safety equipment.
- Educate employees about potential hazards and the safe work practices to follow that can reduce their risk of injury.
- Know and follow all OSHA standards, rules, and regulations.
- Properly label, handle, use, and store all hazardous materials.
- Inspect your jobsites regularly to identify potential safety hazards and promptly correct any hazards.
- Require trade contractors to establish their own safety program and to have adequate insurance.
- Require workers to report all accidents immediately.
- Investigate accidents to determine exactly what happened, why, and how to prevent them in the future.
- Periodically evaluate the effectiveness of your safety program.

program. Use the NAHB/OSHA training materials for trenching and excavation, working on scaffolding, and for overall jobsite safety. Reinforce safety training at regular meetings. Conduct and implement frequent inspections of your jobsite to ensure compliance.

Assuming Risk

Builders will, as part of doing business, assume certain risks. For example, they will take responsibility for a loss or injury that might result from a risk. Assuming risk is reasonable in the following situations:

- The risk is very small.
- The business could cover the potential loss.
- Insurance coverage, if available, is too expensive.
- There is no other way of protecting against the loss.

Shifting Risk

Perhaps the most common method of managing risk is to shift or transfer it to another party. Builders who use *cost-plus contracts* transfer much of their speculative risk to the buyer. Buying insurance is another way to transfer pure risk.

Insurers, typically insurance companies, agree for a fee to assume financial responsibility for losses that might result from a specific risk. Most types of pure risk generally are insurable. Most types of speculative risk generally are not.

Types of Insurance

You can choose from many types of insurance designed to shift risk. After you analyze your potential risks, speak with an attorney and an insurance agent to investigate the best types for you and your business. State and local laws may require you to carry specific types of insurance.

Injury and Property Damage

Commercial general liability insurance (CGL) insures against bodily injury and property damage that occurs in and from the builder's operations. The initial premium is based on estimates of

- the builder's payroll for the term of the policy, which is typically one year;
- work the builder performs by category, such as carpentry, concrete, roofing, and painting; and
- work the builder subcontracts by category.

An audit of the builder's payroll at the end of the policy period determines the actual premium cost. For contracted work, the builder provides a certificate of insurance for each contractor who has worked during the policy period. If a trade contractor has no insurance, or if the builder has not obtained a certificate of insurance, the insurance company may charge the builder for the amount of the trade contract. Builders should have trade contractors add the builder/general contractor as an *additional insured* (AI) on the trade contractor's CGL policy.

Workers' Compensation

Builders should require trade contractors to carry workers' compensation and provide proof of coverage as part of the contract. Often referred to as "workers' comp," this insurance provides coverage for work-related injuries. Workers' comp covers medical expenses and provides salaries for employees who are injured while at work. It also pays benefits to dependents of workers killed on the job. Every state requires employers to provide some form of workers' comp insurance, but the benefits injured workers may receive vary by state. If your company conducts business in more than one state, know the requirements for each state where you conduct business.

Workers' comp estimated premiums are determined and paid similarly to CGL premiums—by estimated payroll by category. As with CGL, a payroll audit determines any adjustments. Workers' comp generally covers all employees, including family members.

Workers' comp is available from most insurance companies or through a group self-insured fund, which often offers lower initial premiums. If a self-insured fund pays out more benefits than anticipated, however, the fund may levy a retroactive assessment on participating builders. State regulations govern whether a builder may participate in a self-insured fund.

Builder's Risk Insurance

Builder's risk insurance covers property damage to projects under construction. Builders can add options such as coverage for damage to building materials in transit or for materials stored at a temporary location.

There are two basic methods for purchasing builder's risk insurance: a specific policy for each project or one policy that covers all projects. If you purchased a single policy to cover all projects, you would submit monthly reports on started, finished, and ongoing projects.

Builder's risk premiums are based on the completed construction costs of the properties. Typically, you must insure a property for 100% of its completed value, minus land cost.

If you are a custom builder who builds on the owner's property, you, rather than your client, should carry the builder's risk insurance. If owners carry the insurance instead, make sure you are named as an additional insured on their policy.

Property Insurance

Property insurance protects you from loss or damage to your structures and their contents. Most property insurance policies contain a *coinsurance clause* that requires the policyholder to purchase coverage at least equal to some specified percentage (typically 80%) of the property value. If you don't maintain the required coverage, only part of a loss will be reimbursed. For example, if you own a building valued at $50,000 but only insure it for $40,000 (or 80% of the property value), and then incur fire damages valued at $20,000, the insurance company will pay the full amount of $20,000. However, if you insure the property for only $37,500 (75% of the property value), the insurance company generally would pay only 75% percent of the loss, or $15,000.

Builders can insure themselves against the risk of loss from employee theft, forgery, or embezzlement by purchasing fidelity bonds for some or all employees.

Understand Risk

Residential construction can be a risky business but its potential rewards—being your own boss, doing what you love, earning a profit—can outweigh the risks. Knowing the risks inherent in operating your business is the first step in dealing with them. Understand your alternatives for handling each type of risk—financial, speculative, and pure—and then choose the best option for managing it.

5

Understanding Contracts and Other Legal Documents

Legal issues affect virtually every aspect of a home builder's business. From contracts with customers, suppliers, and trade contractors to applying for a zoning change from the local government, every business decision has a legal component. Because the law evolves continuously, your legal documents must change as well. That is just one reason why all builders—all business owners, for that matter—need to hire a trusted attorney to draft documents and consult with him or her periodically. An attorney can offer his or her expertise in matters of legal organization, accounting and tax preparation requirements, and employment policies.

Contract Basics

A contract is an agreement between two or more parties that creates legally enforceable duties or obligations. It need not be a formal, written document nor include the word "contract" to be a legally enforceable promise.

As a home builder, you may enter into hundreds of contracts each year with buyers, trade contractors, lenders, suppliers, and landowners. These contracts may include loan agreements, sales contracts, employment agreements, subcontracts, and leases. A purchase order also might be considered a contract—one that promises materials within a specified time period at a certain price.

Contracts perform two primary functions:

1. They provide builders with the means to describe and formalize agreements with buyers, subcontractors, landowners, suppliers, or other individuals or companies. Think of a contract as a tool to define a mutually beneficial relationship rather than a means to force parties to perform their obligations.

2. Contracts also allocate responsibilities and risks among all the parties so that everyone understands the risks they are assuming. If you take on more risk, you need a higher potential return to justify it.

Five Elements of a Contract

An enforceable contract contains five essential elements:

1. **Agreement.** One party extends an offer, and the other party accepts it. The agreement reflects the mutual assent, often referred to as the "meeting of the minds" between the parties.
2. **Contractual capacity.** All parties to a contract understand the general nature of the contract.
3. **Lawful objective**. An agreement fails to satisfy this requirement if it is prohibited by statute or violates public policy.
4. **Consideration.** A promise by one party and an acceptance of that promise by another do not, by themselves, constitute an enforceable contract. The party to whom the promise is made must give up something in return, which the law refers to as consideration.
5. **Proper format.** Many contracts that contain the elements discussed above are valid and enforceable regardless of how they were created. However, some types of contracts must be in writing to be enforceable.

Types of Contracts

Although it is wise to put contracts in writing, the law also recognizes oral and *implied contracts*, as well as agreements that give signers the right to future options.

Oral versus written contracts. Most builders have entered into oral contracts at one time or another, but written contracts are almost always preferable. Written contracts identify the rights and obligations of each party to the contract. This can reduce personal liability, manage risk, and ensure compliance from all parties. If a dispute arises, it may be difficult for a court to determine the parties' true intent in an oral contract or even to identify the promises that were made. A well-written contract provides an accurate, objective, and specific record of an agreement.

Each state has a *statute of frauds* that requires certain types of contracts to be written. Four types of contracts covered by these statutes are particularly relevant to home builders:

1. Contracts governing activities that cannot be performed within one year after the contract is made
2. Real estate sales contracts or those that govern the transfer of interest in land
3. Promises to pay, or be responsible for, another party's debts
4. Sales of goods valued at $500 or more

Contracts involving the sale of goods valued at $500 or more are now covered by requirements in the Uniform Commercial Code § 2-201. Make sure you understand your state's UCC requirements. Written contracts are subject to the *parol evidence rule.* The rule states that when parties reduce their agreement to a detailed, complete writing, that writing is recognized as the complete agreement. Spoken words (parol evidence) that add to, alter, or vary the terms of the contract are not admissible evidence in court. The parol evidence rule follows the theory that when a written contract exists, the writing should embody all the terms agreed upon at the time the contract was written. However, courts sometimes will admit testimonial evidence of terms that are not part of the written contract. That testimony may be allowed to fill gaps in incomplete agreements, clarify ambiguities (two or more reasonable interpretations), correct obvious clerical errors, or show that a contract is void or voidable.

Express and implied contracts. In a written or oral *express contract,* the parties have, through their words, created contractual obligations. In an implied contract, the parties' actions, rather than their words, provide evidence that a contract exists.

Bilateral, unilateral, and option contracts. A contract in which one party extends an offer and another party accepts the offer and promises something in return is called a *bilateral contract.* In contrast, a *unilateral contract* contains only one promise: that one party engage in certain conduct. The contract is formed only upon completion of the required conduct. For example, in listing a piece of property with a real estate agent, the property owner promises to pay a commission if the property is sold while the listing agreement is in effect.

An *option contract* gives one of the contracting parties the right to enter into another contract later. For example, a builder and a landowner may enter into a contract that gives the builder the right to purchase the land at a specified price within a certain time. If the builder exercises the option, the landowner must sell according to the agreed-upon terms. If the option is not exercised, it expires.

Rather than entering into an option contract, one party may give another party the right of first refusal, which requires that the first offer be made to the party having the first refusal rights. In the above example, the landowner may be unwilling to sell the property when the contract is written, but may reconsider selling later. By giving the builder a right of first refusal, the landowner agrees that if the land is offered for sale, the builder has the right to buy the land, generally at a predetermined price or at a price matching a good-faith bid by a third party. Once the land is offered for sale, an option is created that gives the builder the right to buy or not buy.

Interpreting Contracts

If each party is satisfied with the other's performance under a contract, then no problems arise in interpreting its terms. For cases where disagreements exist, courts have devised rules to help interpret contracts. These rules encompass the following factors:

Parties' intentions. Courts seek to determine the expressed intent of the parties, evidenced by their words and actions. Generally, courts limit their interpretations to expressed intent and give no weight to secret or undisclosed intentions.

Overall interpretation. The agreement is read and interpreted as a whole, and the parties' intentions are determined from the entire agreement, not from isolated words or phrases.

Order of precedence. Contracts often consist of a number of documents containing, for example, printed forms, typed text and attachments, and handwritten notes and corrections. When conflicts exist among various documents and the conflicts cannot be reconciled, courts generally will use the following order of precedence to interpret the contract:

1. Handwritten changes and inserts
2. Typed changes
3. Typed agreement
4. Printed terms

Word usage and ambiguity. When analyzing the wording of an agreement, the courts accept definitions provided in the agreement. Otherwise, ordinary words are given their ordinary meanings and technical or trade terms are interpreted according to the area of technical knowledge or trade from which they were taken.

When the wording of an agreement is so unclear or ambiguous that the court cannot determine the true intent of the parties, it may look beyond the written agreement to oral testimony. If oral testimony does not eliminate the ambiguity, the courts generally find against the party who prepared the agreement.

Plain Language

Contracts traditionally have been written in extremely complex language. For a document to be legal, it had to sound legal. This resulted in contracts that were unfathomable, even by the people signing them.

Now contract drafters try to replace legalese with plain language. In fact, a number of states have passed readability legislation, and more are expected to do so. If the agreement between or among the parties cannot be written so others understand it, the parties themselves probably do not understand what they are agreeing to.

Contract Performance

Courts generally recognize three degrees of contract performance: complete, substantial, and material breach.

Complete performance. Complete performance occurs when parties to a contract have fulfilled their duties under the contract. A party that performs completely is entitled to expect the same behavior from the other party and may sue to enforce this right.

Substantial performance. It is not unusual for a party to fall short of a complete performance. Substantial performance occurs when a party essentially performs his or her contractual obligations but with minor deviations.

Consider, for example, a builder who has contracted to build a custom home for a client. The specifications call for a particular brand and model of vanity bowl. For reasons beyond the builder's control, the particular vanity bowl specified in the contract is not available, requiring him or her to substitute a bowl with similar features and quality.

If the builder has acted in good faith, courts generally will hold that the builder substantially complied with the contract's obligations, particularly in cases where the deviation is relatively minor. Thus, the buyer cannot refuse to pay for and take possession of a home because of a relatively minor deviation from the contract.

The courts may, however, award the owner damages because of deviations like this example.

Material breach. A material breach occurs when a party fails to perform important contractual duties. When a material breach occurs, the non-breaching party may be discharged from further performance and may have a right to damages because of the breach.

Liquidated Damages

Contracts often state that specific damages will be awarded in the event of contract breach. This *liquidated damages* clause reduces uncertainty over what happens if a party fails to comply with specified obligations. Liquidated damages often are included as penalties for breaching a contract. They may include a high liquidated damage amount as a warning.

However, courts enforce only "true" liquidated damage clauses, not what they consider penalty clauses. The court will try to decide whether the damages specified at the contract's signing were a reasonable representation of the losses that could result from a breach of contract.

Resolving Contract Disputes

No matter how carefully an agreement is prepared or how diligently the parties attempt to execute the agreement, disputes can arise. Most disputes are settled by the parties involved. When that fails, one or both parties may decide to litigate. However, litigation often is not the best approach. Attorneys' fees, court costs, travel expenses, and lost work time quickly can exceed the amount of damages sought. In addition, litigation may take months or years to resolve and permanently damage relations between the parties.

There are alternative dispute resolution procedures. Mediation and arbitration are the two most widely used.

Mediation. In mediation, the parties voluntarily engage a neutral third party. This mediator will not render a decision in favor of one party or the other. Instead, he or she assists the parties in negotiating a mutually satisfactory agreement. The American Arbitration Association (AAA) has developed a set of rules, the Construction Industry Arbitration Rules and Mediation Procedures, which can provide a structure for this process. Mediation does not guarantee a resolution, so the parties ultimately may have to seek some other means to resolve their dispute. However, if the parties do reach an agreement during mediation, that agreement may be written and become an enforceable contract.

Arbitration. In arbitration, the parties in a dispute submit their cases to a third party who considers the evidence, applies the law, and renders a binding decision. The arbitrator is typically either a single individual or a three-person panel. Most states recognize and are willing to enforce arbitration agreements. Courts generally refuse to rehear a case that has been arbitrated.

Often, a formal dispute resolution organization such as AAA will supervise arbitration. The parties concerned can choose the group they want to oversee the proceedings.

Successful mediation or arbitration depends largely on the quality and expertise of the neutral third party. The disputing parties should feel confident that the mediator or arbitrator is knowledgeable about standard construction practices. In most cases, the disputing parties should attempt to resolve their dispute through mediation and move to arbitration only if the dispute remains unresolved.

Study the costs and time required for alternative dispute resolution procedures. This will help you select the best dispute resolution tool for a particular situation.

Sales and Trade Contracts

Two contracts builders frequently use are sales contracts with buyers or owners, and trade contractor agreements. A contract performs these three functions:

1. Documents understandings and agreements
2. Manages expectations
3. Controls risk, shifts liability, or both

Most building-related contracts use terms that are recognized and have common definitions in legal circles nationwide. There are exceptions, though, so consult an attorney whenever you are drafting contracts. You will include specific language depending on whether the contract is with a buyer or a trade contractor.

Defining Property

Property usually refers to a piece of land, a thing, or an object. Builders regularly deal with real property—interests in land and anything firmly attached to it. As a legal concept, real property refers to various rights an owner has related to the possession, use, enjoyment, and disposal of a land parcel. However, an owner does not have absolute, unlimited rights. Public and private rules govern land use and transfer.

Public Limitations

Public limitations on ownership balance the needs and rights of the community with the needs and rights of the individual property owner. For example, a city develops a set of zoning regulations concerning the use of land within its boundaries. A local government can thereby plan and manage the growth and development of its community. Zoning attempts to provide orderly regulation of various property uses by essentially transferring some of a landowner's rights to other residents of the community. These residents, through their local government, determine acceptable uses of property within the community.

Although zoning affects property rights and may limit owners' rights, property owners generally do not receive compensation when these rights are restricted. To prevent landowners from shouldering an inequitable burden, the courts limit the extent to which government may regulate land use. For example, if a court finds that excessive regulation has resulted in an unreasonable loss in property value, the government may have to pay the property owner just compensation for the loss.

Zoning ordinances classify land use. Regulatory bodies determine the most appropriate use for each geographic area within their respective communities and assign classifications to these areas. Classifications vary from city to city but usually include residential, commercial, industrial, agricultural, and office categories. Each of these typically includes subcategories. Zoning classifications dictate the type of development allowed and set limits on unit types, number of units, building heights, and setbacks. If a land parcel's zoning classification changes, existing improvements that no longer meet zoning requirements are considered a *nonconforming use.*

Property owners generally can continue to use these improvements but cannot add to them and, in many cases, cannot make extensive renovations. Moreover, if the landowner discontinues the nonconforming use, he or she generally cannot have it reinstated. If the intended use of a piece of property does not match its current zoning, the builder must ask for a change in classification. Builders should familiarize themselves with the local rezoning process.

Private Limitations

Ownership of real property is subject to private as well as public limitations. Common private limitations on ownership include easements, *restrictive covenants*, and liens.

Easements

An easement gives a person or entity the right to use another's land. This right may convey to a specific individual or to whoever owns the land. A *utility easement*, for example, may be necessary to maintain infrastructure and equipment. An access easement may allow people ingress to or egress from an adjacent property. Generally, an easement must be written to be enforceable to satisfy the statute of frauds. Because an easement is recorded in the land records, often as part of the deed, it is difficult to remove. Accordingly, once an easement is established, the granting party cannot revoke it absent one of the following conditions:

- All the parties grant their consent.
- Grantor can show that the reason for the easement ceases to exist.
- Circumstances have so changed that the easement is no longer necessary or allowed.

Restrictive Covenants

When property is transferred from one owner to another, the seller (or grantor in the case of a gift) may limit how the property is used. These limitations, or restrictive covenants, generally are placed in the deed. They also are called deed restrictions. Once they are included in the deed, restrictive covenants "run with the land"; that is, they remain in effect forever unless they are removed by the party who created them, that person's heirs, or a court. Developers often use restrictive covenants to limit buyers' options related to building setbacks, construction materials and methods, and the purposes for which the property is used.

Mechanics' Liens and Lien Laws

A *lien* is a legal claim on property for the payment of a debt or obligation. Under state laws, providers of materials or labor for a construction project may place a mechanic's lien on the property where the project is located. Because a lien results in a cloud on the title to the property, lien holders must comply strictly with state statutory requirements to file and collect the debt secured by the lien. Once a lien is recorded, if the party owing the debt or obligation fails to pay, the lien holder has the right to file a civil suit, called foreclose, to force payment. Liens are powerful tools for collecting money owed on a construction project. Builders may use them to ensure that customers pay. Builders also can have mechanic's liens placed on their property by suppliers or trade contractors to whom the builder owes money.

Each state has specific requirements for mechanic's liens. For example, a number of states require a preliminary notice, sometimes called a prelim notice, early in the construction process or even in the original contract with the customer, before starting construction. The language and timing of the notice generally is specified in the statute. In general, it states that a mechanic's lien will be filed unless the builder or trade contractor is paid. Whoever files the notice must do so within a specified time after the last materials or labor have been provided. Because each state has different lien requirements, including filing deadlines, notice requirements, and eligibility to file, builders must become familiar with their own state laws. If you are conducting business in more than one state, do not assume that all states have similar legal requirements.

Sales Contracts

Contracts between builders and buyers or owners, generally referred to as sales contracts, can be effective tools that can prevent problems both during and after construction. Sales contracts have two major sections: the agreement and the general conditions.

The agreement. The agreement describes the specific project (house, office, etc.) for which the contract is being written. In general, the agreement embodies the scope of work, timing, price, and method of payment. Use objective criteria by describing the work according to plans and specifications. Avoid subjective terms such as "best," "good," "workmanlike," "first-class," and "diligent."

A sales contract typically includes the following items:

- **Names.** Include the full legal names of all parties to the contract in the first section. The names of all contracting parties should appear on all other contract documents.

- **Location.** Describe the location and provide the legal description of the property.

- **References to contract documents.** Provide descriptions of all documents relevant to the contract, such as drawings, specifications, or warranties. Referenced documents become part of the contract, just as if they were attached.

- **Start date.** Specify the date that work shall begin or a specified period of time following the signing of the contract.

- **Completion date.** Specify the date by which the work is to be substantially completed. The contract may spell out that work is to be completed by a specific date or within a specified time, in days or months, after the start of work. The parties should define and include in the contract what constitutes substantial completion. If no completion date is specified, courts will use a "reasonable" standard to identify a completion date based on the extent of the project and compared to similar projects in that geo-

Sales Contract Guidelines

Limit your role to building. Don't claim, or try to be, an expert on everything. Specify the following:

- You rely on third parties regarding site suitability and the foundation. Have an engineer certify, take concrete samples, and use a level stick to measure the foundation.
- The builder does not control land use.
- The builder is not responsible for environmental risks (such as radon).

graphic area. Be cautious in using a completion date that does not allow room for unexpected or unavoidable delays.

- **Price.** The amount the builder is to be paid for performing the work should be expressed in both numbers and words. This may be a total fixed price, cost plus a fixed fee, or cost plus a percentage. If the price is cost-plus, explain what comprises cost.

- **Payment schedule.** Specify how payments are to be made. Include both the amount and scheduling of each payment. Buyers should pay earnest money at contract signing and a nonrefundable fee to begin construction (if you are building a custom, rather than a speculative home). The fee protects the builder if a buyer backs out after construction begins. To increase your chances of retaining the fee if it is challenged in a lawsuit, it is best to base it on cost only (no profit margin). A jury is more likely to uphold the fee if it represents the builder's true cost.

- **Liquidated damages.** Specify the amount of liquidated damages, if any, and what circumstances will prompt liquidated damages. Courts will not enforce a liquidated damages clause if the amount is unreasonable.

- **Ownership of plans and specifications.** Specify which of the parties has legal rights to the plans and who is responsible for any defects or mistakes in the plans or specifications. When necessary, determine who owns the copyright on the plans. If the builder hires an architect or drafter to draft the plans, unless the builder buys the copyright, the architect or drafter owns them. Without a written agreement transferring ownership of the copyright, the builder will generally only have a one-use license to the plans. If the customer provides the plans, ensure he or she has the right to use them, or obtain indemnification from the owner in the event the copyright holder sues for infringement.[3]

---

[3] David N. Crump. *Copyright Law for Home Builders, Second Edition.* Washington, DC: Builder Books.com.

- **Signatures.** Provide a space for all parties to sign the contract. The parties should sign all contract documents. Some states may require a separate place to initial or sign an arbitration clause, which signals that the parties have read that clause and agree to it. Be sure to check the applicable state's laws to ensure your contracts comply with any such requirements.

General Conditions

The general conditions are those elements of the sales contract that are not project specific; that is, they are general provisions that apply to all contracts. The general agreement either may be a separate document or it may be combined with the agreement into a single document. The contract should document that the buyer has obtained, or will obtain, any required financing. The contract also should specify that any financing provided by the buyer or owner will be placed in escrow. All costs associated with financing, such as fees and closing costs, should be allocated among the parties. Specify what closing costs the builder and buyer pay, avoiding ambiguous terms such as "normal," "routine," or "customary."

Allowances

An allowance is a budget for a specific element or elements of a construction project, such as flooring, light and plumbing fixtures, and appliances. You can include allowances in a contract to reduce your risk while giving the customer some flexibility in product selections. By establishing allowances for certain items or activities, you and your buyer can sign the contract, and you can start construction before the customer makes product and materials selections. The contract should describe how the allowances work and note their specific dollar amounts. It should state, for example, whether any unused allowance amounts are refunded to the buyer.

The home buyer is responsible for determining whether allowances are adequate. However, to maintain a positive relationship with your buyer, do not set unrealistically low allowances. Also, explain to the customer how you have determined the allowance(s). For example, if your buyer knows that you set the carpet allowance based on $30 per sq. yd., they can use the information either to request an adjustment before signing the contract or to shop for their carpeting once the contract is signed. If the customer wants a higher priced carpet, you can increase the allowance and, of course, the contract price, before signing the contract. Regardless of how you establish the allowance, though, the contract should state a lump sum, rather than a per-unit amount, such as square foot or square yard, to avoid discussions about how areas are measured. An allowance may include only the materials or it may include related costs such as sales tax, delivery, installation, and labor. Explain to the customer what is included.

Other Contract Provisions

The contract should explain or specify additional terms or provisions. It should allocate responsibility for obtaining and paying for any required permits, licenses, fees, or other costs associated with the project. Your sales contract should address the following specific areas:

- **Insurance.** Identify the insurance coverage each party must carry.
- **Site conditions.** Site conditions that differ from those expected at the time of the agreement can increase the cost and duration of a project substantially. The contract should outline how unexpected and unknown/unknowable site conditions will be handled. A physical characteristic of the property that was unknown when you signed a contract can materially change the construction techniques.
- **Change orders.** Outline the procedures buyers must use when requesting and paying for changes to the scope of work, if permitted, after the contract is signed. Remember that a change order is a modification to an existing contract and documenting the change will protect the builder and the customer. All change orders should be written, describe the nature of the change, and specify the cost of making it. They should be dated and signed by all contracting parties before any change order work begins.
- **Waiver of lien.** In general, you should not waive your right to assert a lien. However, many banks now require partial lien waivers before subsequent construction draws. Do not sign lien waivers until you receive payment for completed work.

Change Orders

A completed change order form should include

- Date of issue
- Job name
- Change order number
- Detailed description of change
- Monetary impact to home contract
- Impact of change on schedule for completion of home

- **Inspection, acceptance, and possession.** The contract should define possession and identify activities, such as inspections required before the buyer can accept the project and take possession of the home.

- **Representations and warranties.** Explain any warranties in the contract. For example, if you use NAHB's *Residential Construction Performance Guidelines,*[4] specify which edition of the book applies to the project, and maintain a copy of that edition in your records. The buyer should sign the warranty section separately.

- **Alternative dispute resolution.** The contract should specify dispute resolution procedures the parties have agreed to. These may include mediation or binding arbitration.

- **Termination.** The contract should specify the circumstances under which the contract may be terminated, either by mutual agreement or for breach of the agreement by one of the parties. Breach of the agreement can occur when the customer refuses to continue to make payments or refuses to allow the builder or contractor on the jobsite. Also, specify each party's remedies if either party breaches the contract.

- **A bank draw schedule.** Depending on how you finance a project, your lender or the customer's will provide the schedule based on *percentage of completion*, which is discussed in chapter 14.

- **Other clauses.** The builder and buyer also may want to include clauses to cover issues such as cleanup, the builder's right to display a sign on the site, and customer access to the jobsite during construction.

Reducing Risk

Builders can reduce risk and potential liability by taking preventive steps before developing the sales contract. For example, if you are building on the customer's lot, you should require them to provide evidence of a clear title to the property and a survey that includes any easements or deed restrictions. Also, ensure that local ordinances and zoning requirements are compatible with the planned project. Finally, ensure that your company's capabilities fit the customer's expectations.

Trade Contracts

Have a signed agreement with each trade contractor that defines the scope of work and allocates responsibilities. As with all other contracts, you should consult an

---

[4] *Residential Construction Performance Guidelines, 4th Edition, Contractor Reference,* National Association of Home Builders. Washington, DC: BuilderBooks.com, 2011.

attorney to draw up these agreements. In general, though, they should address the following areas:

- **Price.** As discussed previously, a contractual agreement consists of an offer and an acceptance. In a trade contract, the proposal from the trade is the offer. When the builder accepts this offer, the contract is formed.
- **Scope of work.** This should be specified in detail to prevent overlap or omission in trade contractor duties. For example, does the framer or the roofer install felt paper on the roof?
- **Change orders.** As with your sales contracts, your trade contracts should discuss procedures for making changes, how changes will be priced, and who is authorized to approve changes. Change orders unsigned by the customer may be extremely difficult to enforce. Therefore, consider requiring all change orders to be processed through one person, and prohibiting any change unless and until the general contractor and the customer sign a change order.
- **Liability and insurance.** The contract should include a provision to indemnify the general contractor for liability for construction defects caused by the trade contractor's work. Require the trade contractor to carry sufficient insurance to cover damages for which they might be liable as well as general liability and workers' compensation insurance. Require trade contractors to submit certificates of insurance before they begin work, and have them include the builder (general contractor) as an additional insured on the trade contractor's CGL.

Warranties

A warranty is an enforceable promise that the home you deliver to a customer will meet certain standards. Consumers increasingly expect more value for the price they pay for a new home, and they will go to great lengths to ensure that they get the value they expect. Therefore, warranties are becoming more and more important. Warranty-related issues can cost you money and sully your good reputation.

Implied Warranties

Implied warranties are assumed promises sellers make about their goods or services. The warranty takes effect when the product or service is sold. All states have an implied warranty of habitability, regardless of whether the builder makes specific guarantees. Under this implied warranty, the home must be habitable or fit for its intended purpose. As a tool for limiting liability, consider including a clause in your contract that waives implied warranties. Recognize that courts do not favor waivers of implied warranties and often have requirements that such waivers are conspicuous and can be seen clearly (i.e., not written in fine print and hidden in other clauses). In addition, some states—Texas and Massachusetts are two examples—do not allow implied warranties to be waived. Check your state's laws for requirements or restrictions.

Express Warranties

Express warranties are specific promises made by builders to buyers. They may be written or verbal. An express warranty on a product that costs more than $10 must be clearly and conspicuously designated as either a full warranty or a limited warranty.

Full warranty. Under a full warranty, the seller is obligated to repair or replace a defective product, within a reasonable time, at no charge to the buyer. If the defect is not fixed after a reasonable number of attempts, the buyer may receive a cash refund or a free replacement of the product. Companies that offer full warranties cannot place limitations on or obtain waivers of implied warranties. In some states, full warranties apply to subsequent as well as original purchasers. Given these stringent requirements, it is not surprising that builders seldom provide full warranties.

Limited warranty. Any warranty that does not provide the complete protection of a full warranty is a limited warranty. Limited warranties must be identified conspicuously as such, and all limitations must be described clearly in the warranty document. Builders commonly provide limited warranties on materials and workmanship for one year.

Warranty Provisions

Builders' warranties should include at least the following information.

Purchasers' names. Write the names of all purchasers in the first paragraph. They should match exactly the names on the property title and the purchasers' signatures at the end of the warranty document.

Assignability. Specify whether any remaining warranty may be transferred from the original owner to a subsequent owner.

Items covered and excluded. Clearly specify which items are covered and which are not. Specifically list all excluded items. Do not provide a warranty beyond a manufacturer's warranty, such as an additional warranty on appliances. This could subject you to the *Magnuson-Moss Warranty Act* and expose you to additional liability.

Remedies. You can decide how warranty problems will be addressed. Builders typically will replace, repair, or pay a reasonable cost to have covered defects repaired. You should educate buyers about what constitutes a defect for covered items. Home builders use the *Residential Construction Performance Guidelines* to manage customer expectations.

Length of warranty. Specify the length of the warranty period.

Claims procedures and owners' obligations. The written warranty should specify the procedures buyers use to make warranty service claims. The warranty also should outline owners' obligations, such as providing normal maintenance.

Insured Warranties

You can purchase insured warranties from third-party providers. These providers require that builders meet certain criteria related to home building experience, financial stability, and customer service history.

Insured warranty companies charge builders a fee for the warranties they provide. The builder typically pays a one-time membership fee and then pays a fee for each home sold. The fees are based on factors such as the builder's annual sales volume, experience, length of time in the program, and the loss experience in the geographic region in which the builder operates. Warranty coverage is similar from provider to provider. During the first year, the builder is responsible for workmanship and materials that do not conform to performance standards set by the warranty provider. The builder guarantees the home will be free of major system defects during the second year, including wiring, piping, and ductwork.

If the builder is unable or unwilling to fulfill warranty obligations during the first or second year, the insurer must do so. Insured warranties cover major structural defects for 10 years. After the second year, responsibility for structural defects moves from the builder to the insurer.

The specific benefits an insured warranty offers vary among warranty providers, but benefits typically include:

- Marketing. You can distinguish yourself from competitors and reduce any perception of risk a buyer may have.
- Financial support. You can defend against a warranty-related lawsuit.
- Waivers on certain inspections required by federally insured mortgages, such as FHA or VA.

Questions to Ask About Warranties

Who is the insurance backer for the program? An insured warranty is only as good as the person or company behind it. The warranty provider should be able to provide evidence of sound financial backing.

What is the acceptance or rejection rate of builders into the program? This data reveals which warranty providers use stringent screening processes. Typically, the more selective the screening process and the higher the rejection rate, the lower the potential losses and less chance of *default* for the warranty company.

Is the warranty provider able to offer warranties in all states in which the builder operates? Some insured warranty companies operate only in specific geographic regions. Builders generally need a single insured warranty company that can cover all of their homes, regardless of location.

The Magnuson-Moss Warranty Act

The Magnuson-Moss Warranty Act is the primary legislation governing product warranties. The act established criteria for written warranties and applies to consumer products. The act does not cover a new home or, in general, remodeling work done to an existing home. Instead, it encompasses only items that are considered consumer products, such as appliances.

The Magnuson-Moss Act does not require that builders provide written warranties. Accordingly, builders should be sure to include copies of any manufacturers' warranties for the buyer. Don't provide warranties beyond what is required. Doing so will incur unnecessary liability.

6

Developing a Strategy and Business Plan

In most small businesses, the owners are so busy taking care of urgent issues that they never set aside time to craft a plan for their businesses. Whether your business is running at 100 mph or you are in a period of recession, you must allocate the time, energy, and focus to develop a strategic plan. Strategic planning creates a blueprint to guide the daily building of your business.

Planning is the entrepreneur's core function. If you own a small business and you are not devoting time to strategic planning, you are behaving like your company's highest paid employee, rather than as an entrepreneur. You may be the captain of the ship, but you are on a ship without a course or destination. To remain profitable, you must manage your home building company strategically. This means thinking beyond next month and even next year. The starting point for any strategic plan is a vision.

Your Vision

To formulate a strategic vision, you must be able to answer the following three questions:

1. Who are you?
2. What is your desired legacy or mission?
3. What distinguishes you from the competition?

Creating a vision will help you focus your energy on defining and capitalizing on your unique strengths in the market. Then you can build a brand and secure market share, even if you are in a competitive situation where your competition has more land, more options, and more capital than you have. A vision will help you be pro-active. You can focus your efforts on growing your reputation and your profit margins rather than wasting time trying to react defensively to changes in the market.

Unlocking High Performance

Five factors generally explain why some firms consistently perform better than others:

1. They have long-term, simple, and consistent goals.
2. They understand their competitive environment.
3. They objectively appraise their resources.
4. They formulate and implement strategies to use resources effectively and efficiently.
5. Their strategies are flexible and adjustable to respond to changes in the market.

One way to start the strategic visioning process is to fully appreciate that, as a home builder, you are not merely in the construction business. Rather, you are providing lifestyle options to an increasingly diverse universe of potential home buyers. People closely tie their identity with where they live. Their homes and communities are the foundation upon which they create their lives. So, what is your vision of where your company fits into the array of lifestyles that home buyers may represent? And have you fully explored all the possibilities for finding your niche in this dynamic marketplace? The goal is to identify market segments that are underserved, that have depth and sustainability, and which your company can serve better than other builders. With a well-defined strategic vision, a company can create a mission statement and then a strategic plan. This plan will be your pathway toward realizing your vision.

The Business Plan

A business plan guides your daily work. Planning confers at least five benefits:

1. **It helps you manage proactively rather than reactively.** Proactive builders have a vision for their companies and work to create it. Reactive builders respond to problems as they arise.

The Mission Statement

A mission statement defines a company's distinct attribute(s) by identifying who its customers are, what needs it satisfies, and its values and philosophy. Once you have a mission statement, you can develop your strategic plan with objectives that support it. To manage strategically, builders must balance long- and short-term concerns. For example, although investing company profits in land may pay off in the end, it ties up cash you may need to meet current obligations.

2. **It provides direction.** Answer three key questions: What are we going to accomplish? How are we going to do it? What tools do we need?

3. **It allows your company to coordinate effort.** Planning helps you develop a team of employees, suppliers, trade contractors, and investors/lenders, and then coordinate their activities to reach the company's goals. This discourages team members from working against each other.

4. **It reduces uncertainty.** Planning forces builders to look ahead, anticipate changes, consider the impact, and develop appropriate responses. In effect, planning allows you to master change by helping you define your expectations and then cultivate strategies that will help you realize your vision.

5. **It stimulates critical thinking.** Planning forces you to evaluate and reexamine your goals, the methods to achieve them, your strengths and weaknesses, and your competitors. Successful builders thoroughly understand their business, their competitors, their customers, and their industry.

Establishing Objectives

Objectives that flow from the strategic plan provide both short- and long-term direction. They will be your performance benchmarks. You may want to develop objectives for profitability, employee safety, market share, productivity, public responsibility, physical and financial resources, employee satisfaction, quality, and customer satisfaction.

Effective objectives possess four key characteristics:

1. **They are written.** Use clear, unambiguous language to help employees understand and commit to them.

2. **They are measurable.** Instead of writing, "We want to increase profits," write, "We want to increase profits by 10%."

3. **They have a deadline.** Specifically state that, "We want to increase profits by 10%," and add, "in the next 12 months."

4. **They are challenging but attainable.** Setting unrealistic goals leads to frustration. At the same time, setting the bar so low that it doesn't require team members to reexamine their work provides no motivation to improve.

Analyzing Your Situation

Before you can achieve your objectives, you must understand how your internal organization stacks up against your competitors' and your current position in the marketplace.

External Analysis

The external environment encompasses everything outside the organization that influences your decisions and your company's performance.

- Study the market you will build in.
- Identify what market segment can afford and will purchase your product.
- Identify your price point.

Look at the factors that directly determine the supply and demand for housing in your market. These include demographics, economics, political and legal factors, competitors' actions, social and cultural trends, and technological change.

- **Demographics.** Is the population growing or declining in your area? What is the breakdown by age groups of your population? What is the household size?

- **Housing economics.** What are current interest rates? Are they rising, falling, or stable? What is household income? What is the unemployment rate? Are prices rising?

- **Income and disposable income.** What can the market afford? What percentage of the available market will be able to buy your home?

- **Political and legal concerns.** Laws, regulations, and the changing political winds can expand or constrain your freedom to build and develop land. Pay attention to planning and zoning regulations and decisions, environmental regulations, and who is contributing to political campaigns.

- **The competition.** You must study key competitors' strengths and weaknesses to be able to accurately predict their strategic moves, but keep in mind you cannot control the competition, you can only control your company. Understand your competitive edge—what your product will provide that creates more perceived and actual value than other builders' offerings

Your external analysis will help you identify potential opportunities and threats. You may discover a market that nobody else is serving, one that is underserved, or one that is being served but is still growing, which will allow you to enter that market. You also may discover trade contractor shortages, labor shortages, or both; environmental regulations; or economic conditions that you will need to overcome.

Internal Analysis

An internal analysis identifies and evaluates the company's strengths and weaknesses. A strength can be a skill, expertise in a critical area, or a significant resource. Your strengths might be a construction superintendent who has long-term relationships with quality trade contractors, a prime piece of property, an established reputation for building quality homes, or a strong financial position.

Typical weaknesses for home builders include the lack of managerial talent, insufficient capital, or below-average marketing skills. You can overcome these weaknesses without incurring more overhead. Successful builders carefully review strategies with financial and business associates and partners to expose blind spots. These associates may include local lenders and brokers that know the market, your legal and financial counsel, political and business leaders in the area, and experienced builders. Do what successful people do.

A thorough internal analysis will encompass both company resources and activities. The various stakeholders in your organization include customers, suppliers, trade contractors, employees, investors, and the communities in which each of these operates. Evaluate your financial strength, access to capital, reputation, human resources, management systems, trade contractor base, and equipment. Then assess your company's activities. Look at your target market, geographic area, and the types of work that employees and trade contractors perform. Your own experience, information from employees, and company records, such as budgets and other financial reports, are helpful data sources.

Developing a Strategy

Typically, a builder's strategy should encompass what the company will do and the resources it will use over the next two to five years. Your strategies should advance your objectives, given the opportunities you have identified and the resources your company has.

The following questions will help you develop your strategy:

- Will you develop your own lots, or will you purchase developed lots?
- Will you target one or multiple market segments?
- Will you employ your own crews or use trade contractors?
- Will you build inventory homes or require that all starts be presold?

These general questions apply to all builders, but you want your strategy to create an advantage over your competitors. You can gain this competitive advantage through differentiation, price leadership, or both.

Differentiation

Differentiation means offering customers unique products or services that are more attractive than your competitors'. You differentiate your company with unique attributes such as superior design, outstanding customer service, a distinguished reputation for quality, or a combination of these.

Price Leadership

Price leadership is not haphazardly slashing sales prices to undercut your competition and unload unsold inventory. Rather, builders develop a competitive pricing advantage by always offering their homes at lower prices than competitors while they achieve above-average margins. If you decide to pursue price leadership as a strategy, you must be able to produce homes at a lower cost than your competitors can.

Implementing a Strategy

Before you can accomplish your strategy, you must do these three things:

1. **Assemble a team.** Hire or align yourself with employees, trade contractors, suppliers, brokers, and lenders who have the knowledge, skills, and abilities to achieve the organization's objectives.

2. **Set goals.** Help each team member develop specific goals that support the company's objectives. Assume, for example, that a company objective is to reduce variances in framing material costs by 20 percent. To achieve this objective, your estimator's goal could be to improve estimating accuracy by 10 percent, and your construction superintendent's goal could be to reduce waste by 15 percent.

3. **Allocate resources.** You will use project budgets and schedules to allocate resources so employees can achieve their goals and the company can achieve its objectives.

Writing Policies and Procedures

Because builders operate in a constantly changing environment, they continually must reevaluate, update, and modify their plans, and reengineer procedures. Some policies, however, seldom change. They provide consistency and standards for employee behavior. You must establish policies for areas such as marketing, customer service, personnel, and production. Following are sample policy statements:

- We will do whatever we must to ensure customer satisfaction.
- We will not shop trade contractor bids.

- Employees and trade contractors are not permitted to drink alcohol while on the job.
- Everyone must wear safety goggles when operating power tools.

A procedure is a series of steps that accomplishes a specific project or endeavor. It may evolve over time. Your procedures govern activities such as the following:

- Comparing invoices with purchase orders
- Handling trade contractor requests for draws
- Performing a customer walk-through

Monitoring Progress

Because planning is ongoing, you must develop systems to monitor progress and take corrective action as needed. Therefore, you must establish performance indicators to help determine whether your company is achieving its goals. Your company must have an information system that provides data relevant to the performance indicators and budgets and schedules to guide and evaluate progress toward reaching goals.

Writing a Business Plan

After you have established your mission, objectives, and strategies for accomplishing them, you need a written plan. This plan will be your guide for running your business and a tool for others you rely on:

- **Employees.** They will use the plan to guide their actions and decision making.
- **Lenders.** Attach a summary of the plan to your loan applications so your bank knows you are a professional with a sound business strategy.
- **Potential investors.** Venture capitalists will look to the plan to help them judge whether they will receive a return commensurate with the risks they will assume.

Ideally, a written business plan is well organized, neatly typed, grammatically correct, and in general presents a professional company image to outsiders. Hiring a professional editor to read your plan is a wise investment. Your written plan should be written and organized so a reader can digest the information at a glance. You can include supplemental pages with additional information. A well-developed written business plan will include each of the following elements:

Cover page. Include the business name, address, phone number, and the names of the principals of the company.

Executive summary. Concisely and convincingly summarize key elements of your plan. Many readers will evaluate the entire plan based on the executive summary. It should grab and hold the reader's attention, and convey credibility and integrity.

Company overview. Detail the company's structure, staff, and operations, including reporting relationships and the company's philosophy toward employees and customers. Explain:

- The company's history, including how long it has been in business
- Financial information for at least the previous two years
- Descriptions of the company's previous projects, including styles, sizes, and prices
- Descriptions of the company's current and proposed projects
- Whether you develop your own lots or purchase developed lots
- Markets and customers the company serves
- The number of projects completed annually and the amount of revenue they generate
- Background, education, and experience of key employees
- Descriptions of the company's major competitors

Marketing plan. Identify the target market and describe its geographic location, demographics, and psychographics. Discuss major competitors' strengths and weaknesses and explain how your company will compete effectively. Address the four Ps of the *marketing mix*: product, promotion, price, and place.

- Describe your home types, sizes, and styles.
- Discuss promotional plans. Explain how you will create customer awareness and motivate customers to buy. Include plans for advertising, sales promotions, publicity, and sales.
- Detail your pricing strategy. Specify how you determine prices based on your costs and competitors' prices.

Financial plan. Forecast the company's financial results, or *pro forma financial statements*, for at least the next five years. Use *balance sheets*, income statements, *cash flow statements*, and *break-even analyses*. You can make monthly projections for the first year, quarterly for the second and third years, and annually for the remaining years.

Support your assertions, particularly cash flow projections, with well-substantiated assumptions and explanations. Include construction loan payments and the owner's salary as well as direct construction costs in your projections. You should be able to answer the following questions before beginning any development or construction work:

- If administrative and project overhead is fixed at $20,000 per month and it takes 12 months to improve a lot and build a home, how much cash do I need?
- If my overhead is $20,000 per month and I sell two homes per month at 25% gross profit, what will my net profit be?
- If I reduce my sales price to increase velocity to three homes sold per month, will I still make enough to cover my costs and earn a profit?
- How much would I earn by raising gross profit from 25 to 28% and reducing construction costs by 6%?

Developing scenarios like this on paper before you begin building must and will become second nature as part of the way you do business. Whether your plan is an internal management tool or an introduction for potential lenders or investors, it must demonstrate that your company will generate enough cash to pay bills on time.

Plan to be Successful

Review your business plan regularly to ensure that the daily challenges of earning a living do not derail your long-term goals for your company. Your plan is a map for getting to the business you envision. Refer to it often in analyzing alternatives, making decisions, and taking appropriate steps to finance, market, and maintain or grow your company.

7

Marketing

By Daniel R. Levitan, MIRM, IRM Fellow, CAASH, CMP, CSP, CPB
President, Levitan & Associates, Fort Lauderdale, Florida

Most builders equate marketing with advertising. Although advertising certainly is one important facet of marketing, the marketing process begins well before bringing a home to market and includes a number of other essential elements.

Marketing encompasses all activities and processes for creating, communicating, and delivering products to consumers. For home builders, these activities and processes include the following:

- Identifying viable purchaser segments and their specific needs, wants, and desires
- Creating the correct housing products in the right location that can be sold at the right price
- Informing prospective purchasers about available homes and features and maintaining their interest in and desire for them
- Creating a process to transform interest into sales
- Forming long-term relationships that will increase brand awareness and create referrals and repeat business

To compete effectively in today's environment, builders must develop a marketing orientation to advance the company's purpose: to survive and prosper by satisfying customers' needs and desires while earning a profit. To do this you must first identify your target market and pinpoint its needs, wants, and desires. Then you must satisfy the market more efficiently and effectively than your competitors can. Your competitors include not just other builders offering new homes but also resale and rental inventory.

Marketing Functions

Identifying target markets and developing an appropriate marketing mix for each requires a number of specialties, including the following:

- Marketing research
- Land planning
- Design
- Merchandising
- Public relations
- Advertising
- Graphic design

You can perform these functions yourself, hire other professionals to do them, or combine approaches. Your approach will depend on your areas of expertise and available time. Because finding and capitalizing on a niche and developing an appropriate marketing mix are vital to your success, you must ensure that whoever performs these marketing functions is professional. He or she must develop an independent and unbiased strategy based on fact-finding research.

Market Driven: Four Principles

A market-driven company

- understands its customers;
- focuses on customer satisfaction;
- seeks long-term profitability rather than short-term profits or sales volume; and
- integrates marketing processes with all other company functions, including land acquisition, design, and production.

Understand your customers. You cannot offer the right product in the right place and at the right price without understanding customers' current and future needs and desires. Ask yourself the following questions:

- Who are my buyers?
- How many people will live in the home? How are they related to each other?

- What are their financial limitations both for an initial investment and monthly payments?
- What are their recreational choices?
- What psychological factors influence their purchase decisions?

Focus on customer satisfaction. Market-driven companies develop products and services with the customer in mind. They provide their customers with a superior value proposition by satisfying customer needs better than their competitors. You can accomplish this by providing lower prices, superior features, unique styles and designs, or a combination of all of these attributes. For example, Lennar's *unique selling proposition (USP)*, "It's all included," provides an array of features within a base-price home.

All company activities must focus on the customer's well-being. This includes not only delivering a quality housing product but also one that is appropriate for the buyer's needs, pocketbook, and comfort. Marketing superior service may be as important as attractive design and efficient home construction for a high-end custom home builder, for example.

One home builder successfully turned delivery of a "defect-free" home into a branding opportunity. This builder attracted repeat business, referrals, and high resale values by having no punch list items at closing and making warranty repairs the first priority for the company and its trade contractors. The positive reputation lowered the company's advertising costs.

Build long-term profitability. A marketing orientation stresses long-term profitability rather than short-term profits or sales volume. Sales volume is not the goal; if it becomes the driving force behind your company, you will be forced to increase your advertising budget, accept low margins, or both.

Integrate marketing efforts. Marketing does not occur in a vacuum. It is only one part of an integrated, company-wide effort. Market-driven builders involve the whole company—land acquisition, design, production, finance, accounting, human resources, and of course, sales and marketing—in satisfying customer needs. The details—your signs, vehicles, and employees' and trade contractors' attitudes and work ethic—convey your company's philosophy and principles. They will influence your success.

One builder developed a training program for his trade contractors to educate them about why his homes were better than competitors'. In one of his communities, the electricians working on his homes were so impressed by his professionalism that they referred friends and relatives, which resulted in five home sales.

Identifying Markets and Developing a Plan

Once you have identified markets, or market segments, you can create products and a marketing plan to target prospective purchasers and appeal to their emotions. No one home design will appeal to all market segments any more than there is a standard restaurant to appeal to all palates. Similarly, a home and community's location, home price, and home size determine which markets will respond to it. Therefore, homesite and home design selection are fundamental to effective and successful marketing.

Before you begin to market your homes, you must have a thoughtful marketing plan. Your plan should answer the following questions:

1. Who are potential customers?
2. Where are they, and how will you reach them?
3. What marketing efforts have you used successfully in the past?
4. Which marketing efforts did not work?
5. Who are your competitors, and what are their advantages and disadvantages?
6. What competing products are available and at what prices?
7. What is the market's attitude toward competitors' products?
8. What marketing techniques do your most successful competitors use?
9. What marketing techniques do your least successful competitors use?
10. What are your company's strengths and weaknesses?
11. What are your overall company objectives for the next year?
12. What are your company objectives for the next five years?

Identifying a Niche

As a builder, you cannot be all things to all people. Your chances for success increase dramatically when you choose a market segment and serve it exceptionally well, so identify potential markets, choose one, and position your company to compete effectively in it. Builders commonly serve a specific geographic area, a particular demographic, or both. You can divide a market by geography, demographics, psychographics, and behaviors. Ask the following questions before deciding which market(s) to target:

1. Is it large enough to support the anticipated level of activity?
2. Are competitors already serving the market well?
3. Do you have, or can you acquire, the knowledge, skills, and resources needed to compete in the market?

Geographic Segmentation

Divide the market into different geographic areas—regions, states, counties, cities, or neighborhoods—to determine the areas in which to build and the styles, features, and amenities that are popular in each one. Most small-volume builders segment their market geographically by building only in two or three towns or neighborhoods within the metro area and designing and building homes appropriate to their locality.

To understand market segments, you can look at a population's age range, family sizes, income, and where households fall within the family life cycle. Housing needs align closely with these demographic variables. Following are eight classifications that embody life cycle, although methods to project housing needs are as varied as marketing theories:

1. Singles—unmarried individuals living alone
2. Tandems—two persons who share a dwelling but are not a couple
3. Single parents—separated, divorced, widowed, or never-married people who have one or more children living with them
4. Professional couples—married or cohabiting couples who are both employed income earners
5. Traditional couples—childless married couples with one spouse working
6. Empty nesters—older, traditional married couples with one spouse employed and no children living with them
7. Seniors—retired or semiretired couples and singles
8. Couples with children—one- and two-income earners with children living at home

Positioning the Company

Position your company and its products to compete effectively in the marketplace. Your competitive position reflects how potential customers perceive you and your products compared with competitors. Consumers typically choose products that provide the greatest value. Thus, the key to winning and keeping customers is to understand customer needs better than your competitors do and to use that understanding to add value. You could offer a home comparable to your competitors' at a lower price, or you could provide a higher-priced home with more benefits. To maintain your position in the marketplace, you must deliver what you promise. If you say you build the highest quality homes, you must do it.

Ongoing Market Research

Marketing research provides objective data on which to base your business decisions.

Because consumer tastes are changing constantly, home designs that were successful in the past may not attract today's or tomorrow's buyers. Therefore, reassess your market regularly. Your market research should help you answer these six important design and location questions:

1. Where are the current "hot" market areas?
2. Who is my competition?
3. What is currently selling and why?
4. What is my market willing to pay today?
5. What do my home designs (styles, sizes, room sizes, and functions) need to provide to compete both with other new homes and with resales?
6. What features do my customers want included as standard?

To answer these questions you can use two types of research: primary and secondary.

Primary Research

Primary research is conducted specifically for your use and typically comes directly from the source. The following three strategies exemplify primary research:

1. Shopping the competition. One of the most effective and cost-efficient ways to learn about housing supply is to visit area new home developments and model homes periodically. Get information on available homes, homesites, recent sales, and builders' marketing programs. Bring a camera and a checklist to record the following information objectively and systematically:

   - Sales prices
   - Home types and styles
   - Square footage
   - Prices per square foot
   - Number of bedrooms and baths
   - Included and optional features
   - Lot sizes and densities
   - Amenities
   - Details about the sales environment and sales process

Although geographic market areas vary widely, in general, you should collect information on projects within your submarket—either a specific town or, in larger metro areas, within a 5–10-mile radius of your property. You can use Microsoft® Excel to chart or graph quantitative information and show trends. Builders should use the comparative shopping process to identify what their competitors are doing as well as what they are not doing. What customer needs are not currently being satisfied?

2. Focus groups. If you have the resources to convene a focus group, it can be a viable alternative to a large-scale survey. The NAHB Research Center has experienced facilitators who run focus groups, which typically consist of 3 to 10 individuals who fit a target market profile. Focus groups can provide useful information on location, product features, building materials, prices, and other preferences. You should present these groups with a limited number of choices and prices to get useful feedback. (When the sky's the limit, buyers usually will choose designs and features that cost more than what they actually are willing to pay.)

3. Customer and visitor surveys. You should gather information regularly from your visitors using e-mail, direct mail, telephone calls, and personal visits. One builder in central Florida required his sales team to visit his buyers in their homes 90 days after closing to solicit feedback on what the company could be doing better. Buyers could demonstrate "live" the areas that could be improved. The sales associates provided a thank-you gift to the buyers and asked for referrals.

Ask your buyers the following questions:

- Why did you purchase a home from us rather than from another builder?
- What do you like best about your home? What do you like least?
- What would you do differently if you were buying your new home today?
- What do you think about the quality of your home?
- How was the service you received?

Secondary Research

Secondary research is information gathered from an existing source that usually has been prepared by and for someone else. Consult multiple sources for a comprehensive view of the market:

Professional Associations. Join NAHB to receive *Nation's Building News* and *Builder* magazine. Join the National Sales and Marketing Council to learn about other builders' successful marketing programs. Subscribe to HousingEconomics. com to receive regular information about regional and national housing trends. Local HBAs also can provide valuable information or refer you to other good sources.

Government statistics. Consult your city or county building departments for information on housing starts or check the permit information for any county at http://socds.huduser.org/permits/index.html. The U.S. Department of Labor has information on state and local employment. Local planning departments have your area's master plan for land use and zoning, population projections, and plans for new or improved infrastructure and developments.

Real estate professionals. Real estate agents know what buyers are looking for in a home and the niches your competitors already are filling. They are also familiar with other new homes and communities in your area. Real estate appraisers have detailed information about home sizes, features, and prices. Because each individual may be familiar with only a limited part of the market, you can piece together a more comprehensive picture by developing relationships with many agents and appraisers. If your local Realtor® belongs to the Multiple Listing Service (MLS), he or she may provide sales statistics that may include new homes as well as resales.

Lenders. Banks and other mortgage lenders often study their market area and can provide current information.

Creating a Marketing Strategy

Share your written marketing strategy with your team, which should include your architect or home designer, land planner, engineer, estimators, construction staff or trades, sales associates or real estate agents, advertising agency, home merchandiser or interior designer, warranty service staff or company, and anyone else who helps construct and deliver homes to buyers. A comprehensive marketing strategy includes sharing a written document with all team members to ensure everyone is following the same program. Everyone on your team should understand precisely who your targeted home buyer is and what will satisfy his or her physical and emotional needs. Without this coordinated approach, you risk designing a home for one type of buyer, furnishing it for a second and entirely different demographic, and advertising it to a third group that does not fit the profile outlined in your marketing strategy.

You can pay consultants to develop your marketing strategy, but doing it yourself is worth the time and effort it takes.

Two key elements lay the foundation for your marketing strategy:

1. Researching the market, competition, properties, and players
2. Developing a logical and comprehensive program based on the results

Consider each of the following factors in developing your marketing strategy. They influence what consumers do and how successful you will be.

Economic factors. Understand both local and national trends. Both should influence your strategy. Answer these three questions:

1. Is the economy growing or shrinking?
2. What is the local and national employment picture? What kinds of jobs, if any, is the economy creating?
3. What are interest rates and underwriting requirements for loans?

Beyond these numbers, though, your strategy must acknowledge and address a critical factor that influences home sales: the buyer's perception of the facts. Even if a prospect has a secure job, he or she will be skittish if there is a barrage of bad employment news. Similarly, if a consumer knows someone whose loan application was rejected, he or she may fear being turned away as well. Skilled sales associates understand how to ask questions that will identify buyer concerns and allay fears.

Demographics and psychographics. Notice changes in the following three areas:

1. Population trends (births, deaths, in- and out-migration)
2. Household formation and composition (family size, age, income)
3. Consumer motivation (who the potential buyers are, how they live, and what they think)

Housing activity. Observe current permit and construction activity as well as activity during the previous 10 years to determine the normal levels of housing absorption. What product has the local market preferred? Single-family detached homes? Townhomes? Condominiums? Rental apartments? Observe pricing trends. Gather sales data for the past 4–5 years from personal research and observation, from a friendly Realtor's MLS data, from a housing service report, or all of these sources. Divide sales into quintiles by price. Notice whether the prevailing price points in the market are selling by looking at average time on market (90 days or fewer indicates a hot market) for resales.

Competition. Observe which builders and products are selling in the residential market, and who is buying. Analyze home sales by location. Most markets have developed strong preferences for—and prejudices against—specific locales (town, school district, side of town, urban, suburban). Which market segments are buying homes? Which builders are active in the market? Examine existing homesite inventory (improved and approved) and entitled developments to see your probable future competition. Shop individual builders. Determine which home styles, designs, and plans are selling, and why. Look at the sales office, gallery, staff, brokers, and product.

Company capacity. What is your financial capacity? What is your construction and development experience and capability? What are your short- and long-term professional and personal goals? These factors should influence your marketing strategy. After you assemble this data and analyze the research, you can see where the sales opportunities are and start to build your marketing program. A strategic marketing program will maximize opportunities identified in your market research as follows:

Target a market. There is no universal housing product. To target a market, consider the following factors:

- Age
- Household size
- Household composition
- Lifestyle
- Financial capability
- Current housing status

Create the product. After you identify the target market, create a product the market will buy, considering the following factors:

- Price
- Home type and style
- Floor plan
- Included features and options
- Site orientation
- Exterior design

Develop a USP. What differentiates you from your competition? Your USP can focus on price, quality, or differentiated market position. Your target market determines the focus, but to market your product successfully, you must choose one.

1. **Price.** You offer the lowest price, typically by reducing design elements and limiting features and finishes included in your standard product line.

2. **Quality.** You provide above-average design elements, features, and finishes within the standard product line.

3. **Differentiated market position.** You create a unique product for your market or locality, such as duplex homes where the prevailing product is single family, an age-restricted community, a themed or service-included community, or a certified green home or development.

Any of these market positions is valid as long as your research uncovers an unmet need and a viable target market.

Implement. How will you inform your market about your product and stimulate interest, instill desire, and prompt prospects to visit your sales center or model home(s)? How do you present yourself and differentiate yourself from the competition? What must you do to provide an effective sales environment and process to maximize sales?

Developing the Product

Once you have positioned your company and selected a target market, you must choose where to build, design products to meet the designated price points, and price the product so you can market it.

- **Location.** Evaluate possible locations according to whether they satisfy your target market's needs and expectations. Consider:
  - Proximity to shopping areas
  - School quality
  - Community facilities
  - Area amenities
  - Terrain and other physical property features
  - Utility availability
  - Legal entitlements

- ○ Traffic patterns
- ○ First impressions (what your buyers will see when they arrive at the location)
- ○ Existing neighborhood characteristics, including type, price, and age of existing housing
- ○ Demographics of existing population

You can create your own community, build in a larger development that includes other builders, build on scattered sites including infill locations, or build custom homes on a home buyer's land.

- • **Homes.** Builders typically focus on their products' physical characteristics, such as framing lumber, paint, windows, and cabinets. These features, although important, often have little effect on how customers view your homes. Customers buy *benefits* that satisfy their needs, rather than sticks and bricks. Your prospects probably will ponder the following questions before they purchase a home:
  - ○ How long can I comfortably live in this house?
  - ○ Will it maintain its value?
  - ○ Will it accommodate my growing family?
  - ○ Is this an area where my family wants to live?

You must demonstrate how your product will satisfy a prospect's needs before you attempt to sell (or build) them a home. In developing your USP, consider both the tangible and intangible benefits of owning one of your homes. Tangible benefits could include comfort, safety, prestige, convenience, and financial advantages. Intangible benefits might be better health, education, community, and marital harmony.

No matter how much you invest in building homes, your customer defines "quality." It is a subjective term. The best quality kitchen floor could be vinyl, ceramic tile, or wood, depending on the home buyer's need. Likewise, the best countertop could be laminate, another synthetic, or granite. On the other hand, a home that has not been designed to meet home buyers' needs is not a quality product, even if it incorporates top-of-the-line flooring and countertops.

One approach to exceeding customer expectations and differentiating your product from the competition's is to include as standard a feature that consumers want, but which other builders in the market consider an option or an upgrade. You can accomplish this strategy by eliminating, or making optional, other features that most home buyers do not want or need.

Price. Price is the ultimate amenity. You may have designed and built the most attractive home with the best features in a great location, but if your market cannot afford it, you have built a monument, not a profitable home. In marketing terms, prices should never be based on your cost, which is irrelevant to the consumer. Instead, your market research, including competitors' prices, should determine the price of your homes. Although sales prices, obviously, must be high enough to cover all *direct* and *indirect costs,* overhead, and profit, you must consider the sales volume you need to achieve your annual profit goal (not just the profit on one home).

The following factors also determine prices:

- Initial investment (down payment), monthly investment (monthly payment), and appraised value. All buyers ultimately base their buying decisions on cost. Even cash buyers consider the monthly cost of ownership. Typically, lenders will loan a percentage of the sales price or appraised value, whichever is lower. An appraisal that is lower than the sales price will lower the loan amount and increase the required down payment, thereby reducing the attractiveness of a home.

- Special factors. If you obtain homesites in an exceptionally desirable location, you may be able to add a premium to your prices. Conversely, if you are new to a market, temporarily pricing homes lower than the competition's may help you establish your company and gain name recognition.

Promotion

If you have a great product in a super location that is a good value but nobody knows about it, what good is it? You must promote your product using the appropriate marketing channels and collateral opportunities. Before you can persuade them to buy your homes, buyers must know they exist. Your *promotional mix* includes traditional and online advertising and promotion, and personal selling.

Internet Marketing

As few as 10 years ago, the Internet was merely an afterthought in housing marketing. Today more than 85% of home purchasers use the Internet during their home search and more than half do so to the exclusion of all other media. Your online presence today must incorporate a website, blog, social media site, and online directories.

Effective marketing on the Internet begins with a professionally designed and optimized website. It is the front door to your company and an essential sales tool today, as a burgeoning number of consumers prefers online communication. Your website should appear in the top 10—or at least the top 20—search results when your target market types keywords into a search engine such as Google™, Yahoo!®, Bing®, Ask®, or AOL®.

Successful e-marketing campaigns also include, minimally, your own blog or at least regular posting on other blogging sites your prospects visit, a Facebook® page, a Twitter® account, and a YouTube™ channel. E-marketing requires not only time, but specialized skills, so most builders of all sizes rely on independent marketing professionals to run, or at least assist with, their e-marketing. You also may consider taking a course on e-marketing at a local community college.

Advertising

Effective advertising captures attention, maintains interest, fosters desire, and spurs action *(AIDA)*. Regardless of the specific media you use, your ad must

- grab consumers' attention and make them aware of your company and its products;
- hold their attention long enough for them to develop interest in your company and its products;
- arouse desire for the company's products; and
- elicit consumer action, including visiting the model home or sales office.

Advertising should reflect your brand with consistent logos, layouts, colors, and copy that consumers will identify with your company and its products. You can choose from many vehicles in creating your advertising campaign.

Websites

One method for small builders to dramatically and cost effectively expand their Web presence is through paid listings or advertisements on new home or real estate websites. As of the date this book was published, the following websites were available to list new homes:

- http://www.newhomesdirectory.com
- http://www.newhomesource.com
- http://www.newhomeguide.com
- http://www.trulia.com
- http://www.realtor.com
- http://www.zillow.com

Most local markets offer additional Web portals worth investigating, such as the Chamber of Commerce, and state, county, and municipal sites. Search the Web for a city or town name, and see what pops up.

Periodicals

Newspaper and magazine ads should be concise, simple, and straightforward, never wordy. Although newspapers and magazines have online versions of their publications, be aware that newspaper readership continues to decline. The greatest proportion of newspaper readers is 47 or older, so although they can be part of a comprehensive strategy, you should consider other media to reach younger audiences. Nevertheless, home seekers historically have searched for a new home in the newspaper and newspapers continue to offer opportunities for selling homes in many markets. For example, most newspapers host their own real estate websites. Magazines offer the same benefits as newspapers and also target specific market segments that may include your prospects.

Television

TV allows builders to combine sight, sound, and motion to show home exteriors and interiors to a broad audience, but as with newspapers, its audience continues to age. Prime-time audiences for network programming are, on average, older than the U.S. population and older than the 18–49 age group most advertisers covet. However, audiences naturally vary widely by programming. With the advent of cable and the wide array of channels available, including local channels, you can pinpoint the audience you are trying to reach and better target your ads. Although TV remains the highest-priced medium and offers only fleeting exposure as you compete with other on-the-air advertisers, you can purchase time on local channels affordably. Local access channels with real estate programming offer small-volume builders a cost-effective way to take advantage of the benefits of television advertising.

Radio

A minute of radio advertising during peak listening times can cost less than a comparable minute of TV advertising, making it a cost-effective alternative for small-volume builders. As with television advertising, though, your message will be fleeting and can be forgotten easily among all the other ads. Successful radio campaigns typically include several spots per day over a two- to three-week campaign. Radio ads are often most effective when they accompany an on-site promotion, such as a grand opening or an open house.

Signage

Signage includes two elements—billboards and directional signs. A home or development's location determines the type of signage needed. If you are visible from a main highway, you may only need to post price ranges and directions or arrows pointing to your location. For a remote location, you may need more elaborate and prominent signage to deliver traffic. In most cases, signage is not your primary advertising medium but a supplement that reminds prospects of your presence and helps them find you.

Signs must be located in high-traffic areas. But avoid arraying your signs on "popsicle sticks" along with other builders' on an unkempt highway median that also may include advertisements for junk hauling, garage sales, and babysitting services. That is not the image you want to portray. Be sure your signage reflects well on your brand. Keep your messages simple, brief, and easy to read. Use the colors that identify your brand.

Direct Marketing

Advertising sent only to members of a specific target market is called direct marketing. Letters, brochures, pamphlets, postcards, flyers, and mini-CDs are all examples of direct marketing. This media either can be an effective and cost-efficient advertising option, or end up in the wastebasket. To maximize cost efficiency, you must target direct mail pieces appropriately—to a specific zip code or only to apartment dwellers in your area, for example. You can generate your own mailing lists or purchase lists from a company that specializes in direct mail. Incorporating a special, limited-time offer will increase the effectiveness and response from direct mail.

Sales Promotion

Sales promotion includes activities other than personal selling, advertising, or public relations, although often it combines these other efforts to maximize visibility. Typical sales promotions include preview showings, grand openings, broker parties, resident recognition activities, and periodically offering special included features, free goods, or trips to both consumers and real estate brokers.

Public Relations

A public relations strategy helps builders promote their positive reputation. It also provides the public with information about the company's products, policies, and personnel. If you have company information that a local newspaper, website, or TV or radio station deems newsworthy, the media may communicate it for free.

You will not have to pay for the message as you do to advertise, and you will not be identified as the message sponsor, which enhances the information's credibility. In addition, both free and fee-based websites are available to distribute your press releases online. You can distribute press releases about activities or events such as model home openings, promotions, and company milestones. Specially designated days, weeks, or months provide an angle for your news. Write about your green homes for Earth Day, your kitchens for Better Breakfast Month, your home office spaces for Home Business Month, and safety features for Baby Safety Month. Several builders offer special pricing, discounts, or both, to military personnel, public school teachers, police, firefighters, and other municipal employees. A public relations strategy encompasses much more than distributing press releases, though. Consider sponsoring youth athletic teams, fashion shows, cultural events, automobile shows, or local organizations such as museums and zoos. You also could teach a continuing education class on a familiar topic, such as green building, energy efficiency, building a custom home, or home maintenance.

The Marketing Budget

A realistic marketing budget includes the following items:

1. Start-up costs
2. Sales center or model home expenses
3. Sales center or model homes operating costs
4. Advertising and promotion
5. Collateral materials, such as brochures, newsletters, letterhead, business cards, and thank-you notes
6. Broker sales commissions
7. In-house sales commissions
8. Signage and billboards
9. Referral fees
10. General and administrative marketing expenses, such as market research

Base your budget on your desired objectives. For example, if your *conversion ratio* is 5%, and you want to sell 12 homes per year, you must generate an average of 20 inquiries per month. What marketing activities will generate 20 inquiries and how much will they cost? Most builders budget for these expenses by allocating a specific percentage of their revenue or a specific amount of money per unit sold by actual revenue, units sold during specific periods, expected revenues, or unit sales.

Free Marketing Help

Consider the following free materials, services, and resources in developing your marketing plan and campaigns:

- NAHB's website (http://www.nahb.org) offers members ready-to-use downloadable marketing materials, including ads, TV spots, consumer handouts, and materials for your website.
- The International Builders' Show includes experts who will review and critique your marketing materials.
- The Institute of Residential marketing offers 30-minute phone consultations.
- Local colleges and universities sometimes seek local businesses where students can serve as interns and gain practical marketing experience. Typically, a team of two to five students will work with a local business to identify a problem or an opportunity and develop a plan to address it.

Building and Maintaining Brand

Consistency is the key to developing and maintaining an effective marketing program. To build a powerful brand, marketing should be strategic and ongoing, rather than ad hoc and sporadic. Consistently communicating your message to consumers will ensure that you become a recognized leader in home building, rather than just another local builder. Coordinate everything, and leave nothing to chance. Keep your name fresh in the minds of former customers, prospective buyers, and real estate and other industry professionals. Marketing does not stop after customers buy a new home. Fostering an ongoing relationship can lead to positive word-of mouth advertising, future purchases, and referrals.

8

New Home Sales Management

By Daniel R. Levitan, MIRM, IRM Fellow, CAASH, CMP, CSP, CPB
President, Levitan & Associates, Fort Lauderdale, Florida

Buying or having a new home built is both joyous and stressful for the future home owner. For most of us, purchasing a home is the most significant purchase of our lives. It is emotional because a home is not merely a consumer good; it is the place where we will live and raise our families.

The home purchase decision is all about choices. First, the prospective purchasers must find what is available. Then, they continuously refine and narrow their choices before settling on a single home and then contemplating whether to purchase it. In seeking a new home, buyers consider location, community, the home style, layout and design, features, amenities, the builder's reputation, price and terms, and warranty. The average home seeker initially may consider more than 30 homes, visit more than 15, and return to their favorite homes several times before deciding on one. Buyers may begin searching as early as 4–6 months before finally deciding to buy. The sales process can take several hours and several visits.

Using the Internet, home purchasers now can start the sales process before they actually visit a home. Web concierge and web sales services offer live representatives to chat with prospects in the comfort of their homes, offices, or elsewhere before and after normal business hours. Younger buyers, Millennials (people born in the 1980s and 1990s) and even older Web-savvy purchasers, such as Gen Xers, may eliminate builders from consideration before visiting homes or sales offices if builders don't offer these convenient services.

Moreover, home shoppers today are well prepared and informed. Most search the Internet, read the newspaper, or both, before visiting builders' websites. This makes them more like returning customers than first-time visitors when they visit models, inventory homes, and sales offices. That is, they probably have already eliminated unsatisfactory choices, may be ready to begin serious negotiations, and are unwilling to tolerate a salesperson who will try to sell them with canned presentations that focus on the builder's needs, rather than their own. Sales associates must be able to *qualify* a visitor quickly, identify his or her needs, and develop a presentation that specifically addresses them on the spot. The *critical path*, *relationship selling*, and *interview selling* are all proven techniques that will enable you to sell more homes.

You have three options for selling homes: sell them yourself, hire an in-house sales force, or use real estate brokers.

Selling Your Homes Yourself

There are advantages to selling your homes yourself. No one knows the home better than you. You can point out and explain a home's construction, features, and design, and answer customers' questions. Many customers feel more comfortable working directly with the builder, and builders who sell their own homes may not incur the costs of salesperson salaries and/or broker commissions. However, there are disadvantages to selling your own homes. You must be available at the customer's convenience, which typically will involve weekends and evenings. Also, as discussed above, the process may require several hours and many meetings. For someone lacking a natural affinity for and training in sales, the process can seem long and tedious. Although you may save money by handling your own sales, these potential savings are meaningless if you cannot make a sale. Therefore, most successful builders rely on professional sales associates or real estate agents to handle sales, and they budget for this as a standard cost of doing business.

If you decide not to sell your own homes, then you must choose between creating an in-house sales operation or using a broker. A broker can work with you on a contract basis to provide dedicated full-time sales staff and, other factors being equal, will cost the same per home sale as maintaining your own sales department. Therefore, builders usually base their choice on their philosophy, company structure, and economic model. Among the factors to consider in deciding on a strategy for selling your homes are the following:

- Annual dollar volume of homes sold
- Number of home sales in a year
- Anticipated traffic by day of the week and time of day
- Housing product (presale, speculative, custom, production)
- What competitors offer in their sales facilities, numbers and types of models
- Anticipated life of the development, community, or operation

Although larger builders normally will choose in-house sales operations to maintain operational and procedural consistency, they may use brokers when entering new markets. The latter option reduces overhead and supervision, provides an immediate sales force, and maximizes the broker's existing contacts and established reputation within the local market. Smaller builders may have to use brokers.

Training the Sales Staff

Every sales team member should enroll in the NAHB Certified Sales Professional (CSP) course, an essential introduction to selling new homes as an on-site representative. Advanced CSP programs like "House Construction as a Selling Tool" and "Essential Closing Strategies," can augment their education.

Fortunately, the new home industry also has many excellent professional sales trainers who will work with your staff in a variety of ways—privately in off-site seminars, in on-site presentations, and in one-on-one training. The NAHB International Builders' Show also offers sales education. You can supplement these live training opportunities with books, audiotapes, and video presentations.

Training should increase both selling skills and motivation, but each company must create a program that reflects the individual personality of that company. The sales manager is responsible for daily training. A comprehensive sales training program incorporates the following strategies:

- Before opening a new development, schedule time for the architect, land planner, and interior merchandiser to meet with the sales staff to explain the community, home designs, and special features. Visit homes under construction and walk through several with the construction manager to examine the construction techniques and quality. Demonstrate the homes' livability and the unique benefits they offer.

- Ensure that each member of the sales team individually shops every competitive development and prepares a written analysis of each one to be reviewed and discussed in a group meeting. Repeat these surveys at least quarterly to ensure that your sales team is aware of new products, sales performance, and traffic at your competitors' communities.

- Have each sales associate walk through your community and each home in it, and then prepare a written list of every positive and negative attribute they find. Use the list of negatives to train the sales staff to respond to objections. Turn each potential negative into a strong selling feature.

- Review sales associates' telephone skills or, for new salespeople, schedule a sales training session on telephone selling skills.

- Spend several days role-playing the selling process in the sales office and model homes. It may be uncomfortable for the sales staff to perform in front of the sales manager or peers. But if an associate cannot properly handle the process when there is no sale to be lost, how will they handle a customer when a commission is on the line?

- Videotape a sample sales presentation for each salesperson, and give the tape to that individual to take home and study, looking for opportunities to improve mannerisms, posture, expressions, and voice.

- Hold weekly company-wide sales meetings, alternating the location between a central facility (company or sales office) and a model or production home. Rotate leadership of the meeting among salespeople and have them select the meeting topic. Manager-led meetings should focus on motivation, training, or both, and may include a speaker such as a lender, supplier, trainer, or motivational speaker. Save discussions of sales goals or performance for another time and place. Weekly meetings should provide a positive atmosphere and opportunities for personal improvement.

- Hold weekly meetings in each sales office with that office's sales team (or person), reviewing the traffic and sales for the week and analyzing each visitor to plan the proper approach to generate a return visit and purchase. Work with each salesperson on an individual basis in ongoing role-playing.

- Use mystery shoppers to provide sales associates with a buyer's view of their performance. Record these shopping experiences and give them to the salesperson with the sales manager's report to review and discuss privately, concentrating on opportunities for improvement.

- Hold company-wide sales training meetings semiannually, preferably at an off-site location, featuring an outside sales trainer or motivational speaker. If your company budget will not allow for this, cooperate with other local builders, and pool your resources to pay the best trainer or speaker.

- Require your salespeople to participate actively in their local HBA Sales and Marketing Council (SMC), serve on committees, and regularly attend SMC programs and functions. SMCs provide excellent networking and referral opportunities and useful information about the housing market.

- Require your salespeople to be active members of their local Board of Realtors, serving on committees and regularly attending programs and functions. Like SMCs, these boards provide networking, referral, and information opportunities.

If you manage your sales training well, your staff will perform with confidence. Proper sales management requires the sales manager to be in the field at communities regularly, personally assisting the sales staff in making each sale, rather than sitting in the home office doing paperwork.

In-House Sales

Hiring a sales staff allows a builder to concentrate on other facets of growing a business, knowing that a competent professional is working full time selling his or her homes. Having a dedicated sales staff also will benefit your company because your salespeople

- thoroughly understand your product designs, features, options, pricing, community, location, and your operations;
- know the competitive marketplace and are committed and skilled in selling the benefits of a new, rather than a used, home;
- are available, willing, and able to sell your homes to prospects as they arrive at your model homes or sales offices;
- have a sense of ownership in the home building company that is the sales associate's only source of income from home sales; and
- may save you money, depending on sales volume and compensation structure.

The disadvantages of having your own sales staff include the following:

- Commitment of time and money. There are fixed costs to hire, manage, and maintain your own sales staff. The sales staff must be able to earn acceptable income or the quality of the sales operation will suffer.
- Increased costs per-unit sold as home sales volume declines. Without sufficient sales volume to cover these additional costs, an in-house sales force may cost considerably more on a per-sale basis than outside brokers.
- Required commitment to ongoing training. As with any professional, sales associates require regular professional development to upgrade their skills in selling and ongoing training to keep abreast of the company's products, competitors' offerings, and mortgage sources and rates.

Broker Sales

The advantages of using real estate brokers include the following:

- They are affiliated with the local multiple listing service (MLS) and, usually, with national real estate companies. Although in most markets anyone can list a home with the MLS (for a fee), brokers are familiar with the processes and the specific skills necessary to create and promote a listing, ensure it is current, and maintain its visibility to other brokers.

- They know and understand the local real estate market and have well-developed networks of contacts. Brokers are familiar with competitors' offerings and may have tips about potentially profitable markets that are not being served adequately.

- They understand how to qualify buyers. They work with real estate purchasers every day and are familiar with both the process and the documentation required.

- They have relationships with mortgage lenders. These relationships may provide additional funding, special programs, and incentives because of the loan business they generate.

- They generate less front-end expense compared with an in-house sales associate. Although brokers may get a partial commission with a non-contingent sale, you typically don't compensate a broker until you close a home. Therefore, there is no cost of sale until a home is sold.

- They can assist with design, site selection, procurement, pricing, and marketing research. Although your staff might be able to perform these functions, brokers probably have more expertise in these areas. They are familiar and experienced with a wide range of products and companies in the marketplace and have the background to recommend choices.

The disadvantages of using brokers include the following:

- You will have less control. Whether they concentrate solely on new homes or on both new and resale homes, brokers represent many clients. Brokers and their sales agents are independent contractors who schedule their own activities. Ease of sale, commission rate, and length of time to closing influence which clients or homes they focus their attention on. New construction typically is more complex to sell, takes longer, and offers a lower commission.

- You may not have a dedicated sales representative. Depending on the size and scope (dollar volume) of the builder's operation, brokers may have to rotate staffing among several individuals who will not know the builder's product and operation as well as a full-time salesperson.

To have a workable relationship, the builder and broker must agree in advance who will perform each marketing activity. Some brokers assume most of the marketing responsibilities, handling both promotion and sales. In other cases, the

Selecting a Broker

Evaluate brokers according to the following criteria:

- Experience in new home sales
- Market leadership in sales and with your specific product type
- Professional reputation. What do your competitors say about them?
- Sales history. What percentage of their own and other brokers' listings they have sold. Are they "sellers" or just "listers"?
- Agents' attitudes. Are they friendly and personable?
- Professionalism and presentation. Are the agents knowledgeable and skilled? Is their presentation appropriate for your market?
- Facilities. Will the sales office reflect well on your brand? Is it appropriate?

builder handles promotions and the broker handles only sales. Broker compensation varies depending on how marketing responsibilities are divided between the builder and the broker.

Interview several brokers and the agent(s) they propose to assign to your development to verify compatibility with your operation. Once you agree, negotiate a formal agreement detailing the specific responsibilities and obligations of the parties.

There is no perfect scenario for selling your homes. Assess your situation, evaluate the advantages and disadvantages of each option, and select the method that works best for your company.

Written Agreements

Your written agreement with a broker should specify details in the following areas:

- Staffing
- Compensation
- Advertising
- Promotion
- Cooperative programs
- Marketing strategy
- Systems and reporting

Broker Cooperation

No matter how you decide to staff your sales operation—with in-house sales associates or with agents provided by a real estate broker—you need an effective broker cooperation program to maximize sales. Here's why:

- 80% of home sales are resales
- Brokers handle almost all resales
- Brokers control much of the prospective buyer traffic
- Most major employers use relocation services that include local real estate brokers
- Prospects who already own a home often have their own real estate agent

Therefore, if your marketing and sales strategy does not include brokers, you are not selling as many homes as you could be. Your advertising campaign will have little impact if you don't include real estate brokers or if brokers are steering traffic away from your new homes or communities. Although first-time home purchasers and self-motivated pre-retirees, retirees, or vacationers may investigate new homes on their own, the real estate brokerage community controls the traffic needed to generate new home sales.

Effective cooperative arrangements with brokers can account for 25%–75%, or more, of the total sales in a new home development. Use the following strategies to maximize your relationships with brokers:

- Mail information (snail mail and e-mail) regularly to all MLS agents.
- Schedule on-site broker events (breakfasts, brunches, holiday parties) for each brokerage office in addition to larger events where you include all agents.
- Participate in caravan tours of communities conducted by each major brokerage in your area at least twice a year.
- Distribute flyers announcing new homes or special promotions at brokers' weekly sales meetings.
- Present information about your communities at monthly real estate board meetings.
- Deliver flowers or candy when a cooperative sale is signed or holiday gifts to the brokers who promote the new home community.
- Prominently mention cooperating brokers' activity, such as community visits and sales, in blogs, and on social media sites such as Facebook® and Twitter®.

Managing Broker Relations

- Create a written procedure for broker cooperation.
- Register all prospects who visit your sales office and homes.
- Follow up with agents to confirm registration of their clients.
- Keep the referring agent updated on home construction progress and the projected closing date.
- Allow agents to refer a prospect by phone.

Broker Incentives

Bonuses and contests create excitement and provide an extra sales incentive for brokers. Programs should have seasonal or special appeal; give away something that the agents might not purchase on their own. There must be a realistic opportunity to win the grand prize. Offer several smaller prizes so everyone is a winner.

Local licensing laws typically forbid paying an agent directly. Most state real estate laws require paying commissions directly to the broker who then may distribute the commission money or, in this case, the prize, according to its own internal policies. To maximize agent involvement, brokers must agree to pass bonuses or contest prizes to the agent.

Another option for encouraging broker cooperation is to advance part of the commission payment to the cooperating broker—generally one-half—after receiving a signed purchase contract with no contingencies and with a nonrefundable purchase deposit.

Your goal is to draw agents to your sales office and model homes, build trust with the on-site sales associate, and show them that selling your homes is easy and lucrative.

Model Homes

If your volume can support them, consider staging model homes as part of your sales strategy. Model homes should demonstrate the superior quality of your construction and attention to detail. A model should highlight your homes' special features, reflect a particular lifestyle, demonstrate that rooms are spacious and livable, and show prospects that they would be comfortable living in one of your homes. To highlight your homes' benefits in a model, consider lighting, color, optional features, furnishings, and accessories.

- Scale furniture correctly for room size.
- Accent doors and windows to make rooms appear spacious.
- Include built-in storage to demonstrate efficient use of space.
- Choose color palettes that exude warmth.
- Spark buyers' emotions with accessories.

Your model should invite visitors to "try on" one of your homes.

Poor staging can turn a good product into a white elephant, so merchandise your models appropriately to your target market. They should appeal to the budget, age, and taste of your prospects. Budget enough for design, furnishings, landscaping, and home maintenance as well as construction. The cost of the furnished model can vary dramatically, but typically you should plan to spend 25%–40% of the retail price of the home. A professionally merchandised model home should generate a premium when you sell it. When you sell the furnishings, you should be able to recapture 50% of the initial cost. You also will need to calculate the following into the cost of maintaining a model:

- Utilities
- Property taxes
- Regular cleaning
- Repairs
- Insurance

Finally, don't underestimate the opportunity cost of using capital to provide a model. It must generate enough incremental sales to be a good investment, perhaps a minimum of two additional sales per year. However, if your competitors display furnished models, and your market expects to see them, consider model homes a cost of doing business.

When a physical model is not financially feasible, many builders today use virtual models created by a professional home merchandiser. They cost a fraction of what a model does in the initial investment and ongoing expenses. If a virtual model is not a good investment, you can use inventory homes or even one of your buyer's homes as a sales tool.

Building new homes and residential communities can be fun and profitable, but there is no profit until you close a home sale. The vitality and viability of your home building company begins and ends with your ability to sell what you build. Invest the time, money, and commitment to convert leads into prospects and, finally, into home buyers.

Managing for Success

Builders are responsible for educating salespeople about the design and construction of homes, the builder's operation, and the benefits of features the homes provide. To generate peak performance and maximize sales, sales management must extend far beyond an initial orientation to include regular coaching, training, and retraining in sales skills, customer follow-up, financing, new consumer markets, and other areas. Brokers usually will include sales management in their service contract. When you commit to running your sales operation in-house, you also must act as a sales trainer, coach, and motivator.

In addition, you must be able to analyze all visitor and sales activity to create performance standards based on historical data and to judge your sales effectiveness weekly.

- Is your advertising generating adequate numbers of visitors?
- How many visits does it take to create a sale?
- How much time elapses from first visit to signed purchase agreement?
- Is the traffic from the target market profile you originally anticipated, or are you attracting new buyer segments that warrant an adjustment to your advertising?
- How many homes have you sold, and what do you need to do to improve results?

Request referrals. Ask prospects and buyers who else might like living in your community or in one of your custom homes. Simple, well-timed questions can lead to prequalified prospects and more sales.

9

Estimating

Your success depends heavily on producing timely, accurate cost estimates. With volatile material costs and market uncertainties, your risk will decline significantly when the actual costs of your projects align closely with estimates. Developing accurate estimates is the first step to bringing a project in on budget.

Whether the project is an inventory home or a high-end custom home, the key to maximizing profitability is creating an accurate cost estimate before construction. If estimates are too high, you will not be competitive, and you may lose jobs. If estimates are low, you may win jobs but sacrifice profit.

Here are additional reasons to ensure your estimates are accurate:

- If you build custom homes, your project bids to potential clients rely on accurate cost estimates.
- If you are contemplating a speculative project, you need an accurate estimate to determine whether the expected costs are commensurate with the projected selling price.
- Estimates contain details vital to scheduling, purchasing, cost control, and cash flow projections.
- You can use estimates to provide lenders with key information to evaluate a project.
- Estimates provide information architects can use in designing projects.

If your estimates are within 3% (higher or lower) of the final cost of a home, your methods are working well.

Principles and Practices

To create accurate estimates, you must understand basic construction principles and local construction practices thoroughly. Builders stay on top of construction information and trends by investigating new methods and materials; finding dependable, cost-effective sources of materials and labor; and knowing applicable building codes and site restrictions. Estimates are useless if they overlook or omit important items.

To develop accurate estimates, you must be able to read drawings and specifications, perform basic mathematical calculations, and know how to use an architect's scale. The scale allows you to translate measurements on scaled drawings into full-scale measurements. Accurate estimators are detail-oriented individuals who check their work.

Some builders who subcontract construction activities omit estimating. Instead, they merely obtain bids from trade contractors, total them, and add a percentage or a lump sum to cover overhead and profit. If this is how you operate, you cannot evaluate trade contractor bids properly, and even builders who use trade contractors extensively must develop at least some portions of their estimates.

Three Types of Estimates

Builders use different types of estimates, depending on the situation. There are three types of estimates:

- Square foot
- Unit cost
- Detailed

The level of detail, accuracy, and the time required to develop them distinguish each type of estimate.

Square foot estimates are the quickest and easiest to complete. They provide "ballpark" costs. Unit cost estimates generally require more information and time, but in some cases provide a more accurate estimate. Detailed estimates require more time and information, but they are the most precise.

To choose the appropriate method, you must evaluate trade-offs between speed, detail, and accuracy. For example, if a client merely needs to determine whether a proposed house plan falls within a particular price range, you can provide a square-foot or unit-cost estimate. However, if a client expects a firm bid, or if you are estimating the cost of a speculative project, a detailed estimate can reduce risk significantly. It is worth the extra time and effort.

The level of detail in the documents you start with often dictates the estimating method. Square-foot estimates typically rely on design drawings, perhaps from a plan book. Detailed estimates generally use detailed construction documents, such as finished architectural renderings and allowances for customer selection items.

Builders who provide ballpark estimates should protect themselves by informing customers that the numbers may change after a final detailed estimate is prepared. Keep in mind that customers will focus on the lowest figure in a price range. Their selective recollection can come back to haunt you.

Square Foot

You can complete the square-foot estimate in a few minutes by multiplying the home's dimensions in square feet by the expected cost per square foot. The following factors limit the usefulness of square-foot estimates:

Determining the appropriate cost per square foot. You generally rely on the costs of previously completed homes. Therefore, the accuracy of your square-foot estimate depends on how closely the project you are estimating matches previous projects. Small-volume builders' projects may not be similar enough to one another to develop meaningful square-foot cost information. Even if you use just a few select designs, perhaps you modify the elevations or substitute materials significantly to add variety. Builders who create a unique product with each new home, but use square-foot estimating, may be taking unnecessary risk.

Cost variations from one area of a home to another. Kitchen and bath costs are much higher than costs for a family room or bedroom. Because costs in the high-ticket areas are spread over more square feet, larger homes will have a lower overall cost per square foot. Consider a builder accustomed to building homes in the 1,800-square-foot range. He or she might underestimate the cost of constructing a 1,500-square-foot home significantly.

Nonliving spaces such as porches, garages, and unfinished basements. The sizes and construction details of nonliving spaces vary greatly from plan to plan, which reduces the accuracy of square-foot estimates that lump the costs of all areas together. You could calculate the cost of nonliving spaces at one-half their actual area. However, keep in mind that the costs to do framing and foundation work do not vary according to the ultimate use of a space.

Outdated cost records or price escalation. If cost information is old, or if labor, materials, or trade contractor prices have changed substantially, historical costs are irrelevant. Builders not only must use current cost data, they must be confident the costs will not escalate during the project.

Unit Cost

The unit-cost estimate, which computes the cost of each home component separately, may yield a more accurate estimate. These *assemblies* typically are the floor system, roof system, exterior walls, interior walls, and cornice. You can create other assemblies depending on your construction methods and materials.

After identifying all assemblies, you select a unit of measure for each. You measure an assembly that varies in only one direction, such as a standard 8-foot-high exterior wall, in linear feet. Other assemblies, such as floor systems that vary in two dimensions, are measured in square feet. Figure 9.1 shows a sample list of assemblies and corresponding units of measure.

After you identify individual assemblies and select the appropriate measurement, you develop a complete list of materials, labor, and trade contractors for each. A footing, for example, includes concrete, rebar, and trade contractor costs.

Each assembly has its own unit measurement.

Next, determine unit costs for all materials in the assembly. Based on your experience, published cost information, trade contractor bids, and supplier quotes, you determine a per-unit cost for the material in each assembly. You can obtain

Figure 9.1 Typical Assemblies

Assembly	Typical Unit Measure
Footing	Linear Feet
Foundation	Square Feet
Floor Framing	Square Feet
Wall Framing	Square Feet
Roof Framing	Square Feet
Insulation	Square Feet
Roofing	Square
Windows	Each
Exterior Doors	Each
Brick	One Thousand
Siding	Square
Cornice	Linear Feet
Interior Doors	Each
Interior Trim	Square Feet
Cabinets	Linear Feet
Floor Covering	Square Feet
Painting	Square Feet
Drywall	Square Feet
Heating, Venting, and Air Conditioning	Square Feet
Electrical	Square Feet
Plumbing	Drain Outlets
Lighting	Allowance
Appliances	Allowance

labor costs from trade contractor bids, previous jobs, and published compilations of construction costs.

Compute the cost of each unit by multiplying the assembly's unit cost by the number of units required for the job. Finally, total the costs of all assemblies to arrive at a total cost for the project.

After computing the cost of each assembly, the estimator totals all, adds other construction-related costs such as permits, fees, and *indirect construction costs*, and includes overhead and profit.

Because the unit-cost method allows the builder to pinpoint costs for individual components of a house, it generally is more accurate than a square-foot estimate. It has a number of limitations, however. The estimate is accurate only if the builder has sufficient information to determine accurate unit costs. Finding these is time consuming and requires a significant amount of construction experience with the type of house being estimated.

Many builders like the unit-cost estimate because once you calculate a per-unit price for a specific assembly, you can reuse it without recalculating. But unit-cost estimates, like square-foot estimates, often use historical information that may or may not reflect current market prices. Changes in costs for any of the materials, labor, or trade contractors that comprise an assembly will throw off the estimate.

Detailed

A detailed estimate lists each item to be part of the home and provides an estimated quantity, price, and total cost for each item. You compute the total estimated cost for the project by adding up all the item costs. These estimates typically include the following:

- Materials
- Labor
- Trade contractors
- Equipment
- Cleanup
- Temporary utilities

Depending on a job's complexity and the tools or technology used to create an estimate, a detailed estimate can take from a few hours to several days. Computer programs, including Microsoft® Excel, have dramatically reduced the time requirement for complete detailed estimates. If it is done correctly, a detailed estimate is the most accurate type of estimate. Therefore, it will reduce risk. It increases your control over the job. Always use a comprehensive and detailed estimate to develop bids.

- Identify each item of material, labor, trade contract, equipment, or fee required to complete the job.
- Determine the quantity (in measurable units) of each item.
- Apply the current market price per unit to each item.
- Multiply the estimated quantity (total units) by the unit price for each item.
- Add the costs for all items to obtain the total cost for the job.

Detailed estimates offer three distinct benefits over square-foot and unit-cost estimates.

1. With a little experience, most builders can produce estimates that consistently predict actual costs with a narrow margin of error.
2. Detailed estimates compile a complete list of materials, labor, and trades. This information is used in budgets, purchasing, and scheduling.
3. Detailed estimates allow the builder to identify and investigate variances, or discrepancies, between estimated and actual costs. You can use this information to help control costs and improve future estimates.

Of the three types of estimates—square foot, unit cost, and detailed—only a detailed estimate provides an accurate picture of each specific cost associated with a project. Detailed estimates also help ensure that each item is specified, which can reduce oversights and keep costs in check. You can use Microsoft® Excel or another program to improve the efficiency and accuracy of your estimating.

Materials and Labor

The first step in estimating is to identify each type of material, labor, trade contractor, equipment, and fee required. Solicit multiple quotes for every job. You probably will need to consult working drawings, job specifications, and site inspections to complete this step. This is often the most time-consuming part of estimating.

Working Drawings

Typically, working drawings include site, foundation, floor framing, floor, and roof framing plans; elevations; sections; and door and room finish schedules. Wall sections, room finish and stair details, and door schedules are part of the floor plan rather than separate drawings. There may be separate drawings and details for cabinets, bookshelves, or specialty woodwork such as mantels or wainscoting.

Plan Review Questions

- Do I have all drawings I need to complete the estimate?
- Do any items seem unusual?
- Am I familiar with all techniques, methods, and equipment required for the job?
- Do the dimensions seem to be correct?
- Are there any discrepancies between written dimensions and scaled dimensions?
- Are there any discrepancies between plans and specifications?
- Are any materials or methods incompatible with local building codes or standard practices?

Site plan. The site plan should show where to locate the home and how to position it on the lot. It also should show the location and dimensions of the driveway, walkways, detached buildings, swimming pool, and other site features. It may include specifications for the initial and final grades.

Foundation plan. The foundation plan provides details about concrete footings, foundations, the height of foundation walls, and basement walls. It typically includes dimensions of footings, grade beams, types and sizes of concrete blocks, locations of thickened slabs, and reinforcing materials such as wire mesh or rebar.

Floor plan. A floor plan shows the location of interior and exterior walls, doors, windows, bath fixtures, kitchen and bath cabinets, and features such as fireplaces or decks. Floor plans generally are drawn from a perspective of four feet above the floor, with a separate plan for each floor in the house. In residential construction, the floor plan customarily includes electrical details as well. Plumbing and heating, ventilation, and air conditioning (HVAC) details may appear on the floor plan, or they may be shown on separate plans.

Sections. Sections show the home as if it were sliced vertically at a given point. Sections include wall-to-ceiling heights, cornice details, insulation type and thickness, air and vapor barriers, flashing details, and miscellaneous structural information.

Framing plans. These plans show structural information about floors and roofs. The floor framing plan includes the size and placement of sills, girders, joists, bridging, and subflooring. The roof framing plan shows the size and placement of ceiling joists, rafters, trusses, bracing, and roof decking, along with details about roof pitches, valleys, and hips.

Elevation plans. Elevations show one or more views of the home's exterior as it will look when completed. The elevations provide specifics about such items as siding, brick, window and exterior door trim, and roofing. Most builders develop a standard method for reviewing plans. One commonly used method is to review drawings in the order of construction as follows:

1. Site plan
2. Foundation plan
3. Floor plan
4. Framing plans

Having a standard procedure for reviewing plans expedites this step and reduces likelihood that you will overlook or omit important items. Therefore, many builders have developed checklists to standardize plan review.

As you review plans, note unfamiliar materials or methods specified. Thoroughly checking for errors in drawings and dimensions can prevent overlooking important details that cost money. The earlier you find errors, the less money and effort you will have to spend correcting them. Carefully check all lines on drawings, particularly if plans are not prepared by the builder, so you don't misconstrue other lines as dimension lines.

For example, a builder was using plans drawn by an engineer. What looked like a dimension line over the staircase actually denoted a particular angle that was part of the design. After the drywall was finished, the engineer pointed out the mistake and the builder had to remove and reframe the ceiling over the staircase.

On another project, the architect's dimensions on a hand-drawn plan were not calculated correctly. The mathematical errors resulted in a front door that was not centered between the posts of a front porch.

Learning from these mistakes, the builder now

- draws his own plans or includes contingencies for plans drawn by others;
- requires the customer to sign a statement that the architect is responsible for the drawing and dimensions; or
- charges the customer for the time and other costs of redrawing plans on the builder's computer if the architect states on plans that the contractor is responsible for the drawing and dimensions.

Residential builders often have less than a full set of working drawings for developing estimates. If you don't have all the necessary drawings for estimating, note what information is missing and take steps to obtain or supply it. If you must make assumptions, put them in writing and attach them to the estimate. Clear communication about all aspects of the project helps ensure the accuracy of the estimate and prevents problems during construction.

Finally, most customers cannot visualize a finished product just by looking at specifications or plans. They need to see photos, or even touch products, to select items and finishes. Control this selection process because an experienced sales associate can persuade customers to choose materials that will exceed your allowances. The home buyer may then think you priced their home using "cheap" materials.

Specifications

The specifications detail materials, methods, and workmanship, including information such as the size, type, brand, and finish of materials. Flag unusual items that might increase costs, compromise quality, or complicate the schedule. Standard practice dictates that when discrepancies arise between working drawings and specifications, specs supersede plans. However, reconciling discrepancies before completing the estimate will save you from potential rework.

If possible, builders should develop their own specifications using materials and methods they are familiar with. The builder also should review thoroughly any specifications supplied by a designer, architect, or owner.

If you encounter vague or incomplete specifications, contact the person you are preparing the estimate for and ask for clarification. If you choose instead to make an educated assumption, stipulate in writing that the estimate is based on one or more assumptions, and attach a detailed, written explanation about each qualification. Builders who enter into contracts based on qualified estimates should address those qualifications in the contract.

The degree of detail in the drawings and specifications often reflects whether you are submitting a bid to a customer or building an inventory home. For inventory projects, builders usually complete the estimate and may start construction before all decisions are made on plans and specifications. However, to protect your profit margin, it is important to finalize as many elements of the project as possible before you break ground or shortly thereafter. With completed plans and specifications to inform your estimate, you can determine whether you can build, sell, and earn a profit on the project in the relevant market. A detailed, accurate estimate also provides a sound basis for comparing actual and budgeted costs.

Site Inspection

Inspecting the building site early in the estimating process, preferably before performing quantity take-offs, helps prevent costly surprises. After starting a job, many builders have been surprised to discover serious complications on a site that was presumed ready for construction.

For example, although residential site plans typically include details about building setbacks and improvements such as driveways and sidewalks, many do not contain information concerning grades, drainage ditches, tree removal, and other critical costs. Walk each site and thoroughly inspect it to identify features omitted from the site plan that might affect the estimate.

Even with a thorough site inspection, some conditions, such as poor soil compaction or subterranean rock, are not obvious. However, you can obtain this information from other sources. Ask for soil tests. If soil tests are not available, area utility companies may have firsthand knowledge of soil conditions, rock, and other considerations. As a last resort, qualify the estimate for soil conditions.

Fees

The estimate should identify all costs associated with required permits and fees and include the ones the builder is responsible for. Typically, fees include:

- Mortgage inspection
- Other inspections
- Utility (water, sewer, electricity, gas, telephone, and cable)
- Permits

Questions about Site Conditions

- Will a road need to be constructed to gain access to the site? If so, is the builder responsible for estimating the cost?
- What culverts or drainage tiles are required?
- How much excavation is needed? Will fill dirt or topsoil have to be brought in or hauled off?
- Does the soil have sufficient stability and compaction?
- Does the site drain adequately?
- Will the soil conditions require special methods or equipment?
- Will trees, boulders, structures, or other objects on the site need to be removed?
- Will preserving trees require special care in accessing the site with heavy equipment?
- Will overhead or underground utilities interfere with the job?
- Are there utility lines or utilities to the site? Not all sites are developed, even in developed neighborhoods.
- What flood zone is the site in for foundation elevation?
- Does the site require specialty foundation, such as pilings, if soil is less than 1,500 psi?

Measurements

Before identifying quantities, take measurements from the working drawings. For example, the number of linear feet of a particular type of wall provides information about the quantity of studs, sheathing, insulation, and drywall. Sometimes you must combine two or more measurements to get all the information you will need. For example, multiplying floor length by floor width to calculate square footage provides information about floor decking, HVAC requirements, and floor covering.

Most working drawings use scales of either ⅛":1' or ¼":1'. Details typically are drawn to larger scales such as ½":1' or ¾":1'. You can use an architect's scale to take measurements from working drawings. Double check all measurements and resolve any questions that remain. An error in one measurement will cause inaccurate estimates for all items associated with it.

Take-offs

A take-off identifies the types and quantities of materials, labor, and trade contractor activities for the project. Each builder must find a take-off method that is accurate, timely, and consistent with his or her method of construction. One option that works well is to follow the sequence of construction steps for the project.

Checklists

As with plan reviews, using checklists to standardize take-offs can help you catch omissions. The take-off should include quantities for each material, labor, equipment, or trade contractor the job will require. Many builders develop a master checklist and add or subtract items from it according to the project. Some builders create separate checklists for materials, labor, and trade contracts. Use computerized spreadsheets and word processors to create your master list.

Checklists should conform to your method for performing take-offs. Performing take-offs and using checklists in the same order and manner every time minimizes the chance of overlooking items or elements of a job.

As you build a project, compile and review variances to improve estimating and construction management on future jobs. Analyze variances to determine whether an inaccurate estimate or another issue caused them. Do not change prices without getting a written quote from a supplier or trade before estimating a job.

Assigning Work

To compile a detailed estimate, you must decide who will do each phase of the work—your own crews or trade contractors. The final estimate should conform as closely as possible to how you plan to complete the project.

You can estimate portions of a job using both quantity take-offs and trade contractor bids. Test multiple scenarios to choose the most appropriate work plan for the project and to minimize costs. Take-offs help you monitor trade contractor prices.

Trade Contractor Bids

You may be able to get trade contractor bids in a few minutes, but you also may have to wait several days. You can save time by compiling, in advance, a database of costs for many commonly used materials and trade contractors. You can fax or e-mail drawings to contractors to expedite their estimating. Allow trade contractors sufficient time to prepare their bids, but set a deadline.

Trade contractors may provide a lump sum, unit price, cost plus, or hourly rate. Their prices rise and fall with work availability. If you are loyal to trade contractors, they are more likely to perform warranty work promptly. For example, you might negotiate with a roofing trade to establish a labor price per square foot to install various types of roofing within a specified period, such as in the next six months. This strategy also works for many other standard materials and trade contracts as long as costs for materials and labor remain fairly stable. Frequently update your databases. Both material and labor costs fluctuate according to supply and demand, not just with inflation. Lumber prices, for example, vary daily.

Lump sum. An offer to perform a specified scope of work for a predetermined price—either materials and labor, or labor only—is a lump-sum bid. To prepare the bid, the trade contractor needs complete information about the job and detailed specifications for materials and workmanship.

Unit cost. The trade contractor offers to supply both material and labor, or labor only, on a per-unit basis. For example, a framing trade contractor may offer to furnish labor to frame a house for a certain number of dollars and cents per square foot.

For unit-cost bids, the builder and trade contractor must agree on the method for determining the scope and pricing of work to be completed under the contract.

For example, the builder and trade contractor must agree on the number of square feet that will determine the total price for framing labor. You should ask whether square footage includes only living area or also porches, breezeways, garages, and similar areas, and at what cost.

Cost plus. The trade contractor offers to supply materials and labor, or labor only, at the trade contractor's cost, plus a specified markup. Ask about quantity and cash discounts, labor burden, and other factors that may influence the trade contractor's cost. Some builders view this method as a blank check.

Hourly rate. An hourly rate bid is an offer to supply labor or equipment services at a specified rate per hour. An excavating trade contractor who offers to provide a bulldozer and operator for $50 per hour is offering an hourly rate bid. Paying trade contractors by the hour increases the possibility that the IRS may classify them as employees rather than independent contractors. Therefore, consult your attorneys and/or tax accountants about the possible implications of accepting this option.

To ensure consistency among bids from multiple vendors in the same trade, you must provide each with the same information and the same proposal form. This helps you make valid comparisons. You also should request—and verify—that bids and quotes comprise all costs, including sales tax, special order charges, and delivery charges.

Pricing vs. Take-off Units

Many items, such as windows, wall studs, and doors, may be priced as individual units. However, the take-off units and pricing units differ for many items. For example, concrete for a garage floor is purchased by the cubic yard, while the floor area typically is measured in square feet. To calculate the amount of concrete required to pour a garage floor, you must use a formula to convert square feet of floor area to cubic yards of concrete.[5]

After you account for materials and tasks, and have the bids, you can assign a cost to each take-off item. Prior preparation time, the quantity of special or non-standard materials, and the time frame for trade contractors' bid submissions will determine how long this step takes.

---

[5] Jay P. Christofferson. *Estimating with Microsoft® Excel, Third Edition.* Washington, DC: Builder Books.com, 2010.

Calculating Total Cost

To determine the *extended price*, multiply the total units by the unit price for each take-off item. Confirm that you are recording each take-off quantity and its corresponding unit price using the same unit of measure. For example, ensure that all calculations for framing lumber are in linear feet.

Next, total all costs, set the estimate aside for a few hours or a day, and then review it with fresh eyes for errors and omissions.

The procedures discussed so far apply to estimates of direct construction costs (costs easily identified with a specific project or job). A complete estimate also should include indirect construction costs and an amount sufficient to cover operating expenses and profit.

Indirect Costs and Profit

Indirect construction costs, or "soft costs," are costs not attributable to a specific project. They include superintendent salaries, construction vehicle expenses, and jobsite offices. The *NAHB Chart of Accounts* provides a comprehensive listing of indirect construction costs.[6]

You can allocate these expenses among projects in many ways. Many builders apply indirect costs to estimates the same way they allocate indirect costs to their completed projects.

Profit is the amount the builder expects the company to have left after covering all construction and overhead costs. Builders decide how much profit to include based on the nature of the job and market conditions.

Contingencies

Most builders also budget a percentage over the estimate amount for unplanned events that may increase the actual cost of the project. The percentage may vary from estimate to estimate, depending on the complexity of the job, construction methods or materials the builder is not familiar with, expected price fluctuations, or other factors.

---

[6] Emma Shinn. *Accounting and Financial Management for Residential Construction,* 5th Edition. Washington, DC: BuilderBooks.com, 2008. 189–90.

Combining Estimating Approaches

In practice, builders may use a variety of estimating approaches to balance the desire for speed with the need for accuracy. For example, you could use the detailed approach to estimate framing lumber, foundation blocks, windows, and doors. Then, if you know the cost of materials and labor required per square foot of exterior concrete, you could estimate a unit cost for this item. After you complete an estimate, you can calculate the expected overall cost per square foot, which you then can compare with the square-foot costs of similar projects.

Computerized Estimating

Automating your estimating using an off-the-shelf or customized product will save time and increase accuracy. Estimating programs enable you to store databases of materials, labor items, and costs, which enhances organization, operational control, and productivity. The computer helps you link estimating information to other key business functions, such as accounting and financial management, scheduling, and purchasing. Using the computer to perform calculations decreases mathematical errors and increases estimating accuracy so you can predict your profit margin with confidence.

A number of computerized estimating programs are available to small-volume builders, and the hardware needed to run them has become more affordable.

Two Ways to Automate

Generic spreadsheets. Electronic spreadsheets are organized around rows and columns similar to an accountant's ledger. They provide a means to organize and automate estimating. A typical estimate has columns for the item description, take-off quantity, unit of measure, unit price, and total item price. You can write formulas to convert take-off quantities to pricing quantities, and to compute total costs.

Construction estimating program. Dedicated estimating software is designed specifically for construction estimating. Some programs suit both commercial and residential construction projects. Others are tailored specifically to home builders. Unlike generic spreadsheets, which require the estimator to develop checklists, populate databases, and develop all formulas and conversion factors, dedicated systems may come with ready-made checklists, price books, conversion factors, and formulas.

Although each estimating package has its own unique design, capabilities, and output, they all share basic attributes. They perform complicated calculations quickly and accurately, store vast amounts of data, and retrieve and manipulate data quickly. Many also integrate estimating with other business functions. No estimating program, however, can eliminate the need for good estimating skills and sound judgment.

Program Features

Most computerized estimating programs contain the following basic features:

Checklists. Checklists increase both speed and accuracy. Estimating software automates the development of checklists and enables you to store and retrieve these lists for future use. Many programs create sample checklists you can modify for your needs.

Automatically calculated take-offs. Estimating programs can simplify and improve the take-off process. You group items into an assembly or *work package*, and then enter a quantity for the assembly to develop an estimate. Once you create them, these assemblies are stored electronically so you can use them again in the future.

Many computer estimating programs offer the option of performing take-offs electronically. Computer peripherals such as digitizers and electronic measuring devices let you transfer measurements and quantities directly from the drawing into the estimating program.

Price lists. Perhaps the most important feature of estimating software is that it enables you to develop and maintain a master list of items required to complete your estimates. Each item in this master list will have an identification number, item description, unit measure, and unit price.

Many programs also allow the builder to develop a vendor list that includes suppliers and trade contractors. The price list is linked to the vendor list, providing multiple prices for each item. You can generate requests for bids from suppliers or trade contractors by activity, job, material type, or vendor.

Frequently used formulas. Many programs include formulas that convert take-off units to pricing units. For example, they will convert square feet of drywall to number of boards, or linear feet to cubic yards of concrete. You can also write and store your own frequently used formulas.

Structure and organization. Perhaps one of the most important functions of a computer estimating program is its ability to provide structure and organization to the estimating process. By standardizing checklists, assemblies, price lists, and formulas, you can be confident that you are creating estimates using the same approach every time.

Reports. You can generate reports on take-offs by job, activity, type of material, trade contractor, or vendor. You can generate price lists by vendor, type of material, or trade contractor.

Estimates typically are generated with the following columns of data: take-off item description, take-off quantity, unit price, and total cost. Estimate reports are organized by phase of construction, type of work, work location, or other criteria.

Some estimating software also will generate cash flow reports, schedules, and estimate histories, which are summaries of previously developed estimates for comparison with new estimates.

Program integration. Computer estimating programs may be self contained or integrated with other functions. Integrating estimating with computer-aided design (CAD) programs, which allow the user to design and draw, enables information to flow from the CAD program to the estimate, saving time and reducing errors. Integrating estimating with scheduling provides basic information to develop your schedule.

Cost control. Computer estimating programs also can facilitate cost control. You can categorize estimated items and job cost information using the same classifications in order to compare budgeted and actual costs.

Selecting a Computer Estimating Program

- **Compatibility.** Look for a computer estimating program that approximates how you compile your estimates currently. Even if it requires adjustments, the program should be flexible enough to accommodate your preferred methods and organization.
- **User friendliness.** A program should be relatively simple to operate and easy to learn, yet powerful enough to meet your needs. A complicated computer estimating program does not serve most small-volume builders very well.
- **Ability to upgrade.** Look for programs that have features or related programs you can add as needed, as your company grows and changes.

Profitable Estimating

Creating accurate estimates doesn't have to consume all of your time. You can use spreadsheets and databases to eliminate repetitive work and capture historical information that will improve your estimating capabilities. Reliable estimates will help you maintain your profit margin, build a positive reputation, and reduce risk. Choose the appropriate estimating method at each step of a project and you will increase your efficiency and improve your bottom line.

10
Purchasing

A purchase order is a list of materials or services a supplier or contractor furnishes. If you do not already use one, adopting a purchase order system as your way of doing business is the single most significant change you can make to control costs. Purchase orders

- Help you identify billing mistakes more easily;
- Force you to plan and organize projects;
- Require you to identify the materials and services you need for each construction activity and assign costs to them before beginning construction;
- Allow you to compare the quantity and price of materials and services delivered with what was ordered;
- Enable you to better control materials by specifying in writing delivery times and methods, how materials should be stacked, and where to place them on the site;
- Increase your control over purchases by reducing incidental purchases by employees; and
- Provide price records to reference for change orders.

Your purchase orders should contain at least the following information:

- Job or project name
- Cost code
- Detailed listing of materials or services purchased
- Quoted price of the materials or services
- Payment terms, including discounts and finance charges
- Delivery schedules and other delivery instructions

Figure 10.1 is a sample purchase order.

Company size and organizational structure impact the design and use of a purchase order system. Small-volume builders often use a three-part purchase order. Part I goes to the vendor, Part II goes to the superintendent, and Part III goes in an office file. When a vendor delivers the material or a trade contractor completes his or her work, the superintendent (or perhaps the builder in a small company) compares the material received or work completed with the purchase order. He or she notes any discrepancies, and approves the purchase order for payment. The accounting department or relevant staff member compares the vendor's invoice with the purchase order. If they match, the invoice is paid. Some home builders don't pay invoices at all; they only use POs and VPOs.

A purchase order system is a valuable cost-control tool.

Variance Purchase Orders

If there are variances between the purchase order and the materials or labor required for an activity, the superintendent or another relevant staff member writes a variance purchase order (VPO). This "tags" the transaction for further attention by the builder. A variance purchase order (fig. 10.2) should list the variance, explain it, and suggest ways to prevent its recurrence. Documented correctly, it can tell you what went wrong on a jobsite and prevent the problem in the future.

Examining variances and tracing them back to their source, with VPOs, provides valuable insight for improving construction systems and future estimates.

A VPO is useless, though, if it omits details, if no one uses the VPO to correct future estimates, or both. For example, a $132.50 VPO ultimately cost one builder $1,800. Because the VPO, which was for additional materials, included only a lump sum, with no quantity or pricing information, it took 3½ months to track down the reason for the materials discrepancy and correct it. Most VPOs are for significantly more than $132. Moreover, the time required to research a poorly documented VPO is time you could instead spend adding value to your business. By drilling down to the details in the big picture, you can dramatically decrease costs and rapidly increase efficiency.

Figure 10.1   Purchase Order

Purchase Order
DAN SMITH CONSTRUCTION
2400 Main Street
Anytown, Anystate 00000

P.O.# _____

Date: _____   Vendor: _____

Terms: _____

Delivery Date: _____

F.O.B.:_____   Deliver To: _____

Cost Code: _____

Qty. Unit Item_____

Qty	Unit	Item	Description	Unit Price	Amount

Subtotal _____

Tax _____

Total _____

Figure 10.2   Variance Purchase Order

Variance Purchase Order
DAN SMITH CONSTRUCTION
2400 Main Street
Anytown, Anystate 00000

To:					P.O.#:		
Vendor #							
C/C#:					Project/ Lot:		
Date: Orig.							
P.O. #							
Variance Code	Qty	Unit	Item	Description		Unit Price	Amount
Explanation:					Subtotal		
					Tax		
					Total		
Action Taken to Prevent Future Variance:							

Variance Codes:

1. Plan Error	6. Site Conditions	11. Code Requirement
2. Quantity Estimation	7. Theft/Vandalism	12. Weather Conditions
3. Price Estimation Material	8. Poor Workmanship	13. Design Change
4. Incorrect Material	9. Superintendent	14. Inferior Material
5. Price Change	10. Customer-Requested Change	15. Subcontractor Error

Keys to an Effective PO System

- **The superintendent is your frontline person.** As your eyes and ears in the field, he or she should be the one responsible for approving POs or writing variance POs.

- **Details, details.** A VPO should not just include a date and a lump sum, but also specifics about the lot involved; an account code; materials, quantity, and price; and any of the 30 or more reasons for the variance.

- **Don't pass the buck; close the loop!** If the VPO was caused by an estimating error, go back to the estimating department and let them know about it; if it was an error in sales, go back to that office. Use the VPO to help you improve your employees' knowledge about the business and your own processes.

- **Monitor variances monthly.** Analyze variances by superintendent, community, plan name, cost code, vendor or trade, and variance code.

- **Set a benchmark.** Define an acceptable level of variance—1% or less is the generally accepted industry standard.

- **Document everything.** Don't expect an electronic system to work magic for your purchasing system. You need to have a system in place before you can improve it.

11

Scheduling

Successful builders agree that developing a realistic schedule is essential to managing cash flow, trade contractors, vendors, and customer expectations. Your schedule should be detailed, listing the activities required to accomplish an objective, resources to be allocated, and a timetable with intermittent deadlines. The schedule answers who, what, when, and where. "Schedule by the day, and you will get results in a day," says Joe Pfeiffer of Business ROI Inc.

Maintaining Control

An effective scheduling system will help you manage production proactively as the size, complexity, and number of your projects increase. A schedule will help you

- see when each crew or trade contractor is to begin;
- know how long each activity should take;
- adhere to lead time requirements for material orders and trade contractors;
- develop and maintain professional relationships with suppliers, trade contractors, and lenders;
- decrease construction delays;
- maintain and manage financing costs and cash flow;
- pay bills on time; and
- manage customer expectations.

Activities

For many builders, "schedule" refers to the timing and coordination of on-site work activities. A comprehensive, well-developed schedule, however, also includes other activities. A well-developed schedule shows when various activities can begin, when they should be completed, and the resources you will need to accomplish them.

Start-up activities. Start-up activities are completed before construction begins. They include

- drawings;
- permits;
- utility hook-ups;
- on-site sanitary facilities;
- locating lot corners;
- customer financing; and
- customer deposits.

Material orders. Ensure that materials are available when you need them by ordering well in advance. Lead time (the amount of time between when an order is placed and materials are delivered) can be less than an hour for a few sheets of plywood or several months for a custom door. Builders should incorporate this information into the scheduling process.

Trade contractor notification. Notify trade contractors in advance. Although small-volume builders often have little control over material lead times, they may have input about trade contractors' lead times. Negotiate with trade contractors to determine mutually acceptable lead times.

Material deliveries. Schedule the delivery of materials before crews will need them and at a convenient time so deliveries don't interfere with ongoing work.

Work activities. Identify and schedule tasks, including work by both trade contractors and the builder's crews. Effective scheduling coordinates the work of various trades and ensures that each activity begins and ends on time. Scheduling also can identify potential conflicts. For example, a plumbing trade contractor who has only one crew cannot rough in a house on the same day he or she is expected to lay out another house.

Inspections. Local codes often require inspections at specified points during construction. Typical inspections include the following:

- Footers
- Foundation
- Framing
- Plumbing

- Electrical
- Drywall
- Final
- Customer walk-through

A schedule reduces the possibility of overlooking any of these inspections. It also decreases the likelihood that the next phase of work will start before required inspections are complete. If your drywall contractors start before the home passes required framing, plumbing, and electrical inspections, you may have to rip out the drywall, increasing costs and lengthening construction.

Customer selections. Construction often starts before the customer has selected specific materials and colors. Give clients a schedule with deadlines for making their selections and let them know that missing their deadlines will delay construction. Including these selections on a list of activities that must be scheduled prevents them from being forgotten or delayed.

Cleanups. Each trade contractor's or builder's crew is responsible for cleaning up after it completes its work. Specify this in your contracts.

Project closeout activities. Include end-of-project activities in the schedule, such as disconnecting the temporary electrical service, removing signs, and other tasks associated with closing out the house.

The Master Activity List

A master activity list can improve scheduling accuracy and reduce the time needed to produce a schedule. The master list should contain all activities included in your typical projects. Group activities by project to help organize them into a usable list. Sample project phases used in residential construction might include

- project start-up;
- initial site work;
- footing and foundation;
- framing;
- exterior finish;
- interior finish;
- final site work; and
- project closeout.

Figure 11.1 shows a master activity list.

Figure 11.1   Master Activity List

Project startup
Obtain:
Permit
Approved architecture drawings
Plot of site
Temporary power
Temporary water
Builders risk insurance
Surveyor to locate site
Surveyor to locate building corners
Owner selects
Plumbing fixtures
Light fixtures
HVAC system
Paint
Cabinets
Colors and finishes for all exterior concrete
work
Interior and exterior hardware including
colors and finishes for doorknobs and
locks
Appliances
Roofing colors
Initial site work
Clear site
Grade site
Foundation phase
Install footings
Set batter boards
Dig footings
Set grade stakes
Footing inspection
Pour footings
Install foundation block
Order block or concrete
Deliver block
Order sand and mortar
Sand and mortar delivered
Lay foundation block or pour concrete
Slab-on-grade work
Utility rough-in
Plumbing
HVAC
Electrical
Radon system
Dryer duct
Slab preparation work
Fine grade subbase
Lay out and set batter boards
Excavate turndown edge

Set edge forms
Spread gravel
Termite treatment
Place poly and welded wire mesh
Set grade stakes
Place slab
Inspect slab
Place and finish concrete
Cure concrete
Before backfilling, install downspout and
footing drains with drain tile around
footings
Structure phase
Order framing material
Deliver framing material
Erect rough framing
Floor framing and decking (Some local
codes require inspections of all joists
before decking may be installed)
Walls and sheathing
Deliver roof trusses and roof framing
Roof framing and decking
Complete rough framing
Check plumb and square
Check door openings (size and square)
Install deadwood and blocking and
curtain rod blocking as well as ADA
blocking
Wall insulation
Framing inspection
Clean up waste material
Utility rough-in
Deliver tubs and showers
Plumbing top-out
Plumbing inspection
HVAC rough-in
Install wiring for TV, phones, and music
Electrical rough-in
Prepare home for security system
installation
Install central vacuum system tubing
Electrical inspection
Structure dry-in
Exterior wood
Install fascia and soffits
Order exterior doors and windows
Deliver exterior doors and windows
Install exterior doors and windows
Install siding

Exterior masonry
Order brick
Deliver brick
Install brick
Roofing
Install flashing and felt
Install shingles
Install wall insulation after roof installation
Finish phase
Interior walls
Order paneling
Deliver paneling
Install paneling
Order sheetrock
Deliver sheetrock
Hang sheetrock
Tape and finish sheetrock
Clean up sheetrock waste
Wall finishing items
Paint interior walls
Paint exterior walls
Deliver wallpaper
Hang wallpaper
Paint or stain interior trim
Paint or stain interior doors
Touch-up paint
Interior wood trim
Install locks on all exterior doors and
garage doors
Install interior trim
Baseboards
Chair rails
Crown molding
Install closet shelving and rods
Install interior doors
Finish flooring
Install ceramic tile
Install other hard tile
Install vinyl tile
Install carpet
Install wood flooring
Place wood flooring
Sand and finish wood flooring
Install miscellaneous items
Insulate attic
Order cabinets
Deliver cabinets
Install cabinets
Install bathroom accessories
Order appliances

Deliver and set appliances
Dishwasher
Stove
Compactor
Washer/dryer
Range hood
Finish utilities
Plumbing trim-out
HVAC trim-out
Deliver HVAC equipment
Set grills and thermostat
Test equipment
Electrical trim-out
Install fixtures, devices
Order light fixtures
Deliver light fixtures
Hang light fixtures
Install security, central vacuum, and
music systems
Connect main power
Check and test system
Final electrical inspection
Custom items
Install fireplace items (prior to roofing if
installing a brick fireplace)
Order fireplace
Deliver fireplace
Set fire box (perhaps during framing but
after roof installation)
Set flue and box
Install outside decks
Install hot tub
Order hot tub
Deliver hot tub
Set hot tub
Install alarm system (during wiring stage)
Install telephone wiring (during wiring stage)
Install TV wiring (during wiring stage)
Finish site work
Grade driveway and walks
Form and install concrete driveway
Form and place sidewalks
Site landscaping
Project closeout phase
Remove temporary water connection
Remove temporary power connection
Clean house
Final inspection
Complete punch list work
Install or rekey locks for owners

Figure 11.2 Microsoft® Project Gantt Chart

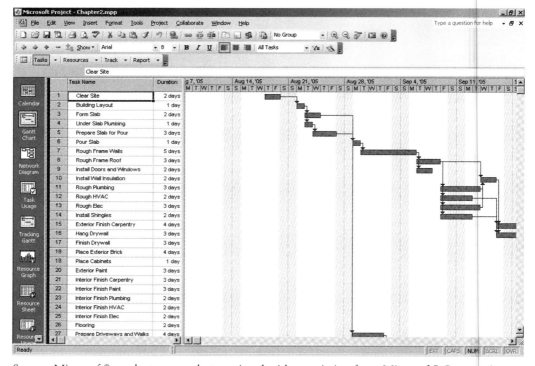

Source: Microsoft® product screen shot reprinted with permission from Microsoft® Corporation.

A master activity list can serve as a template and a checklist to ensure comprehensive project estimates and schedules.

Base your master list on the way you organize your work. Plan and schedule projects so the level of detail matches your project management style. Make the activities list complete without adding excessive subcategories. Too much detail can needlessly complicate schedule monitoring and maintenance.

Select Activities

Draw from the master list to develop a list of phases and activities for each scheduled project.

Activity duration. Once you have identified all activities required for a project, estimate how long each will take. To develop accurate activity durations, follow these three procedures:

1. Accurately record how long it takes to complete each project. Compare the scope of activities on the current project with those of previous projects.

2. Discuss timing with the employees and/or trade contractors who will do the work. They should know how long the activity will take.

3. Identify other conditions that might affect activity durations.

Activity responsibility. The activity list should indicate the trade contractor, supplier, or builder's employee or crew responsible for performing each activity.

Relationship among activities. Relationships among activities are specified in terms of precedence. Each activity typically will have *predecessor activities* that must be completed before the activity can begin, and subsequent activities that cannot begin until the previous activity is completed. Physical constraints (for example, roofing cannot begin until the roof deck has been installed) determine the order of activities in some cases, but in others, your preferences determine precedence. For example, you may prefer to have kitchen floor tile installed before cabinets, rather than after. Once you understand how activities relate to one another, you can be more flexible in managing a schedule.

A Gantt chart helps you visualize the relationships among project components.

Determine the Level of Detail

You will determine the appropriate level of scheduling detail for each specific project by considering the following:

- Project type and scope
- Time required to develop, monitor, and update the schedule
- Who will use the schedule

A construction superintendent probably requires a more detailed schedule than top management does.

Contingencies

How much time should you allow for contingencies? These unplanned events or situations can throw off a schedule. Three common ways of handling contingencies are as follows:

No contingency allowances. This approach does not allow for contingencies in the schedule. Builders who use this approach don't actually believe that no contingencies will arise. But they understand that predicting contingencies is guesswork.

Some builders shy away from contingencies, believing that work will expand to fill the time allotted. Instead, they revise the schedule as contingencies arise.

A drawback to this approach is that even a small project can require extensive scheduling revisions. Employees and trade contractors may become frustrated trying to adhere to a schedule with no allowance for contingencies, so weigh the cost of monitoring and updating this type of schedule with its benefits.

Rain days. A second approach allows contingencies to increase the duration of activities likely to be delayed. For example, rainy weather, the most common reason for delays, can slow down framing but has little effect on interior trim. Building rain days into the time allotted for weather-sensitive activities may yield a more realistic schedule.

Single activity at end of job. A third option is to add a single activity at the end of a job. Although this does not alleviate schedule revision, it provides a cushion for unforeseen events during a project.

Scheduling Tools

Whether you use a calendar or detail-oriented network diagrams, you must record daily activities and overall job progress. Daily activities show you what needs to be done now. Job progress shows you which activities need to be moved up, which need to be postponed a few days, and which ones are continuing on schedule.

To organize the tasks required to complete a home, analyze what works for you now, and what you could improve. Then experiment with a few different types of schedules until you find the right one, or a combination that helps you operate efficiently and effectively.

Calendars

The calendar is probably the simplest scheduling system builders use. You write scheduled activities on calendar days, and the calendar serves as the project schedule. Although a calendar schedule is a better alternative than no schedule, it has limitations. When projects are large and extend for months, calendar schedules can become bulky and difficult to use. There are easy-to-use computer programs to develop calendar schedules.

Bar Charts

Bar charts are a popular scheduling tool for small-volume builders. The bar chart graphically depicts each activity's start date, duration, and completion date.

Figure 11.3   Bar Chart in Spreadsheet

			July 20__																		
		Cal Days	8	9	10	11	12	15	16	17	18	19	22	23	24	25	26	29	30	31
		Workdays	1	2	3	4	5	6	7	8	9	10	11	12	13	14	15	16	17	18
Description	Resp	Duration																		
Slab Prep Work	Concrete Crew	4 days	▓	▓	▓	▓														
Inspect Slab	Inspector	1 day					▓													
Place & Finish Slab	Concrete Crew	1 day						▓												
Erect Wood Framing	Framing Crew	5 days							▓	▓	▓	▓	▓							
Comp Rough Framing	Framing Crew	2 days												▓	▓					
Install Roof Shingles	Roofing Crew	2 days																	▓	▓
Inst Door & Windows	Framing Sub	1 day												▓						
Inst Siding & Cornice	Siding Sub	2 days													▓	▓				
R/I & Trim Electrical	Electrical Sub	2 days															▓	▓		
Paint Exterior	Painting Sub	3 days																▓	▓	▓
Final Inspection	Inspector	1 day																		▓

The bar chart is an effective scheduling tool. *From* Scheduling Residential construction (Figure 2.2), *by Thomas A. Love; Home Builder Press.*

You can develop simple bar charts on spreadsheets. List project activities in the left-hand column. In the second and third columns, list who is responsible for each activity and how long each activity will last. In calculating an activity's duration, include only work days, not weekends and holidays. Label each day's column with both the calendar day and the project workday. Although these simple charts will allow you to show how a job should progress according to the time allotted and compare actual with planned progress, they don't show the effect of one activity's delay on others. They also don't identify *critical tasks*, the work that controls a project's duration.

For example, the bar chart in figure 11.3 shows electrical rough-in and trim completion on July 29. A review of the project's other activities shows that the work probably could be delayed one day without affecting the entire project.

Although it won't have scheduling and project management functionality, you can create a bar chart using spreadsheet software.

Use Network Diagrams

The Critical Path Method (CPM) uses network, or logic, diagrams. These diagrams show not only the start, duration, and completion times for project activities, but also the relationships, or interdependencies, among them. A network diagram allows you to identify a project's critical path—the sequence of activities that represents the shortest amount of time required to complete a project. A CPM diagram allows you to classify crucial and noncrucial activities. Crucial activities, if delayed, will slow down the entire project. Noncrucial activities can be rescheduled without impacting the entire project.

Typically, less than 20% of project activities are crucial, and many of those are designated critical not because of physical constraints, but because of the scheduler's preferences. Understanding which activities are crucial and why is the key to managing the schedule successfully.

Figure 11.2 shows a Gantt chart generated in Microsoft® Project. Because very few projects progress exactly as planned, the program enables you to manage interrelated tasks and easily update the schedule as needed for weather, acts of God, delivery adjustments, trade contractor availability, or other issues.

Communicating the Schedule

You cannot benefit from a well-planned and organized schedule unless you share it with the people who will use or be affected by it. Therefore, if you are starting to use a new scheduling system, alert suppliers, trade contractors, employees, and customers how the system will affect them, where they fit in, and how they will work with it. Tell them what information they will need to provide for the schedule and how to read and interpret schedule reports they receive.

As early as possible, inform each crew, supplier, or trade contractor involved in the project that you are beginning work. One way to do this is to send out all purchase orders before actually starting construction and then provide weekly updates. This will allow suppliers to time orders to receive quantity discounts, reduce freight costs, etc. Trade contractors can adjust their work schedules to reduce conflicts with other jobs and ensure that they are available when needed.

Keeping stakeholders such as customers and lenders apprised of scheduling information enhances your company's professional image and can prevent delays in customer payments on contracts and draws on construction loans.

Monitoring and Controlling the Schedule

A number of factors can alter even the most carefully planned schedule:

- Change orders
- Weather

- Material shortages
- Trade contractors who are late or slow
- Equipment breakdowns
- Employee illness

Although you will need to consider these and other factors in developing and implementing a schedule, don't use them as excuses for deficient scheduling. Create a functional and flexible schedule, and then ensure that work progresses accordingly. The adage, "plan the work and work the plan" is apropos of scheduling.

Someone—a project manager, superintendent, construction manager, or the builder—must be responsible for keeping the job on schedule. He or she needs the resources, decision-making authority, and the documentation necessary to perform the job. Don't get so wrapped up in developing a formal scheduling system that you forget that a schedule is only a tool. The project—not the schedule—must be managed.

Computerized Scheduling

The time and effort required to develop, monitor, and periodically update even simple schedules can become overwhelming. But computerized scheduling packages can assist both large- and small-volume builders' abilities to develop an effective scheduling program. As with any tool, computer scheduling systems are only as valuable as their ability to perform a task effectively and efficiently. Ask the following questions when you are evaluating computerized scheduling programs:

- How does the program enable our construction methods and practices?
- Will the program run on our current or planned hardware?
- What reports can the program generate for the builder, superintendent, and others?
- How much time and effort will the initial schedule and updates require?
- Will the program provide the appropriate details without inundating users with irrelevant information?
- Will the program perform a network analysis and provide related information including project duration, critical path activities, and early and late start and finish times?
- Is the program easy to learn and use?

Matching the Schedule to the Project

All builders should become familiar with available scheduling options and select the most appropriate method for each project. For many builders, simple calendars or bar charts work very well. Builders whose projects are complex or who regularly build more than one project at a time should consider a more sophisticated computerized scheduling system. The key is to match the method used to the project being scheduled.

12

Accounting

To remain competitive and profitable, you must have accurate, meaningful, and timely financial data to make informed decisions. Your accounting system should be able to supply that data. Whether or not you hire an accountant, you must understand accounting fundamentals.

Designing an Accounting System

Accounting is the process of systematically collecting, analyzing, and reporting financial information. A well-designed accounting system should

- provide information to paint a thorough picture of a company's operating results;
- help generate financial statements;
- generate operating reports for both internal and external users;
- allow comparison of the company's financial performance over time with its goals, or with the performance of other companies within its industry;
- permit prompt and accurate filing of local, state, and federal tax returns and other required reports; and
- provide controls to help prevent theft, fraud, waste, and record-keeping errors.

Working with an Accountant

Most small-volume builders cannot justify hiring a full-time accountant, so they contract with one or with a firm to prepare financial statements and tax returns. Builders have found that the additional services accountants provide, particularly their advice, can help reduce risks and improve company performance. Only you and an accountant can determine the most appropriate complement of services for your company.

In selecting an accountant and determining how he or she can best serve your company, consider the accountant's familiarity with the residential construction industry and your own knowledge of accounting. Examples of the type of services accountants can provide include

- designing an accounting system to fit your needs, including software solutions;
- providing expert advice on tax planning, including understanding issues unique to your industry;
- preparing and filing financial reports and tax returns;
- performing audits, reviews, or compilations of the builder's financial statements to verify that they accurately represent the company's performance and financial position;
- analyzing the company's activities and transactions to spot problems or trends;
- suggesting ways clients can improve operations; and
- providing *benchmarking* information and comparing your operations to others.

Who Uses Accounting Information?

Accounting information can be compiled at many levels—for the company as a whole, for a product line, or for a single home. Therefore, accounting provides financial information for a broad range of users. Owners and managers use accounting to study their company's profitability, cash flow, and overall financial health. Creditors and lenders use the information in a builder's financial statements to decide whether the builder can satisfy financial obligations as they come due. Investors examine a builder's financial statements to evaluate whether an investment in the company or a project will generate an acceptable level of return. Government agencies require information about the company's tax liabilities and payroll deductions.

The Accounting Equation

Accounting turns data on revenues and expenses into useful financial information. The *accounting equation* is a simple statement that forms the basis for the accounting process. It shows the relationship between the company's assets, liabilities, and owner's equity as

$$\text{Assets} = \text{Liabilities} + \text{Owner's Equity}$$

The accounting equation must balance. In other words, the left side of the equation (assets) must always equal the sum of the liabilities and owner's equity on the right.

Assets—everything of value that a business owns—are the resources a builder can use or exchange to produce products or services. Assets can be either tangible (e.g., cash, inventories, equipment) or intangible (e.g., *receivables*, deposits, prepaid expenses). Liabilities, which, generally speaking, are claims to or interests in company assets by entities other than the company's owners, are obligations or debts that the builder must pay eventually. Liabilities, such as *accounts payable*, are paid with money, while other liabilities are settled in the form of goods or services. For example, a builder completes a job according to the contract terms in exchange for payment by a customer.

The total claims the owners of a business have on the company's assets, or the amount equal to the company's assets minus its liabilities, is the owner's equity. It is just another way of viewing the accounting equation, as follows:

$$\text{Assets} - \text{Liabilities} = \text{Owner's Equity}$$

Owner's equity is the owner's investment in the business plus profits it generates that the owner has not withdrawn.

Revenues and Expenses

Two other types of accounts, *revenues* and expenses, also affect the equation. Revenues increase owner's equity. They are assets (such as cash or *accounts receivable*) that the business collects from selling products or performing services for customers. Expenses are the costs incurred to produce revenues. They are the assets you must give up or consume in order to produce goods to sell or to serve customers. Expenses decrease owner's equity.

Double-Entry Bookkeeping

Using *double-entry bookkeeping* helps ensure the accounting equation stays balanced (fig. 12.1).

Transaction A. Dan invested $20,000 in the new business and received 20,000 shares of common stock valued at $1 per share. The transaction increased assets (cash) by $20,000 and owner's equity (common stock) by $20,000.

Transaction B. Dan purchased $5,500 worth of office equipment on credit, increasing assets (office equipment) by $5,500 and liabilities (accounts payable) by the same amount.

Transaction C. Dan purchased construction equipment for $2,200 cash. This transaction increased assets (construction equipment) by $2,200 and decreased assets (cash) by $2,200. Note that this transaction did not change the totals in the equation, merely the composition of the assets.

Transaction D. Dan contracted with Sam and Vickie Johnson to build a home on their lot. Upon signing the contract, Dan received a $15,000 payment on contract. This transaction increased assets (cash) by $15,000 and liabilities (deferred income) by the same amount.

Identifying Transactions by Account

Increases and decreases in the accounting equation are identified by the types of assets, liabilities, or owner's equity they represent. Changes in assets, liabilities, or owner's equity are identified by account, the basic unit of the accounting system. An account records the increases and decreases to a specific type of asset, liability, owner's equity, revenue, or expense.

   Asset, liability, and owner's equity accounts are real, or permanent, accounts. Their balances reflect everything that is posted to them from the time the account is initiated. Revenue and expense accounts are nominal, or *temporary accounts*. They temporarily contain the revenue and expense information that will transfer to owner's equity at the end of the accounting period.

Figure 12.1   The Accounting Equation

	Assets		Liabilities		Owner's Equity
A	+$20,000 (Cash)				+$20,000 (Common)
	$20,000	=		+	$20,000
B	+$ 5,500 Office		+$ 5,500 (Accts.		
	$25,500 Equip.	=	$ 5,500 Payable)	+	$20,000
C	+$ 2,200 (Cash)				
	−$ 2,200 (Cash)				
	+$25,500	=	$ 5,500	+	$20,000
D	+$15,000 (Cash)		+$15,000 (Deferred		
	$40,000	=	$20,500 Income)	+	$20,000

This example of double entry bookkeeping shows the relationship between the firm's assets, liabilities, and owner's equity based on the accounting equation.

This example of double-entry bookkeeping shows the relationship between the firm's assets, liabilities, and owner's equity, based on the accounting equation.

Chart of Accounts

Each account typically has both a title and a number. The complete listing of the accounts is known as the chart of accounts. The NAHB Chart of Accounts offers a logical framework for a residential builder or remodeler's accounting system. No matter what chart of accounts you use, it should

- include five general classifications: assets, liabilities, owner's equity, revenues, and expenses;

- provide account classifications that support both fiscal reporting requirements and managerial decision making;

- be consistent and uniform with reports, plans, and budgets;

- allow for integration among the estimating, purchasing, scheduling, accounting, and cost-control systems; and

- be flexible enough to allow for change and growth in the business.

Account numbers within each general classification begin with the same number. For example, asset accounts begin with 1, liabilities with 2, and so forth.

The Accounting Cycle

The process of transforming raw financial data into financial statements is called the *accounting cycle*. It typically comprises five steps:

1. **Analyze source documents.** These receipts, invoices, checks, and other documents show the dollar value of day-to-day business transactions. They represent measurable events that affect a business's financial condition. Analyzing the data in each source document will identify why and how they affect specific accounts.

2. **Record the transactions.** Each financial transaction is recorded in a *journal,* which is the book of original entry, a chronological record of business transactions. Some businesses record all entries in a single journal called the *general journal.* Other businesses use *specialized journals* for specific types of transactions that occur frequently, such as payroll, sales, cash disbursements or receipts, and purchases.

3. **Post transactions.** Information recorded in the journals is posted, or transferred, to the *general ledger.* The general ledger details the increases,

decreases, and current balance of each specific account. Businesses typically use one or more *subsidiary ledgers* in addition to the general ledger. A subsidiary ledger provides a greater level of detail for a single account than the general ledger. Home builders commonly use subsidiary ledgers for accounts receivable, accounts payable, and job costs. The job cost subsidiary ledger contains detailed construction cost information on a unit-by-unit basis.

4. **Prepare the trial balance.** A trial balance summarizes the balances of all general ledger accounts. It determines whether the accounting equation balances. Before financial statements are prepared, the trial balance totals must be correct, and the accounting equation must be balanced.

5. **Prepare financial statements and close the books.** The company's financial statements are prepared from information contained in the trial balance. Financial statements are presented in a standardized format to make them as easy to interpret as possible. After the financial statements are reviewed for accuracy, the company's books are considered "closed" for that accounting period. When the books are closed, revenue and expense accounts are cleared, and the next accounting period begins with zero balances. Income (or loss) is transferred to owner's equity.

Standard Accounting Methods

Accrual. The *accrual* method recognizes revenues when they are earned, regardless of when the company actually receives a cash payment. Likewise, the accounting system recognizes expenses when they are incurred, regardless of when cash is paid out. In the previous example, under the accrual basis, Dan would recognize the telephone expense in December 2010 when it was incurred, rather than in January 2012 when the bill was paid.

For most builders, revenues are earned when a home is completed and the buyer gets the title to the home. For projects built under contract that span two or more accounting periods, there are two specific methods for recognizing revenues.

Completed contract. This method recognizes revenues and corresponding construction costs when the work is completed and the sales contract is fully executed. Revenues and expenses are matched when a house is closed.

Percentage of completion. Builders generally use this method for large custom homes or commercial projects that span multiple accounting periods. It recognizes revenues and construction costs as a project progresses toward completion. At the end of each accounting period, revenues earned to date are calculated based on the estimated percentage of the project that has been completed, using the estimated gross margin at project completion.

Preparing Accounting Transactions and Reports

The primary objectives of every business are profitability and *solvency*. Profitability is the company's ability to generate income. Solvency is its ability to pay debts as they come due. Three standard financial statements summarize a company's profitability and solvency: the income statement, balance sheet, and cash flow statement. Together, these financial statements detail changes in revenues, expenses, assets, liabilities, and owner's equity.

Internal Controls

An accounting system must include internal controls to ensure it operates as it was designed to. Internal control systems vary from company to company. Yours will depend on your company's size, organizational structure, and management style.

Because employees in small companies often perform a variety of tasks, it is more difficult for these companies to establish a system of internal controls. One person may have responsibility for multiple checks and balances in the system. Nevertheless, these basic guidelines will help you improve internal control:

- Keep authority over financial transactions with the owners. For example, the owner or treasurer should sign all checks. Checks written for an amount that exceeds a predetermined threshold should have two signatures.
- Ensure that the owner receives the bank statement directly from the bank and reviews it for unusual transactions.
- Keep supporting documentation with checks presented for signature.
- Number checks in sequential order, and account for all voided checks.
- As much as possible, separate control over an asset from recording transactions related to it. For example, the person responsible for receiving and depositing cash from customers should not be the same person who reconciles bank statements.
- Limit employee access to accounting records to those who need access based on their job function.
- Consider bonding employees to insure against theft or fraud.

Computerized Accounting Systems

Builders use computerized accounting to

- develop more effective internal control structures;
- eliminate many of the tedious manual aspects from the monthly accounting cycle;
- reduce input and calculation errors;
- automatically post data from journals to the general ledger; and
- generate a variety of financial statements and management reports.

Most accounting packages are divided into modules. Each module handles a specific component of the overall accounting process. Many packages allow builders to begin with a basic system (typically the general ledger module) and add modules as needed. In addition to the general ledger, other separate modules typically include the following:

- Accounts receivable
- Accounts payable
- Payroll
- Job costing

Accounting packages range in price from about $100 to several thousand dollars. Builders can choose from generic accounting systems designed for many different types of businesses or from dedicated accounting systems specifically designed for home builders. Although generic systems perform many accounting activities quite well, they are limited in their ability to perform many specific functions that home builders need. Their primary limitation is their inability to integrate accounting with other functions, such as job costing, purchase orders, and estimating.

Builders should understand that a computerized accounting system does not, by itself, correct deficiencies in their manual internal controls. In fact, if a builder's manual internal controls are poorly designed and poorly managed, computerizing the accounting system often creates even more problems. Therefore, builders should have well-defined accounting policies and procedures in place before attempting to computerize.

Job-Cost Accounting

Direct construction costs represent the largest category of a builder's cost of doing business. These construction-related costs are identified with a specific unit of production. Because this account is so crucial, you need an accounting subsidiary ledger—the job cost system—to track, allocate, and analyze each of these costs. The job cost system

- identifies costs by unit of production and by cost category within each unit of production;
- allows the builder to compare actual construction costs with expected costs;
- identifies variances from the original budget; and
- increases the accuracy of future estimates.

By analyzing variances and incorporating the results of the analyses into future estimates, builders can prevent errors made on previous estimates from recurring.

Designing and Using the Job Cost System

Set up the job cost system so each expense is assigned to the appropriate job and the appropriate cost category within that job. Design the system around your method of operation and consider these factors:

- Job type (custom home, tract home, remodeling)
- How much work the builder's crew performs and how much trade contractors do

Base the job cost system on the same categories used for project budgets established from your estimates so you can accurately compare actual costs with estimated costs.

Assign a title and a numerical code, or cost code, to each job category.[7] For example, builders whose plumbing contractor supplies all plumbing materials and labor may use a single cost code to track plumbing costs. Builders who furnish their own materials, however, may need separate cost codes for plumbing materials and plumbing labor.

A typical job cost system for a small-volume builder contains 70 to 80 cost codes.[8] These generally provide an adequate level of detail without being overly cumbersome and time-consuming to administer. Figure 12.2 shows typical cost codes for a small-volume home builder.

For a job cost system to be effective, you must use it for every job. After you use it a few times, it will become a smooth routine.

---

[7] Emma Shinn. *Accounting and Financial Management for Residential Construction,* 5th Edition. Washington, DC: BuilderBooks.com, 2008.
[8] *Appendix E, Direct Construction Costs, Subsidiary Ledger,* National Association of Home Builders Chart of Accounts, www.nahb.org/chart.

Figure 12.2   A Page from the NAHB Chart of Accounts

2900–2990 Owner's Equity
2900 Common Stock
2920 Retained Earnings
2950 Partnership or proprietorship account
2960 Distributions, dividends, and draws

3000–3990 Sales, Revenues, and Cost of Sales
3000–3490 Sales and Revenues
3050 Sales, developed lots
3110 Sales, single-family, production
3120 Sales, single-family, custom designed
3125 Sales, single–family, custom, no land
3190 Sales, other
3370 Design fees collected
3400 Miscellaneous income
3410 Interest income
3420 Dividend income
3450 Earned discounts

3500–3790 Cost of Sales
3550 Cost of sales, developed lots
3610 Cost of sales, single-family, production
3620 Cost of sales, single-family, custom designed
3625 Cost of sales, single-family, custom, no land
3690 Cost of sales, other
3700 Direct construction cost for prior periods

4000–4990 Indirect Construction Cost
4010 Superintendents and construction supervision salaries and wages
4120 Workers' compensation insurance
4265 Mobile phones, pagers, radios, field office
4410 Lease payments, construction vehicles
4420 Mileage reimbursement
4430 Repairs and maintenance, construction vehicles
4440 Operating expenses, construction vehicles
4450 Taxes, licenses, insurance, construction vehicles
4510 Rent, construction equipment
4530 Repairs and maintenance, construction equipment
4540 Operating expenses, construction equipment
4550 Taxes and insurance, construction equipment
4560 Small tools and supplies
4610 Temporary utilities
4620 Trash maintenance
4710 Salaries and wages, warranty
4720 Material, warranty
4920 Builder's risk insurance
4990 Absorbed indirect costs

Develop a Budget

During the estimating process, you will establish a budget for each cost category. Assign a cost code to each take-off item as you price it. When the estimate is complete, calculate totals by cost code. You will have a budget for each cost category you can use to compare actual costs with estimated costs as construction progresses.

Builders may prefer to delay developing a budget beyond the estimating phase because some projects may never reach construction. However, for the job cost system to work properly and to determine whether you will earn a profit, you must prepare a budget before starting construction. Automating your estimating using an off-the-shelf or customized product facilitates estimating, budgeting, and job costing.

Code Invoices

As your company receives invoices, you or your construction superintendent assigns a cost code to each one, and the appropriate person, such as a bookkeeper, posts the costs in the job cost system. Builders must develop procedures to ensure costs are coded by job, regardless of when (in which accounting period) the bills are paid, so you know what your profit margin is for each project. For example, you may complete a home on December 15 but receive an invoice for materials the following year, a different accounting period.

Post Job Costs

As you incur construction costs, record them so you can consolidate costs by job and cost code. Record the date, vendor, check number, and description for each cost item. At any point during construction, you can compute totals for each cost code and compare them with the budget.

Computerized Job Costing

Manual job cost systems are inexpensive and relatively easy to create. However, these systems have limitations and they are cumbersome. Posting information and consolidating costs are tedious and time-consuming tasks. Also, if you make mistakes in calculations, they will impact your estimate and budget.

A computerized job cost system, therefore, is definitely worth investing in. You may choose a dedicated cost-accounting system, or a generic program such as an electronic spreadsheet. The most appropriate format for a particular builder depends on volume of work, staff size, and how employees use the computer to perform other functions.

Dedicated Systems

As discussed in chapter 9, home builders can choose from a number of dedicated computerized job cost systems. Some stand alone, but most are designed to integrate computerized functions such as accounting, estimating, and scheduling. The primary advantage of dedicated systems is that they can provide more information in less time than most manual systems. The disadvantage is that you must invest in software and setup.

Electronic Spreadsheets

An alternative to a customized or dedicated job cost system is to use off-the-shelf software, such as QuickBooks®. With a small investment, you can take a giant leap forward in the speed and accuracy of your accounting and estimating. Once you create them, electronic spreadsheets will perform calculations and update estimates with a few mouse clicks.

Job Cost Reports

The key to a computerized job cost system, as with any management system, is the type of information it provides. Typical programs allow the builder to track costs and variances by project, job, cost center, model, and vendor.

A job cost system should at least provide a *summary variance report* and a *job variance report*. The summary variance report lists the total budgeted costs, actual costs to date, and variances for each job. The system should provide information on jobs in progress and completed. The job variance report lists budgeted costs, actual costs to date, and variances for each cost center within a specific job. By routinely comparing actual costs to what was budgeted, you can adjust expenditures to protect your profit margin.

13

Financial Management, Planning, and Analysis

Accounting and financial management are different but related functions. Although you can hire a professional to do your accounting, you must understand financial management thoroughly if you want your home building company to prosper over the long term.

Accounting primarily collects, consolidates, and presents consistently developed and easily interpreted information about a company's current operations. Financial management helps a builder make decisions based on the information produced by the accounting system. Following are key financial management questions. Answering these questions will further your understanding of your company's finances and operations.

- Are company assets being used efficiently and effectively?
- Is the business generating sufficient cash flow to meet its financial obligations?
- Are accounts payable being managed effectively?
- Will outside financing be required? If so, when and how much?
- Is the company generating sufficient profits, given its investment and level of risk?

With comprehensive information about your company's operations and a solid understanding of how to use it, you can answer these financial management questions.

Financial Planning

Financial planning helps you project the financial resources your company will need to carry out your strategic plan. Financial planning includes both *profit planning* and *cash planning*. Profit planning involves examining expected revenues, costs, and expenses associated with planned activities. Cash planning identifies funding sources and uses of cash, and ensures that the company always has sufficient operating funds.

Profit Planning

Builders use profit planning to develop forecasts and plans to chart their future profit performance and financial position. Profit planning relies on pro forma financial statements, which forecast results.

You can develop a pro forma statement for a single house, a specific phase of production, or company operations during a specific period. Projects that develop in phases generally have a pro forma for each phase. A pro forma statement typically forecasts expected monthly results for a 12-month period.

Pro Forma Income Statement

To develop a pro forma income statement for a specific accounting period, you will need the following information:

- A sales forecast
- Cost and expense estimates
- The company's historical financial statements

The pro forma income statement follows the same format as the historical income statement, but it reflects estimated values based on planning assumptions rather than actual events.

Obviously, sales, or the prospect of sales, provide the basis for all other company activities, so you begin with a sales forecast. Forecast the expected revenues, and estimate construction costs and operating expenses for the period. Remember to include both direct and indirect construction costs, which you can obtain from your project estimates.

Alternatively, you can estimate the cost of sales using the *percent of sales* method, which is discussed below. You then estimate expenses (including marketing, financing, and *general and administrative expenses*) expected during the period. The percent of sales method assumes that the relationships among revenue, construction costs, and operating expenses remain relatively constant over time. Percent-of-sales values for each cost of sales and operating expense category generally are calculated from the builder's historical income statements. To calculate expected profit for the period, you multiply these percentages by the expected revenues and then subtract the construction costs and operating expenses from revenue.

One shortcoming of the percent of sales method is that, as financial advisers remind investors, "The past is no indication of future performance." For example, a trade contractor could suddenly become unavailable or materials prices could spike. When you anticipate changes, such as hiring a superintendent, you can adjust the pro forma statement to reflect those changes. But because a pro forma statement is a best guess about your company's future performance, it should clearly and explicitly state its underlying assumptions.

Cash Flow Planning

The cash budget projects the amount and timing of incoming and outgoing cash. This allows you to anticipate expenditures, rather than trying to figure out, after spending money, where it went. Although builders may have a general sense of the upcoming sales and expense amounts for a specific period, a cash budget provides a more reliable tool for projecting cash needs.

New projects may need infusions of cash, closings may be delayed, or you might need to purchase new equipment. A cash budget will allow you to identify potential cash flow problems and take steps to prevent them. You must update them frequently. Cash budgets also allow builders to anticipate surpluses and develop strategies to invest cash until it is needed.

The Cash Flow Budget

How often cash budgets are prepared and the length of time they cover varies from builder to builder. A small builder generally can prepare monthly cash budgets up to six months in advance. You simply prepare a cash budget for each project and consolidate these individual budgets into a master production budget.

Similar to the pro forma income statement process, you begin the cash budget by developing a sales forecast for the budget period. Armed with information about expected sales and closings, you can project expected incoming cash from customer deposits, payments for work in progress, and receipts from closings. Your cost estimates for each project in progress during the budget period will forecast necessary cash disbursements for construction materials, labor, and payments to trade contractors. The construction schedules will help you determine when payments will have to be made. Include indirect costs and other expenses for the budget period in the master production budget to produce a comprehensive cash flow budget.

Financial Analysis

Financial analysis compares actual performance with expected and past performance, with the performance of other builders, and with industry norms. Benchmarking compares a company's financial performance with other builders and recommendations from industry experts. Using financial analysis, builders can evaluate their operations and assess their financial position. Financial statements provide a wide range of information about a company's current financial position and its operations over a given previous period. You can see how other builders performed in NAHB's biennial *Cost of Doing Business* studies.

The Common Size Income Statement

A *common size income statement* shows the company's costs, expenses, and profits as a percentage of sales. To develop the statement, divide each item on it by the dollar amount of sales. Figure 13.1 shows a typical common size income statement.

Calculate Working Capital

Working capital is the difference between *current assets* and *current liabilities*. It indicates what would remain if you paid off all current liabilities with cash or other current assets. Working capital is calculated using the following equation:

$$\text{Working Capital} = \text{Current Assets} - \text{Current Liabilities}$$

Working capital measures your *liquidity*—your ability to meet short-term obligations as they mature. In other words, can you pay current liabilities with current assets? Current assets normally include cash, accounts receivable, inventories, and short-term investments. Current liabilities include accounts payable, short-term *notes payable*, portions of long-term debt that will become payable within one year, accrued income taxes, and other accrued expenses (principally wages). The closer your working capital is to zero, the more difficulty you will have meeting current obligations with current assets.

A common size income statement shows the company's costs, expenses, and profits as a percentage of sales.

Assets vary in their liquidity; you can convert some into cash more readily than others. In general, the more liquid your assets are, the smaller the risk that you won't be able to pay creditors or that your operations will be strained or interrupted because of a cash crisis. Unfortunately, inventory usually comprises the majority of a small builder's working capital, and generally it is considered the least liquid of current assets. For example, NAHB *Cost of Doing Business Study* data dating to 2004 show that more than 70% of respondents' assets were construction work in progress. When you evaluate your working capital, consider

Figure 13.1 Common Size Income Statement

DAN SMITH CONSTRUCTION
Common Size Income Statement
Percentage of Sales
For Year Ending December 31, 20__

	19x1	%	19x2	%
Revenue				
Sales, Custom	$ 926,352	68.69	$1,032,595	61.11
Sales, Speculative	422,184	31.31	657,032	38.89
Total Sales	1,348,536		$1,689,627	
Cost of Sales, Custom	753,284	55.86	896,325	53.05
Cost of Sales, Speculative	363,497	26.95	555,490	32.88
Total Cost of Sales	1,116,781	82.81	1,451,815	85.93
Gross Profit	$ 231,755	17.19	23,812	14.07
Operating Expenses				
Sales and Marketing	40,561	3.01	52,729	3.12
Insurance	1,564	0.12	2,033	0.12
Office Supplies	2,285	0.17	2,971	0.18
Office Salaries	18,564	1.38	20,150	1.19
Officer Compensation	40,000	2.97	42,568	2.52
Professional Fees	3,250	0.24	3,400	0.20
Vehicle Expenses	16,580	1.23	23,895	1.41
Depreciation Expense	7,843	0.58	5,924	0.35
Travel and Entertainment	7,621	0.57	8,256	0.49
Other General & Administrative	1,695	0.13	2,204	0.13
Total Operating Expenses	$ 139,963	10.38	$ 164,130	9.71
Net Profit Before Taxes	$ 91,792	6.81	$ 73,682	4.36

how quickly you can expect to convert your inventory to cash and the value you would get for a quick liquidation.

Net Profit (Loss)

Net profit (loss), commonly referred to as the "bottom line," is your profitability after you account for all costs and expenses. By measuring net profit (loss), builders can compare their actual financial performance with their expected future and past performances. *The Cost of Doing Business Study* provides industry benchmarks for various types of home building companies.

Ratio Analysis

In addition to making net profit comparisons, you can use *financial ratios* to evaluate your company's performance. Commonly used ratios include *gross profit margin*, net profit margin, *return on assets*, and *return on equity*. Explanations of each ratio, and the equations used to calculate them, follow.

Gross profit margin is the percentage of each sales dollar remaining after deducting the cost of sales.

$$\text{Gross Profit Margin} = \frac{\text{Sales} - \text{Cost of Sales}}{\text{Sales}}$$

Net profit margin is the percentage of each dollar from sales revenue that remains after all costs, expenses, and taxes are deducted from sales.

$$\text{Net Profit Margin} = \frac{\text{Net Profit after Tax}}{\text{Sales}}$$

Return on assets (ROA) reflects the amount of income earned for each dollar invested in assets. It measures how effectively and efficiently the company uses its assets.

$$\text{Return on Assets} = \frac{\text{Net Profit}}{\text{Total Assets}}$$

Return on equity (ROE) reflects the dollars of net profit earned per dollar of owner's capital (invested plus earned capital). ROE reflects how efficiently the owner's invested capital is used.

$$\text{Return on Equity} = \frac{\text{Net Profit after Taxes}}{\text{Total Equity}}$$

Break-Even Analysis

A *break-even analysis* determines the volume of sales required to cover all of the company's costs and expenses. To find your break-even point, you must first determine all your fixed and variable costs. Fixed costs remain constant regardless of sales volume. They may include vehicles and equipment, sales office expenses, and the salaries of owners and construction superintendents. Variable costs, in contrast, vary with changes in sales volume. A builder's largest single variable cost category is direct construction costs.

To find your break-even point, divide total fixed costs by the *contribution margin*—the amount of each sales dollar remaining after deducting variable costs. The contribution margin reflects the amount available to help pay for a builder's fixed costs. Here are the equations used to calculate the contribution margin and the break-even point:

$$\text{Contribution Margin} = \frac{\text{Sales} - \text{Variable Costs}}{\text{Sales}}$$

$$\text{Break-Even Point} = \frac{\text{Total Fixed Costs}}{\text{Contribution Margin}}$$

You can use a break-even analysis to calculate the level of sales volume you must attain to generate a predetermined amount of net profit as follows:

$$\text{Sales Volume} = \frac{\text{Fixed Costs} + \text{Desired Profit}}{\text{Contribution Margin}}$$

The Balance Sheet

A balance sheet, also called a statement of financial position, is a snapshot of the dollar value of a company's assets, liabilities, and owner's equity at a designated time, typically the end of an accounting period. The balance sheet shows that the accounting equation balances. It shows the financial position of the company at the close of business on the date indicated on its heading. Specifically, the balance sheet includes

- the amount the company has invested in assets such as land and construction-in-progress;
- how these assets were financed; and
- who has claims against the assets.

When a balance sheet includes information for two consecutive accounting periods, it is called a *comparative balance sheet*. You can use a comparative balance sheet to view a company's financial position at two different points in time. Figure 13.2 shows a typical balance sheet.

Assets

Although most home builders use a non-classified balance sheet, assets may be listed in order of their liquidity, or the ease with which they could be converted into cash. Current assets include cash and other assets the business will convert to cash or use in a relatively short time—typically one year or less. Cash, the most liquid asset, is listed first. The cash account also may include *marketable securities*—stocks, bonds, and other liquid investments that could be converted to cash quickly.

After cash, the balance sheet lists receivables. The two most common types are accounts receivable—what customers owe the business, and *notes receivable*—promissory notes that customers or others have given the company.

Inventory represents assets that comprise, or will comprise, the products the company will sell to customers. For builders, typical inventory accounts include land slated for development, development costs, direct construction costs, and construction materials inventory. On a non-classified balance sheet, inventory often is listed first.

The final current asset category is *prepaid expenses–assets*. These assets have been paid for but not used. A typical prepaid expense is an insurance premium on a policy that expires sometime in the future.

Fixed assets are expected to be held or used for longer than one year. They generally consist of land, buildings, and equipment acquired for use in the business rather than for resale.

Note that the values of Dan Smith's fixed assets decrease by their *accumulated depreciation*. Depreciation apportions the cost of a fixed asset during the period in which it is used. The amount allotted each year represents an expense for that year, and the value of the asset is reduced by a corresponding amount. In the case of Dan Smith's fixed assets, $33,273 of their value has been depreciated (or used up) since they were acquired. Although your company would maintain a separate accumulated depreciation account for each specific fixed asset category, the balance sheet typically shows only the total accumulated depreciation for all assets.

Liabilities

Current liabilities are debts due in one year or less. You normally would pay them with current assets. Current liabilities are listed according to when they are due. The sooner a liability is due, the higher it ranks on the list.

Accounts payable are the amounts a business owes to its suppliers for goods or services purchased on credit. Accounts payable generally are due in 30 to 60 days. Notes payable are obligations secured with promissory notes. Notes due within one year are considered short-term liabilities.

The balance sheet summarizes in dollars a company's assets, liabilities, and owners' equity accounts for a specific period.

Unearned revenues are payments received for goods or services in advance. They are a liability because the company must perform the agreed-upon services or otherwise fulfill contractual requirements. A home builder's unearned revenues typically come from customer payments made during the construction process. Because the construction is not yet complete, you have not yet earned the revenue.

Figure 13.2   Balance Sheet

DAN SMITH CONSTRUCTION
Balance Sheet
December 31, 20__

Assets		
Current Assets	**20__**	**20__**
Cash	$ 15,170	$ 21,710
Accounts Receivable, Trade	7,680	3,452
Construction Materials	3,425	4,267
Land	68,000	76,000
Work in Process	168,597	225,682
Finished Houses	98,560	179,449
Total Current Assets	$361,432	$510,560
Fixed Assets		
Construction Equipment	35,000	35,000
Trucks and Autos	33,650	33,650
Office Equipment	16,485	17,594
Total	85,135	86,244
Less Accumulated Depreciation	28,860	33,273
Total Fixed Assets	56,275	52,971
Total Assets	417,707	563,531

Liabilities and Owner's Equity		
Current Liabilities		
Construction Loans Payable	165,000	206,000
Notes Payable	20,000	20,000
Accounts Payable	48,237	66,541
Contract Deposits	25,000	40,000
Total Current Liabilities	258,237	332,541
Long-Term Liabilities		
Mortgages Payable	38,684	36,262
Total Liabilities	296,921	368,803
Shareholders' Equity		
Common Stock	20,000	20,000
Retained Earnings	100,786	174,728
Total Shareholders' Equity	120,786	194,728
Total Liabilities and Shareholders' Equity	$417,707	$563,531

Dan Smith shows contract deposits of $40,000, which represent unearned revenues for the company.

Long-term liabilities are debts, such as mortgages or bonds, that are not due for at least one year.

Owner's Equity

The company's legal form or organization determines how owner's equity appears on the balance sheet. A corporation, such as Dan Smith Construction, Inc., would list owner's equity of common stock (the owner's investment in the company) plus retained earnings (accumulated profits that have not been distributed as dividends).

The Income Statement

In contrast to the common size income statement, the income statement summarizes the builder's revenues and expenses during a specific period, which is typically referred to as an accounting period. Generally, that is one year, although it could be a month or a quarter.

The income statement is based on the following equation:

$$\text{Net profit = Revenues} - \text{(Cost of Sales + Expenses)}$$

Figure 13.3 shows a typical income statement.

Revenue. Sales represent the revenues generated during the accounting period. Dan Smith builds both speculative and custom homes, so there is a category for both types of sales.

Cost of sales. This refers to the total cost of the products or services that produced the revenues. For home builders, cost of sales includes land, material, labor, contractors, and all other expenses associated with construction.

Builders incur two types of construction costs: direct and indirect. Direct costs are materials and labor easily identifiable with a specific unit of production, such as framing materials, roofing labor, and HVAC trade contractors. Indirect costs are construction-related costs that you cannot easily identify with a specific unit of production. These include superintendents' salaries, field offices, and construction vehicle expenses.

Gross profit is the difference between sales and the cost of goods sold. It is the amount available to cover operating expenses, pay taxes, and provide a net profit for the builder.

Dan Smith's, gross profit was $237,812.

The income statement summarizes the builder's revenues and expenses for a specific period.

Operating expenses are expenditures a company incurs to support revenues production. Expenses are measured by the costs of assets consumed or given up

Figure 13.3   Income Statement

DAN SMITH CONSTRUCTION
Income Statement
For Year Ending December 31, 20__

Revenue	20__	20__
Sales, Custom	$ 96,532	$1,032,595
Sales. Speculative	422,184	657,032
Total Sales	$1,348,536	$1,689,627
Cost of Sales, Custom	753,284	896,325
Cost of Sales, Speculative	363,497	555,490
Total Cost of Sales	$1,116,781	$1,451,815
Gross Profit	231,755	237,812
Operating Expenses		
Sales and Marketing	40,561	52,729
Insurance	1,564	2,033
Office Supplies	2,285	2,971
Office Salaries	18,564	20,150
Officer Compensation	40,000	42,568
Professional Fees	3,250	3,400
Vehicle Expense	16,580	23,895
Depreciation Expense	7,843	5,924
Travel and Entertainment	7,621	8,256
Other General & Administrative	1,695	2,204
Total Operating Expenses	139,963	164.130
Net Profit Before Taxes	91,792	73,682

during for the period the income statement covers. They include the costs of financing, sales and marketing, and general and administrative expenses.

Financing expenses are the interest charges and other costs associated with borrowing money.

Sales and marketing expenses include advertising, sales commissions, model homes, and the costs of running a sales office.

General and administrative expenses include the costs of office supplies, payments for telephone service, legal and accounting fees, and other expenses of daily operations.

Other expenses are costs that cannot be classified in one of the other four categories.

Net profit (loss) reflects the change in the owner's equity for the period. Net profit increases the owner's equity, and *net loss* decreases the owner's equity.

The Cash Flow Statement

Although the income statement provides important information about your profitability, it may reveal little about your ability to generate cash flows required to meet payroll, pay creditors, or withdraw funds from the business. Many builders have learned the hard way that earning a profit is not always synonymous with having cash in the bank to pay bills. The cash flow statement shows how money flows through your operations.

For example, although purchasing a fixed asset such as a vehicle or construction equipment affects your income statement only to the extent it is depreciated, it may require a significant cash outlay. This will reduce the amount of money you have to satisfy other obligations.

The cash flow statement answers three simple but important questions for a specific period:

1. Where did cash come from?
2. What was the cash used for?
3. What was the change in the cash balance?

The cash flow statement classifies cash receipts and payments by operating, investing, and financing activities.

Cash intakes and outflows from operations result from transactions such as the following:

- Cash receipts from sales and accounts receivable
- Cash purchases
- Payments of accounts payable
- Cash payments for operating expenses

Cash flows from investing activities arise from transactions like these:

- Purchase or sale of fixed assets
- Purchase or sale of short- and long-term investments

Cash flows from financing activities arise from transactions including the following:

- Loan receipts and repayments
- Receipt of capital and disbursement of funds to owners

Figure 13.4 shows a sample cash flow statement.

The statement of cash flows describes how cash was accumulated and spent during a specific time period.

Figure 13.4 Statement of Cash Flows

DAN SMITH CONSTRUCTION
Statement of Cash Flows
For Year Ending December 31, 20__

Cash Flows from Operating Activities	
Net Income	$ 73,682
Adjustments to reconcile net income	
to cash provided by operating activities	
Depreciation Expense	4,413
Decrease in Accounts Receivable	4,228
Increase in Construction Materials	(842)
Increase in land	(8,000)
Increase in Work in Progress	(57,085)
Increase in Finished Houses	(80,629)
Increase in Accounts Payable	18,304
Increase in Contract Deposits	15,000
Net Cash Provided by Operating Activities	$(104,611)
Cash Flows from Investing Activities	
Purchase of Office Equipment	(1,109)
Net Cash Provided by Investing Activities	(1,109)
Cash Flows from Financing Activities	
Construction Loans Obtained	582,371
Construction Loans Paid	(541,371)
Reduction in Long-Term Debt	(2,422)
Net Cash Provided by Financing Activities	38,578
Increase in Cash	6,540
Cash at Beginning of Year	15,170
Cash at End of Year	$ 21,710

Managing Cash

Cash is a builder's lifeblood. Without it, you cannot meet payrolls or pay bills. Without sufficient cash, you have no financial insurance from unanticipated events. If a cash shortage leads to late payments to materials suppliers and trade contractors, these vital partners in your business success will avoid working for you or extending credit in the future. Effectively managing your cash allows you to

- be more selective when choosing jobs;
- take advantage of discounts for early payments to suppliers;
- not feel constantly pressured to hurry a task to receive a draw on a construction loan; and
- have sufficient funds to meet financial obligations.

Managing cash well means you always have enough to meet your financial obligations and excess cash does not sit idle, but is invested wisely.

Cash Flow vs. Profit

The key to developing an effective cash management program is understanding the difference between net profit and cash flow. As discussed earlier, profit is the difference between revenue and expenses over a specific period. Cash flow, on the other hand, is the difference between the cash that flows into the company and that which flows out at given points in time. In the short run, you may experience a substantial discrepancy between net profits and the amount of cash available to meet your financial obligations. Although profit and cash flow are distinct and different concepts, they are closely correlated, and both impact a builder's long-term success or failure.

A builder who earns a profit may not have adequate cash flow, and a builder who has cash on hand is not necessarily the one earning a profit. Many good builders who were poor cash managers have gone out of business. For example, some builders have tried to keep their operations going by shifting cash from one job to another. Borrowing funds from one project to use on another is risky. It can lull you into believing that business is going well when it may not be. Moreover, this strategy may be illegal. Make sure each project has its own budget and don't commingle funds from one to another.

The Cash Budget

Cash management begins with developing a cash budget. Allow for actual cash flows that may differ significantly from what is expected. If your cash budget does not match anticipated cash flow, you will have trouble maintaining your operations.

Separate Personal from Business Cash

Builders should keep their personal cash separate from their business cash. Commingling the two will obscure your view of your company's cash position and may put your personal financial resources at risk.

From time to time, you may withdraw funds from the business (to pay dividends, for capital expenditures, or for loans to owners) or transfer money from your personal bank accounts into the business account (investment). Always use accepted, written legal documents for these transactions. Appropriate documentation helps ensure that owners/officers do not forfeit their limited liability status if they are part of a limited liability company or corporation.

Managing Accounts Payable

If you manage accounts payable effectively, they can be an inexpensive source of funds for financing company operations. On the other hand, if you don't manage accounts payable, they will eat away at your operating funds. To manage accounts payable well, follow these guidelines.

Take Offered Discounts

Suppliers often offer discounts for early payment. For example, *2/10 net 30* payment terms indicate that your company may take a 2% discount if you pay an invoice in full within 10 days of the date on the invoice. The full amount with no discount is due within 30 days.

Some vendors offer a variation of this discount in which the discounted payment is due on the 10th of the following month or the full payment on the 25th. If you think 2% doesn't sound like much, consider that if you pay a supplier who offers this discount on the 25th of the month rather than on the 10th, you are really paying 2% to use the money an extra 15 days. On an annual basis, that is an interest rate of 48%!

Balance Financial Obligations

Suppliers often charge fees for late payments. These late charges typically are 1 to 3% of the invoice amount. They are added to the account balance each month until the bill is paid. Paying late charges, like failing to take discounts, is an extremely expensive form of financing your business. Although you want to make payments in time to benefit from discounts, avoid late charges, and maintain good relationships with your suppliers, you should not pay bills before you need to in order to maintain your cash for expenditures that are necessary.

That said, paying early—particularly when paying small trade contractors—can provide substantial benefits for both the builder and the trade contractor. Small trade contractors often need fast cash turnover to buy materials and pay their employees and themselves. For the builder, consistently paying trade contractors promptly can result in increased loyalty, and sometimes even a better price on future jobs.

Negotiate Terms

Negotiate the best possible terms with your suppliers. The adage "you never know until you ask" applies here. You might find that a supplier who is reluctant to negotiate on price is willing to allow longer payment terms or a larger discount than the customary 2% for early payment. A supplier whose standard terms are 2/10 net 30 may offer an additional discount for payment on delivery. Of course, you need to evaluate the costs and benefits associated with paying early to get the extra discount.

Time Purchases Wisely

Time your purchases to provide the maximum benefit at the least cost. For example, if you are planning a large purchase close to the end of the supplier's billing cycle, consider delaying the purchase until the beginning of the next cycle. This can add an extra 30 days to the payment period. Again, ask and you might receive.

Taxes

Home builders are subject to federal, state, and local taxes. Tax laws often are complex, difficult to interpret, and subject to periodic change. Therefore, few builders—few small businesses, for that matter—have the resources or expertise to deal with them without outside assistance. To ensure that you are complying with the law but not sacrificing profit to taxes, you should enlist a competent tax adviser. You must be able to trust in this adviser's knowledge and expertise because, ultimately, you are accountable for ensuring that your business's income is reported accurately and that you pay taxes accordingly and at the appropriate time.

Nonetheless, business owners should be aware of tax policy changes in order to guide their tax professional to areas of concern to the business. For example, many home builders choose to organize their businesses as pass-through entities (such as LLCs or S corporations). For these businesses, in general, net business income is passed though from the business to the owner and is reported on the owner's individual income tax return. Thus, the effective tax rate for the business is the individual, rather than the corporate, income tax rate.

Home builders whose companies are organized this way need to understand the ramifications, particularly those of the Alternative Minimum Tax (AMT). This parallel tax system can result in higher overall tax liability in certain circumstances. Many tax deductions and credits cannot be applied toward your AMT tax liability. Builders should thoroughly understand their tax-paying status before pursuing certain business strategies, particularly those relying on tax incentives, such as those to encourage low-income housing production and energy-efficient homes. Your tax professional needs to be aware of these details in order to provide you with sound business planning advice.

The Internal Revenue Service (IRS) publishes a comprehensive tax guide for small business, which you can download at www.irs.gov. The guide addresses forms of business ownership and recordkeeping, provides instructions for completing the proper tax forms, and describes accounting periods.

Tax Categories

Four categories of taxes affect home builders:

- Taxes allocable to a business's net profit
- The business owner's personal taxes, including net business income passed through to the owner if the business is a sole proprietorship or pass-through entity, such as a S corporation or LLC
- Estate taxes

Income and employment-related taxes affect virtually all businesses and multiple levels of government can levy these taxes. Because state and local tax laws vary across the country, the following discussion applies only to federal taxes.

Taxpayer Identification

For tax purposes, businesses are identified by their Employer Identification Number (EIN). Sole proprietors with no employees may substitute their Social Security number. However, using a separate EIN for your business facilitates separating personal from business income and expenses.

The Fiscal Year

Each business must identify the month and day on which its accounting year ends, but in practice, most small businesses' tax years will correspond with the calendar year. Sole proprietorships, partnerships, S corporations, and LLCs, in general, must use a calendar year for income tax purposes. Corporations (other than S corporations) have greater flexibility in determining their fiscal years.

Business Structure and Income Taxes

Each business must report its income at the end of the fiscal year. The company's legal organization determines how it must report income and pay taxes.

In a sole proprietorship, the individual owner and the business activity are inseparable. Details of business activity, including sales and revenues, cost of goods sold, gross profit, business expenses, and net profit are included in the owner's personal income tax return. Net profits earned from the business are added to the owner's other income. The combined income, less allowable deductions, exemptions, and credits is used to determine tax liability.

Because the IRS does not want to wait until the fiscal year ends to collect taxes due, sole proprietors must estimate, report, and pay their taxes for the upcoming year. For calendar year taxpayers, partial payments on estimated taxes are due in April, June, September, and January.

As with sole proprietorships, partnership income is passed along to the principals. Therefore, all partners must report their share of the business's profits on their personal income tax returns. In addition, the partnership is required to submit an informational return reporting the results of business operations for the year. Like sole proprietors, partners must pay estimated taxes on their expected income.

Because corporations are legal entities, their tax returns are filed separately from their owners' returns. A corporation pays taxes on its profits and may have to make estimated tax payments. On their individual tax returns, the corporation's owners also must report money they receive from the business in wages or dividends.

As separate legal entities, S corporations must file corporate informational tax returns. Corporate profits are passed to stockholders and reported on their personal income tax returns. Stockholders may have to pay estimated taxes.

Depending on the structure of its operating agreement, an LLC is taxed either as a partnership or as a corporation. Most LLCs prefer to have the IRS treat them as partnerships.

Withholding Employment-Related Taxes

Under federal income tax withholding (FIT), each employer is required to withhold income taxes from an employee's paycheck. The amount depends on the employee's income and information the employee provides about his or her filing status and number of dependents.

Employers also withhold Social Security (FICA) and Medicare taxes for each employee and then match the Social Security amount out of business revenues. By law, upper wage limits are established for Social Security and Medicare taxes each year. Income in excess of the wage limits is not subject to taxation.

Each employer also must contribute to a Federal Unemployment Tax Act (FUTA) fund that compensates employees who are laid off. Employers receive credit if they participate in a state unemployment program.

Employers must periodically deposit income tax and FICA withholdings at an authorized financial institution, usually a bank. The size of the employer's payroll and the amount of withholdings each pay period determine when deposits must be made.

Reporting employment taxes. The employer must submit quarterly and annual reports on wages, salaries, and withholdings to the federal government. At the end of the year, employees receive a W-2 Form that details income and withholdings for the year.

Self-employment taxes. In addition to regular income tax, sole proprietors, partners, and members of an LLC must pay federal self-employment tax. Because these individuals generally are not considered employees, FICA and Medicare taxes are not withheld. The self-employment tax equals the sum of the employer and employee portions of Social Security and Medicare taxes that would have been withheld if the individual were considered an employee.

State and Local Taxes

Although all builders are subject to the same federal taxes, they face a variety of taxes at the state and local levels.

State income taxes. Some states impose a state income tax on their residents. For individuals, state income taxes typically are paid through payroll deductions similar to those for federal income taxes. Businesses generally must pay taxes on their incomes.

State sales taxes. A number of states impose a tax on goods and/or services purchased within their borders. These taxes typically are levied as a percentage of the purchase price. If their state requires it, builders must charge sales taxes on the homes they sell.

Local taxes. Localities may tax wages, salaries, and business revenues or income earned within the locality.

Pulling the Data Together

You have an array of tools for managing your daily finances, judging your company's profitability, and making accurate forecasts about future cash needs. Educate yourself about home building company financial management and be disciplined about reviewing your company's financial statements regularly. When you do, you will be confident that you understand your company's financial position. You will understand your company's current status, strengths, and weaknesses, and you will be prepared to move it in a positive direction.

14
Financing

Builders typically finance their operations with a mix of owner investment, other investors' capital, and bank loans either to their companies or to their home buyers (*construction-to-permanent loans*). Using debt to finance projects or company activities is called leverage. Using debt to pay for projects results in a higher return on investment than using equity (company assets), but at increased financial risk. The key to managing this financial risk successfully is not to avoid debt but to balance the use of debt with the use of company assets.

A common management strategy for small-volume builders is to have customers finance projects and pay the builder for work as it progresses. Buyer financing offers the advantage of debt leverage with less corresponding risk. Instead of taking out a construction loan, this approach transfers the risk of default to the buyer.

Small-volume builders typically use equity, debt, and buyer financing to help pay for their ongoing operations. Although there is no perfect mix, knowing the advantages and disadvantages of each source of capital can help you maximize your profits in robust markets and avoid problems during slowdowns.

Debt vs. Equity Financing

Two basic types of financing are available to builders: debt and equity. *Debt financing* uses borrowed money from a lender such as a bank. You are obligated contractually to repay the lender according to a specified schedule that includes both the loan repayment and the interest. If you default, or fail to meet the payment obligations, the lender may seize your assets or force your company into bankruptcy.

You get *equity financing* by selling ownership in your organization. In proprietorships and partnerships, the owners provide equity funding through direct capital contributions. A corporation may sell shares of company stock to obtain equity financing. Equity financing also is available to limited liability companies, joint ventures, or mergers.

Equity providers expect a return for their investment. For example, stockholders might receive dividends or increases in stock value. Dividends are distributions of the corporation's current or past earnings made at the discretion of the board of directors based on stock ownership. The market determines stock value.

Financing Issues

When you are weighing the benefits and drawbacks of financing with debt or equity, consider each option's impact on risk, profitability, cash flow, and management control.

If you choose to finance through debt, you will have to make principal and interest payments on the lender's schedule, without regard to your cash position or profitability. Interests charges on debt financing increase your company's expenses and reduce net profits. When you are short on cash, making required debt payments can significantly constrain your company's ability to maintain operations. However, these charges are tax deductible, which lessens their negative effect on company profits, compared with equity financing. On the other hand, as your debt increases, so does the possibility of failing to meet principal and interest payments.

Equity financing generally carries no mandatory repayment requirements. Because capital withdrawals and dividends are at your discretion, you can choose not to pay dividends. This is especially important when your profits are lean, or you are short on cash. Instead of paying dividends, you can use your cash to support company operations. On the other hand, dividends or capital withdrawals made to satisfy equity partners reduce the owner's equity. They are not considered expenses and, therefore, are not deductible from the company's revenue. Moreover, although financing with debt does not require builders to relinquish any degree of ownership or control, in contrast, equity investors often want at least some degree of control over company operations. Builders who consider using equity financing should analyze its impact on ownership and control carefully.

Debt Financing Alternatives

The following types of debt financing are common:

- **Unsecured loan.** An unsecured loan is not guaranteed by a specific asset. Because unsecured loans carry a high level of risk for the lender, their interest rates tend to be higher than those on secured loans.

- **Secured loan.** A secured loan is backed by a specific asset. Loans secured by real property commonly are called mortgages. For home builders, secured loans generally take the form of acquisition, development, or construction loans.

- **Small Business Administration (SBA) loans.** SBA loans are a good source of funds for many small businesses. In most cases, the SBA does not make the loan directly but, instead, guarantees a loan made by a private lender such as a bank. To obtain an SBA loan, the borrower must have tried unsuccessfully to secure a loan from a bank or other private source. Currently, SBA will not provide a loan to construct a home unless there is a sales contract.

- **Supplier and trade contractor loans.** Individuals and businesses that provide materials and services on credit are also a source of debt financing for builders. Payment terms vary, usually from 30 to 60 days, with discounts given for early payment, as discussed previously. In some areas, suppliers will wait for payment until a project is completed and closed. A supplier who is willing to extend the credit terms of a builder experiencing a cash flow problem is, in effect, making a loan to that builder.

Lines of Credit

A *line of credit* is the amount a lender, usually a bank, will make available to the borrower to use on an as-needed basis. The borrower pays interest only on the amount of funds used. Lines of credit typically are secured.

You should develop one or more lines of credit so you can access money if your business is short on cash. Unexpected demands for cash or late customer payments can cause a cash shortage. Overdraft protection for the company's checking account is another way to ensure creditors are paid on a timely basis. Maintain contact with two or more banks, even if you need or use only one bank loan at a time.

Lending Sources

There are a number of options for financing a construction company. Your local home builders association can refer you to local lenders. Following are some options:

Commercial banks. In most geographic regions, commercial banks provide most of the construction funds for small builders and developers.

Savings and loan associations. S&Ls used to finance more housing production than they do now. The Financial Institutions Reform, Recovery, and Enforcement Act of 1989 (FIRREA) shifted a significant portion of housing production funding from S&Ls to commercial banks.

Groups of banks or thrifts. Because FIRREA limits the amount banks or thrifts can loan to one borrower, financing for larger developments may come from a group of lenders. Under this arrangement, each lender provides only a portion of the total loan.

Housing trust funds. Housing trust funds, established by Congress in 1990, allow employers to create funds that assist their employees with housing-related expenses. The money can go toward a variety of housing applications, including permanent mortgage financing and funding for, or participation in, development projects.

Federal Finance Laws

Commercial banks and thrifts operate under a number of regulations that impact both their willingness and their ability to make construction-related loans. FIRREA and subsequent regulatory reforms have placed increasingly uniform rules and standards on real estate lending. Major regulations affect banks and thrifts as follows:

Lending policies and procedures. Banks and thrifts must develop internal real estate lending policies and procedures. They must provide written documentation that they conform to lending industry guidelines.

Risk-based capital. Banks and thrifts are subject to risk-based capital requirements. A lender must set aside its own funds, generally 4%–8%, for each construction-related loan it makes. Development and construction loans, usually considered high risk, require the highest set-asides. Because of this, lenders tend to favor loans that carry a lower risk and, therefore, require a lower set-aside.

Loan-to-value ratios. Banks and thrifts must set *loan-to-value ratios* that are equal to, or lower than, national guidelines. The maximum loan-to-value guidelines for various types of real estate loans are:

- Loans on raw land, 65%
- Development loans, 75%

- Multifamily and commercial construction, 80%
- 1–4 family residential construction, 85%
- Multifamily and commercial mortgages, 85%
- 1–4 owner-occupied mortgages, exempt

Restrictions. There are restrictions on how much a lender can loan to one borrower. The type of loan and size and type of lender determine the loans-to-one-borrower limit.

Acquisition, Development, and Construction (AD&C) Financing

The typical builder will, at one time or another, use different types of loans to finance construction activities. The type of loan depends on the activity or resource being financed, and the length of time needed to pay it back.

Acquisition and Development Loans

Acquisition and development loans provide funding to acquire raw land and develop it into finished lots. Acquisition and development can be funded separately or together. These loans typically are repaid on a lot-by-lot basis.

Construction Loans

Construction loans allow builders to buy developed lots and cover construction costs. These loans typically fund a specific project such as one home or group of homes. Loan-to-value ratios for construction loans generally range from 70%–80%. The lowest of the sales price or appraised value determines the value.

The term of a typical construction loan is 6 to 12 months. Sometimes a lender will grant an extension but charge a renewal fee or reduce the loan amount.

Construction loans typically are disbursed in 3 to 6 draws, based on a predetermined schedule. Some terms allow an initial draw to cover a portion of the cost of the lot. The borrower may make the remaining draws as construction progresses. The degree of project completion determines the amount of each draw.

Typically, construction occurs in phases with specific milestones. As the builder reaches each milestone, the lender will release a predetermined amount of money. Not all lenders release funds according to construction phase, how-

Sample Draw Schedule

1. Slab/foundation (15%). This draw is for land if the builder does not already own land, and for permits, septic, and site work. The draw is released at closing. Loan fees, attorney's fees, title insurance, and other loan costs are paid at closing.

2. Framing/rough carpentry (10%). This draw is released when the foundation is poured. It is for the cost of the first-floor walls, subflooring, and exterior wall sheathing.

3. Roof/mechanicals (20%). This draw is released after the second-floor subflooring and walls, roof framing, rough plumbing, electrical, HVAC, and miscellaneous items such as garages and pools are in place.

4. Exterior/interior finishes (20%). This draw occurs after doors, windows, and drywall installation, and completion of exterior siding and/or painting.

5. Trim (20%). After all interior trim, cabinets, paint, plumbing, HVAC, and electrical work are complete, this draw is released.

6. Project close (15%). This final draw occurs when all decks and patios, cleaning, appliance installation, and landscaping are complete, and after final inspection and issuance of occupancy permits.

ever. Some pay percentages that correspond to major construction activities, such as framing, insulation, drywall, and cabinets. When you request a draw, the lender sends an inspector to assess the degree of completion using these predetermined percentages. The lender then pays a portion of the construction loan accordingly.

Draw schedules are designed to match the amount of funds drawn to the amount of work completed. They are intended to ensure that, for the duration of a project, the lender has undisbursed funds sufficient to complete the project.

A construction loan generally costs more than just the total of interest payments. Other costs typically include the following:

- *Loan origination fee* (1% to 2% of the loan value)
- Loan application fee
- Legal fees
- Title search
- Construction survey
- Appraisal
- Inspections
- Document preparation
- *Recording fees*

Combining Construction and Permanent Loans

The combination construction-to-permanent loan, also referred to as a one-time-close or all-in-one loan, benefits both the buyer and the builder. This construction loan converts to a permanent mortgage when the home is completed.

The construction loan also may finance lot acquisition if the buyer does not already own a lot. Combined construction-to-permanent loans have a single closing rather than separate closings for the construction loan and permanent mortgage, which saves the buyer and builder time and money.

Working with Lenders

Many builders, particularly small-volume builders, approach lenders anxiously because they view lending institutions differently from other types of businesses. Although the lending industry has unique characteristics, banks and other lenders are in business to make a profit like other companies, by providing customers with products and services.

Lending Criteria

Lenders evaluate loan applications using a range of criteria. They want to earn an acceptable return on loans without incurring undue risk. In assessing a business's creditworthiness, lenders will evaluate your equity, your company's stability, and your cash position.

The Five Cs of Credit

Lenders consider five factors (the "five Cs of credit") in determining whether to grant a loan to a borrower: capacity, conditions, collateral, character, and capital.

Capacity. Capacity is a project's ability to generate sufficient income to repay the loan. The borrower must be able to repay the principal and pay interest as it becomes due. Lenders typically require builders to demonstrate capacity by providing pro formas that outline the project's expected profitability and cash flow.

Conditions. External conditions also can affect the lender's decision. National, regional, or local economic conditions include current and projected interest rates, employment rates, and inflation. Lenders also evaluate industry-specific conditions such as housing starts and apartment vacancy rates.

Collateral. Collateral is security a lender pledges to the borrower. Home builders' collateral typically includes undeveloped land, developed lots, and construction work in progress. Lenders are increasingly concerned about the value of property pledged. In fact, they may be more concerned about collateral than about your creditworthiness.

Character. Character is your ability and willingness to repay a loan. A bank or other creditor will judge you by your credit history and past relationships with lenders.

Capital. Capital refers to the borrower's financial position and stability. Lenders typically will rely heavily on your balance sheets and income statements to evaluate your company's strength. Lenders often require builders to guarantee their loans personally. A *personal guaranty* is a promise to use your personal assets to make principal or interest payments if your company cannot make the payments. Lenders who require personal guaranties typically evaluate the builder's personal financial condition, as well as his or her professional capacity to honor the terms of the loan.

If you must sign a personal guaranty, make sure it states

- the collateral pledged;
- that it is unsecured;
- liability is limited to principal only (not interest or collection costs);
- the lender will pursue collateral and borrower before the guarantor;
- a deadline for enforcing the guaranty, such as the first or second year of a loan; and
- that the obligation diminishes with each principal or interest payment.

You may place conditions on the guaranty (the more, the better) that may require the lender to lower the interest rate, obtain the collateral, or refrain from litigation for a specified period. Don't sign a guaranty for a company unless you own the company. If you are a partial owner and you must sign, then all other owners should sign, and you should negotiate to cap your liability. Only one spouse in a couple should sign a guaranty. Also, you should not maintain other accounts with the lender for which you are providing the guaranty, and you should avoid providing copies of your tax returns to that lender.

The Loan Proposal

Before applying for a loan, meet with the lender to discuss what you need to include in your application package. (*See* Appendix A for a generic loan application checklist.) Although lenders have standardized loan applications, individual institutions may have some unique requirements. Listen carefully to what they emphasize in your discussion, and then carefully produce all required documents. Most loan requests must include detailed market studies, pro formas, and proof that you have obtained all regulatory approvals, paid impact fees, and addressed environmental concerns. You will need to provide the project location and description, a survey, and title report.

Project Documents

Lenders typically require the following information to process a loan application:

Detailed breakdown of all costs. The lender wants to see the estimated costs of each phase of the project. If possible, include documentation such as trade contractor bids and supplier quotes in your estimates. If you have completed similar projects to the one you are seeking funding for, provide actual costs from those projects. Lenders want reassurance that your cost estimates are comparable to other similar projects so they won't have to provide more money at the last minute to complete a project. They also want to know they will at least break even if they must foreclose.

Pro forma analysis. Include cash flow budgets and income pro formas in the loan application package. The budgets and pro formas should reflect realistic estimates. You may want to include three versions: worst-case scenario, best-case scenario, and most probable scenario.

Plans and specifications. Lenders generally obtain a property or project appraisal. Plans and specifications provide the basis for that appraisal.

Signed contract. If the loan is for a presold home, such as a custom home, include a copy of the signed sales contract. Generally, loans for contracted projects are considered less risky than loans for speculative homes.

Marketing plan. If the loan is not for a presale, include your marketing plans for the project.

Lenders also typically will want the site plan, home plans, and construction schedule.

Personal and Company Documents

Lenders typically also require the following personal and company documents:

Company description and history. You should provide information about your company, key employees, and previous or current projects, particularly when requesting a loan from an unfamiliar lender.

Tax returns and financial statements. Lenders generally want to see the builder's current balance sheet, income statement, and tax returns for at least the previous two years. Because lenders often require builders to guarantee their loans personally, they also may require personal financial statements and tax returns.

Lenders also may want you to document personal collateral, sign a personal guaranty, and provide both personal and business references. They may want to see your partnership and joint venture contracts.

The Professional Presentation

Most builders can convince a lender they are fit to start a project; the challenge is convincing them that you can complete what you start. Go beyond the numbers and required documentation by providing a prospectus of completed projects and discussing your company's vision and goals to demonstrate that you have a plan and marketing acumen. Present a focused, concise proposal that includes a cover page, an executive summary, summary spreadsheets, and detailed annotations of each line item on cost breakdowns.

Maintain Flexibility, Nurture Relationships

If the lender hesitates to fund your project, offer to make changes that will address concerns. For example, you could provide more cash up front, shorten the loan term, or, if you are a land developer, secure lot purchase contracts. You also could offer another guarantor or a second source of repayment.

Above all, cultivate lasting relationships with lenders. Treat them with respect, and try to bring them other business. For example, if a bank lends you money for land acquisition or development, also get your construction loan and mortgage financing for your customers there.

You may want to develop relationships with multiple lenders. Many builders have lost their bank contact and their ability to borrow money when their bank merged with another financial institution. Keep each one informed about what you are doing. Remember, you are in home building for the long haul. Your reputation will precede you in seeking loans in the future. Be trustworthy.

Negotiating the Best Financing Package

Once you have persuaded a bank or thrift to loan money for your project, your negotiating is not finished. Use the following information to negotiate better terms than what the lender offers.

The combination of interest and fees you must pay up front pushes financing costs on the typical residential AD&C loan significantly above the lender's cost of funds—up to 5 percentage points higher. This spread means AD&C loan borrowing costs are 50%–75% higher than those for home mortgages, even though AD&C loans are only slightly riskier for lenders. You should point this out to your bank and try to negotiate lower rates, particularly in situations where the prime rate (to which most lenders tie AD&C loan rates) is significantly higher than other interest rates. In addition, if you are borrowing money to construct presold homes, you can discuss the significantly lower risk for the bank than if you were borrowing to finance speculative construction.

Even if you persuade your lender to reduce the interest rate on your loan, however, the savings from this strategy may be modest. You actually may save more by negotiating the amounts of ancillary fees for appraisal, attorney, inspection, processing, and document preparation.

Managing in a Credit Crunch

The housing recession of the early twenty-first century highlighted the need for builders to have strategies to work with lenders in difficult market conditions. If you are having trouble managing an AD&C loan, you must take immediate steps to talk to your lender. It usually will be in the lender's best interest to negotiate, rather than allow you to default and enter foreclosure. Your first meeting with the lender in this situation will determine the environment, tone, and success of future negotiations.

Meeting with the Lender

Here's how to handle a first meeting with a lender regarding an outstanding loan:

- Have a plan for loan repayment.
- Minimize the number of meeting participants, but include a decision maker.
- Keep the environment positive. Do not argue.
- Use a comprehensive agenda of issues to be discussed.
- Listen carefully.
- Start slowly with small items, reinforcing the joint benefits of your plan for repaying the loan.
- Focus on the future, rather than on past accomplishments.
- Offer a realistic assessment of performance expectations, providing details of your assumptions.

- Weigh options before responding or committing to an offer.
- Be prepared to make reasonable concessions in return for getting more time to repay the loan and continued funding.

Negotiating with the Lender

When you go to meet with your lender, expect negotiations to begin immediately. Before agreeing to anything, assess whether the loan officer is committed to working with you and whether he or she understands the seriousness of the situation. Ask the following three questions:

1. What else do you need to assist with a review?
2. What are your concerns with the business plan?
3. What do you propose we do now?

Although you do not want to agree to any concessions before carefully reviewing their implications, you also want to avoid a stalemate. Everything is negotiable, so you should attempt to receive something in return for every concession. However, you must keep the climate positive and show that you understand the lender's position.

Permanent Financing

Many builders, particularly small-volume builders, do not provide permanent financing to their home buyers. Instead, they often sell homes through outside agents who work with customers to find the best source of permanent financing. Nonetheless, you need to be familiar with various sources and types of permanent financing for the following reasons:

- Builders often must obtain permanent financing for projects such as rental properties, office space, or warehouses.
- Many customers are both unfamiliar with the financing options available to them and apprehensive of the financing process. Builders who can help customers arrange financing that satisfies their needs provide a service that may differentiate them from competitors.
- Familiarity with financing sources and processes helps you qualify your prospects.
- Some types of permanent financing, such as Federal Housing Administration (FHA) or Veterans Administration (VA) loans, impose additional costs on the builder. You should be aware of and allow for these costs.

The Primary Mortgage Market

Lenders who *originate* real estate loans make up the *primary mortgage market.* Today, home buyers have a number of options for financing new homes. Savings and loan associations (S&Ls) and commercial banks provide most loans for home buyers. Other potential sources of real estate loans include mutual savings banks (in the Northeast), life insurance companies, credit unions, and pension funds.

The Secondary Mortgage Market

Another group of institutions plays a key, if less direct, role in providing real estate loans. These institutions comprise the *secondary mortgage market.* They purchase mortgages and resell them to investors, who purchase the right to receive all future payments associated with the mortgage. The secondary mortgage market allows each primary lender to maintain the most appropriate amount and mix of mortgages for its particular situation.

Government Sponsored Enterprises (GSEs)

Fannie Mae and *Freddie Mac* are government-sponsored enterprises (GSEs) that help ensure the availability of credit for home purchases. Fannie Mae and Freddie Mac have substantially similar charters, congressional mandates, and regulatory structures. Both are publicly traded corporations.

Fannie Mae works with mortgage bankers, brokers, and other primary mortgage market partners to help ensure they have funds to lend to home buyers at affordable rates. It funds mortgage investments primarily by issuing debt securities in the domestic and international capital markets.

Freddie Mac supports liquidity and stability in the secondary mortgage market through two principal lines of business:

- A credit-guarantee business purchases residential mortgages and mortgage-related securities in the secondary mortgage market, securitizes these mortgages, and subsequently sells them to investors as mortgage-backed securities.
- A portfolio investment business purchases mortgages for the mortgage-related investments portfolio.

Ginnie Mae is a government-owned corporation within the U.S. Department of Housing and Urban Development that guarantees mortgage-backed securities backed by federally insured or guaranteed loans. Unlike Freddie Mac and Fannie Mae, Ginnie Mae does not purchase mortgages from lenders, nor does it buy, sell, or issue securities. Ginnie Mae provides a secondary market for the federal government's special loan programs, such as low-income or low-interest-rate loans, and guarantees the principal and interest on securities that have FHA and VA mortgages as collateral. Ginnie Mae securities are the only mortgage-backed securities that carry the full faith and credit guaranty of the United States government. Even in difficult times, an investment in Ginnie Mae securities is among the safest investments an investor can make.

Mortgage Insurance and Guaranties

You should understand all available options for insuring and guaranteeing a mortgage for yourself and for your customers.

FHA loans. FHA exists primarily to insure real estate mortgages that approved lending institutions originate. The borrower pays the insurance premium either in full at closing or incrementally, in addition to making regular loan payments.

FHA restricts insurance to mortgages and properties that meet the following guidelines:

- An FHA-approved appraiser must appraise the property.
- The loan amount cannot exceed the maximum established by FHA.
- Only owner-occupied properties are eligible for loans made under the 203(b) program (FHA's centerpiece loan program).
- Seller-paid closing costs may not exceed an amount FHA establishes.
- Construction materials and methods must conform to FHA guidelines.

VA loans. The Veterans Administration established the VA loan program in 1944 to guarantee loans made to veterans for the purchase or construction of homes. Unlike the FHA, the VA guarantees loans; it does not insure them. The VA guarantees only that portion of the loan specified in the veteran's certificate of eligibility, based on his or her length of active service.

A VA-approved lender typically originates the loan for up to 100% of the selling price or appraised value. There is no ceiling on the maximum loan amount.

Farmers Home Administration (FmHA) loans. FmHA, which is part of the U.S. Department of Agriculture (USDA), makes loans to residents of rural areas for the following purposes:

- Homes and building lots for low- and moderate-income families

- Purchase and operation of family farms
- Rural improvement projects

The FmHA guarantees loans made and serviced by private lenders and operates a direct loan program.

Types of Mortgages

When you understand the benefits and drawbacks of particular types of mortgages and can discuss them with buyers, you add value to your relationship and distinguish your company from other builders in your market. The following types of mortgages may be available to your home buyers:

Straight. In a *straight mortgage,* the total loan amount becomes due and payable at the end of the term of the loan. Straight mortgages usually have a short maturity (three to five years) and require periodic payments during the loan term. Straight mortgages are popular for second mortgages and home improvement loans. Before the FHA was established, straight mortgages were the only financing option home buyers had.

Amortized. Most mortgage loans are amortized mortgages. With an amortized mortgage, the borrower makes periodic payments (usually monthly) that include both principal and interest over the term of the loan. These mortgages typically amortize over 15–30 years.

Most mortgages are fully amortized; that is, their payment schedules provide for the entire principal to be paid during the term of the loan. Typically, they are level-payment loans—the payment amount is constant over the life of the loan. The payment amount is credited first to the interest due, and then the remainder of each payment is applied to the principal. As the loan matures, the interest portion of the payment decreases, and the principal payments increase.

A partially amortized mortgage requires periodic payments that do not completely pay the loan principal during the loan term. A final large payment—a balloon payment—pays the remaining balance.

Adjustable rate. *Adjustable rate mortgages* (ARMs) permit the interest rate to vary over the loan term. Interest rates fluctuate according to an index. Most ARMs include limits on interest-rate fluctuations. Periodic rate caps limit the amount of periodic rate adjustments and aggregate rate caps limit the total increase over the term of the loan. For example, an ARM might specify that the interest rate can increase a maximum of 2% at a time and 5% total over the life of the loan.

Interest rate adjustments typically change the loan payment. They also may change the loan balance or loan term.

An ARM also may include a payment cap, a limit on the maximum payment amount. An increase in the interest payment and a payment cap can cause negative amortization—an increase in the principal balance.

Graduated payment. A *graduated payment mortgage* (GPM) allows the borrower to make lower monthly payments during the early years of the loan and higher payments for the remainder of the loan term. This type of loan is attractive for first-time buyers whose income is expected to increase.

Assisting the Lender

Understanding what information the lender needs smoothes the mortgage process for the builder, buyer, and lender. It also can speed up the application process significantly. Lenders analyze the property and the borrower's ability to repay a loan before deciding whether to offer a mortgage. When the borrower provides clear, complete information, the lender can conduct this analysis efficiently.

Property Value

Lenders must feel confident that property pledged as security would garner enough to pay off the loan balance. Therefore, the maximum amount the lender will loan on the property generally is based on the lower of selling price or the property's appraised value. To establish property value, the lender will require an appraisal by a qualified appraiser. As discussed previously, if the borrower is applying for an FHA or VA loan, the property must meet certain minimum federal standards.

Borrower Creditworthiness

The lender must assess the borrower's ability and willingness to make payments over the life of the mortgage. That decision is based on the borrower's current situation and past history.

Borrower's ability to pay. A borrower's ability to make payments depends primarily on income and other financial obligations. Together, the mortgage debt service

Builders and the Appraisal Process

An appraiser should provide an opinion of market value and recognize your knowledge of the market. Insist that your lender uses qualified, designated appraisers. The appraiser should have experience with new construction and understand green building valuations. He or she should be willing to meet with the builder to get information on homes or projects. As the builder, you should provide all relevant data, including

- market, absorption, and sales information;
- property specifications; and
- construction details, including information about materials and why they were chosen.

ratio and the fixed obligation ratio show the lender and buyer what monthly payment the buyer reasonably can afford. These statistics are based on the experience of thousands of other home buyers.

In addition to *ratio analysis*, lenders use balance sheets to assess the borrower's ability to pay. The balance sheet provides information about the borrower's assets and liabilities. The balance sheet also lets the lender know how much financial "cushion" the borrower has and provides information about the source of funds for the down payment and closing costs.

Mortgage debt service ("front") ratio. This ratio indicates the percentage of the borrower's gross monthly income a monthly mortgage payment will consume. The total monthly payment includes the actual loan payment (principal and interest), plus a monthly portion for property taxes and hazard insurance. The ratio is calculated by dividing the total monthly payment—principal, interest, taxes, and insurance—by gross monthly income.

Fixed obligation ("back") ratio. This ratio is the percentage of the borrower's gross income needed to satisfy the monthly mortgage payment and other monthly obligations such as car, furniture, or credit card payments. Lenders have minimum acceptable levels that both ratios must meet for the loan to be approved.

Borrower's desire to pay. The lender evaluates a borrower's desire to pay by examining how the borrower has dealt with past debt obligations. Evidence of the borrower's past financial performance comes primarily from credit reports.

Financing Evolves

The economic and housing recession sparked by lax lending standards that began during the first decade of the twenty-first century will dramatically affect how builders acquire capital and how consumers finance homes in the future. This new environment for financing housing production means builders must work even harder to (1) make their project proposals attractive to lenders (2) understand consumers' ability to get financing, and (3) keep up with lenders' requirements to provide a loan as these prerequisites evolve. No matter how the "five Cs of credit"—capacity, conditions, collateral, character, and capital—change, they will remain important elements of housing finance, and your relationships and communication with stakeholders will be more critical to your success as a home builder than they were in the past.

15

Managing Your Work Force

Builders competing in any given market have access to the same land, materials, and trade contractors. What will set you apart is the quality of your employees. Your workers' enthusiasm and their job satisfaction significantly impacts productivity, customer service, quality, and, ultimately, your company's success or failure. Your employees and trade contractors you work with can propel you from survival mode to stellar performance in the home building industry.

By now you understand that to meet your goals, you must perform a number of distinct but related functions: planning, estimating, scheduling, accounting, financial management, sales and marketing, production management, customer service, and office management. You can

- perform most tasks yourself;
- delegate the responsibility to an employee; or
- contract functions to someone outside the company.

To build a successful company, you must rely on a team with the talent, skill, knowledge, and experience to achieve the organization's goals. To create this team, you must be able to identify, select, develop, and retain qualified workers.

These tasks are easier with an effective human resource program that addresses the following 11 areas:

1. Planning
2. Job analysis
3. Recruiting
4. Selection
5. Orientation
6. Training and development
7. Performance evaluation

8. Compensation
9. Discipline
10. Retention
11. Separation

Human Resources

Human resource planning determines the positions to be filled and the skills, knowledge, personality and experience needed for each one. It also provides a framework for developing strategies to meet future hiring needs. Therefore, it depends on your company's strategic plan.

Job Analysis

Job analysis systematically identifies the components of a job so you can better understand what a team member will need to fulfill his or her role successfully. The analysis defines job tasks and the qualifications (education, experience, specialized training) required to perform them. Ask the following questions when analyzing job requirements:

- What machines and special equipment are required?
- What knowledge, skills, and abilities does a person need to perform the job?
- What are the performance expectations for the job?
- With whom must the jobholder interact to perform these tasks?
- What are the innate personality requirements for this particular job?

The information gathered during a job analysis becomes the basis for a number of other human resource functions:

- **Regulatory compliance.** A job analysis can help the builder comply with government regulations and defend against charges of unfairness or discrimination.
- **Recruitment and selection.** A job analysis helps identify the type of individual best suited for the position based on job qualifications and requirements.
- **Training.** By identifying the required knowledge, skills, and abilities for a job, a job analysis allows the builder to determine training needs.

- **Compensation.** A job analysis helps determine the relative worth of a job by identifying its level of difficulty, duties and responsibilities, and necessary skills and abilities. By understanding the job's worth relative to other jobs, the builder can establish a competitive wage or salary package.
- **Performance appraisal.** To evaluate an employee's performance objectively, the builder must understand exactly what that employee is supposed to do. A job analysis identifies criteria to use in comparing performance.
- **Safety.** A job analysis can identify potentially unsafe working conditions or practices.

Job Descriptions

One function of a job analysis is to provide information for developing job descriptions. A job description details tasks and responsibilities for a particular position and its relationship to other positions in the company. (Appendix B contains sample job descriptions for common positions in a home building company.)

Although there is not a standard format for job descriptions, most contain four parts: job title, job summary, reporting relationships, and job duties and responsibilities.

Job title. A title accurately describes the job and distinguishes it from other jobs.

Job summary. The summary describes the general nature and purpose of the job.

Relationships. This section shows the worker's relationships with others inside and outside of the company, including supervisor(s), subordinates, and colleagues.

Duties and responsibilities. This detailed listing of specific duties and responsibilities also may include how tasks are done and why.

Job Specifications

The job analysis also provides information for developing a job specification for each position. This outlines the qualifications (skills, knowledge, training, education, certification, physical requirements) an individual must possess to perform the duties and responsibilities contained in a job description. It can be a separate document or a section in the job description. The job description

- defines relationships within the company from a professional, rather than a personal, perspective;

- provides a resource for making hiring and promotion decisions; and
- sets clear expectations for employees.

A job description should include physical requirements for the job, such as the ability to bend and to lift heavy objects.

Quantitative

A written job description facilitates setting qualitative and quantitative performance goals such as the following:

- Complete customer service on all lists more than 30 days old.
- Reduce all over-30-day customer service lists to 50% or less of outstanding requests list.
- Get new permits released.
- Develop a professional development plan that includes targeted education opportunities and new work projects.
- Ensure buildable lots are on schedule and within budget.
- Deliver high-quality homes.
- Close homes on schedule.
- Be able to groom employees for promotion.
- Deliver products consistent with the selection sheet.
- Maintain a clean on-site construction facility and project appearance.
- Skillfully manage customers.
- Maintain professional relationships with personnel outside of immediate area of responsibility.
- Provide accurate and timely project and employee status reports.
- Consistently apply company policy.
- Have no
  - outstanding customer service requests older than __ days;
  - punch list items on initial walk-through lists;
  - customer complaints;
  - reported violation of local government regulations; or
  - legitimate repeat service requests from other builders that have purchased lots.

Recruiting the Best

Recruiting—locating, identifying, and attracting qualified applicants—occurs both inside and outside the company. Recruiting from within can offer a number of advantages:

- Current employees understand the business.
- Morale and motivation may increase because qualified employees believe the company offers advancement opportunities.
- Perceived potential for advancement attracts new entry-level employees.
- Recruiting from within often is not as expensive and time-consuming as external recruiting.

Employers naturally want to fill positions by promoting from within to reward employees who have performed well in their current positions. However, you should never promote unless you believe your internal candidate really is the best person for the job.

For example, a builder may promote an outstanding salesperson to the position of sales manager, but then discover the characteristics that made an outstanding salesperson do not transfer well to management. The company not only has lost its best salesperson, it has gotten a poor manager too.

If the vacant position is entry level, or if qualified candidates are not available within the company, you must recruit externally. Recruiting outside the company enables a company to bring in new ideas and people who already possess the required skills and knowledge.

You can find qualified applicants through a number of channels, including the following:

- Referrals from current employees
- Trade contractors
- Referrals from customers and other business associates
- Online advertising
- Public and private employment agencies
- High school, vocational school, and college placement services
- Temporary help services

One method of recruiting is not inherently better than another. However, many builders have found workers by networking with current employees, friends, trade contractors, suppliers, inspectors, and others in the industry. The type of position you are filling, your company's size, and the local labor market will influence your method(s).

Whatever recruiting tools you use, you should continuously be identifying potential candidates to bring into your business and business relationships, whether you have an open position or not. Proactively managing your employees confers a competitive edge as other builders scramble to find good workers on the fly.

Selecting Employees Based on Qualifications

The selection process gathers information about potential employees and identifies the candidate whose qualifications most closely match job requirements. You can use a number of selection devices, including the candidate's job application, written tests, simulations, interviews, background investigations, and physical examinations. However, before you use any of these options, you must understand *reliability* and *validity*. Employment law requires that a selection device be both valid and reliable.

Reliability is the degree to which interviews, tests, and other selection procedures consistently assess what they are intended to. Two or more individuals using the same selection device will reach the same conclusion about a job applicant's qualifications. Assume that a builder uses a specific interview format as a selection device. If two or more managers interview the same candidate, a reliable interview format should lead them to the same conclusions in selecting the right person.

Validity is the accuracy of the selection device in predicting job performance. For a selection device to be valid, it must have a proven relationship with some aspect of job performance. An employer cannot use a test as a selection device unless there is clear evidence that test scores predict how well the individual actually will perform on the job.

Application Forms

An application form allows you to eliminate unqualified applicants and provides basic information for the rest of the selection process. The form should request information about the applicant's education, work experience, and other job-related information. The application should not include questions about the applicant's sex, religion, age, race, color, national origin, marital status, disabilities, or arrests. You may ask whether the applicant is a US Citizen or eligible to work in the United States, and whether he or she has any felony convictions.

Employment Tests

Employment tests generally measure either *aptitude*—the ability to learn or acquire skills, or *achievement*—what a person knows or can do right now. *Cogni-*

Tips for Lawful Testing and Selection[9]

Title VII of the Civil Rights Act of 1964, the *Americans with Disabilities Act* of 1990 (ADA), and the Age Discrimination in Employment Act of 1967 (ADEA), prohibit using discriminatory employment tests and selection procedures.[10]

1. Employers should administer tests and other selection procedures without regard to race, color, national origin, sex, religion, age (40 or older), or disability.

2. Employers should ensure that employment tests and other selection procedures are properly validated for the positions and purposes for which they are used. The test or selection procedure must be job-related and its results appropriate for the employer's purpose. While a test vendor's documentation supporting the validity of a test may be helpful, the employer is still responsible for ensuring that its tests are valid under federal Uniform Guidelines on Selection Procedures.

3. If a selection procedure screens out a protected group, the employer should determine whether there is an equally effective alternative selection procedure with less adverse impact and, if there is, use it instead. For example, if the selection procedure is a test, the employer should determine whether another test would predict job performance but not disproportionately exclude the protected group.

4. To ensure that a test or selection procedure predicts success in a job, employers should keep abreast of changes in job requirements and should update their test specifications or selection procedures accordingly.

5. Employers should ensure that managers are not adopting tests and selection procedures casually. No test or selection procedure should be implemented without an understanding of its effectiveness and limitations for the organization, its appropriateness for a specific job, and whether it can be appropriately administered and scored.

tive ability tests measure mental capabilities such as general intelligence, verbal fluency, numerical ability, and reasoning ability. *Personality tests* assess personal characteristics that tend to be consistent and enduring, such as extroversion, conscientiousness, emotional stability, agreeableness, and openness to experience. *Physical ability tests* measure attributes such as strength, body coordination, and stamina. *Work sample tests* require the candidate to perform tasks that the job requires.

---

[9] *Uniform Guidelines on Selection Procedures* (http://www.eeoc.gov/policy/docs/factemployment_procedures.html), U.S. Departments of Labor and Justice, Office of Personnel Management, and the Equal Employment Opportunity Commission, modified September 23, 2010.
[10] U.S. Equal Employment Opportunity Commission, *Laws Enforced by EEOC* (http://www.eeoc.gov/laws/statutes/index.cfm).

Interviews

The interview is the most widely used method to assess job candidate's qualifications. An interview provides additional information about the applicant and can clarify any questionable information provided on the application. For the applicant, the interview is a way to learn more about the job and the prospective employer.

Ideally, the interview process will include three levels: a 10-minute telephone prescreening, a 20- to 45-minute face-to-face interview of candidates who were not eliminated in the phone interviews, and a half-day interview with 2 to 3 finalists.[11] The final interview is designed to establish rapport with interviewees so they will let down their guard and reveal more about themselves.

Interviews can be structured or unstructured. In a structured interview, the interviewer asks standardized questions in a predetermined format. In an unstructured interview, the interviewer may begin with predetermined questions but may veer from the script in response to answers the candidate provides along the way. As long as questions follow nondiscrimination guidelines, both types of interviews can judge an applicant's qualifications effectively.

Unfortunately, both types of interviews often are conducted poorly and, therefore, provide little useful information for either the interviewer or the interviewee. This problem stems primarily from poor interviewing skills and the interviewer's failure to prepare.

Use the following guidelines to improve the interview process:

- Plan the location and timing of the interview to preclude interruptions.
- Know the job description and job specifications in advance.
- Familiarize yourself with information on the candidate's application form beforehand.
- Develop a framework for the interview.
- Ask questions that require the applicant to give detailed accounts of actual job experience and behaviors.
- Avoid questions that can be answered with yes or no.
- Do not ask questions that are not job related.
- Try to end the interview in a positive mood.

---

[11] Kelly Land and Janna Mansker. *The Ultimate Hiring Guide: 7 Steps for Selecting Great People.* Atlanta: Berke Group, LLC, 2010.

Background Investigations

Unfortunately, some job candidates exaggerate or misrepresent dates of employment, job titles, past salaries, or reasons for leaving a prior position. Background investigations that verify application information and check references are worth the time and effort required. You not only want to confirm previous dates of employment and check education credentials, you want to find out how the candidate performed in specific situations and how they interacted with supervisors, coworkers, and customers.

Because job candidates usually are savvy enough to provide only references likely to discuss them favorably and human resources departments usually will only confirm dates of employment and, perhaps, salary, you will need to dig deeper to get more useful comprehensive and less biased information.

Use your network to verify a candidate's background and experience, and ask the candidate for the names and contact information for three coworkers, three supervisors, and three reports (if they previously supervised staff). You can also use the Internet to find background information; just be sure that you are looking at the correct person when you research online.

Physical Examinations

Physical exams serve two basic functions. For some jobs, they help determine whether an applicant can perform job-related tasks. They also provide information about the applicant's overall health. This information can protect the employer and its insurance carrier against claims for previously existing medical conditions. Under the ADA, a physical examination may be given only after a job offer is made. All candidates for a job category, not just one or some, must be required to take the exam.

Orientation

Employers can alleviate much of the fear and anxiety new employees feel, answer many of their questions, and familiarize them with the company efficiently using a well-designed and properly implemented orientation program. Orientation should introduce and acclimate the employee to your company. It should

- explain job requirements and responsibilities;
- discuss how performance is evaluated;
- include information about the company's philosophy, history, policies, and procedures; and
- introduce the new employee to supervisors and coworkers.

Plan for Training and Development

Employee training can educate new employees and expand the skills of existing workers. Moreover, a small-volume home builder can have an effective training and development program that is neither complicated nor expensive. By devoting as little as an hour every week or two to employee training, you can improve quality, productivity, and employee morale.

Many high-quality, cost-effective employee training options are available to small-volume home builders:

- Education sessions at the International Builders' Show
- NAHB-sponsored webinars
- Local HBA-sponsored programs
- Supplier-sponsored classes
- Courses or seminars at local universities, community colleges, or technical schools
- Training sessions during weekly safety or production meetings
- Articles in industry periodicals such as *Sales and Marketing Ideas* and *Builder* magazines
- Resources available at www.nahb.org and www.nahbrc.org

Provide Performance Appraisal

Because most small-volume builders participate in day-to-day operations, they regularly observe employee behavior and performance and can provide feedback in real time. However, even small companies need a comprehensive performance appraisal system to reduce subjectivity and ensure fair, consistent, and objective employee evaluations. Performance appraisal systems provide the following benefits:

- A structure for evaluating employee performance and offering suggestions for improvement
- An opportunity to distribute rewards such as pay increases and promotions
- Verification that individuals within the organization are working toward organizational goals
- Written documentation of actions the company has taken in response to the employee's performance

A well-designed performance appraisal system should include

- appropriate performance measures;
- designated appraisers;

- periodic performance appraisals (more than once a year); and
- a plan for communicating information about the appraisal to the employee.

Performance measures should

- help accomplish organizational goals and objectives;
- assess observable performance;
- be understood by both employees and managers; and
- address aspects of performance that the employee controls.

Performance appraisal involves three steps: establishing standards, measuring performance, and providing feedback.

Establish performance standards. First, define and communicate the standards for employee performance. A job description by itself often is not sufficient. It is not enough for employees just to know what they must do; they also should understand how well they are expected to do it. Performance standards should translate the company's goals and objectives into job requirements that convey acceptable and unacceptable levels of performance.

Keep in mind that what you measure is what you will get, which may be an unintended outcome. For example, sales associates who are evaluated by the percentage of traffic that signs a contract will sometimes low-ball the traffic count in order to make the percentage goal. Likewise, a superintendent may not list everything on a punch list if the number of items exceeds a performance measure.

Measure performance. Establish a system to measure each employee's performance and to evaluate it according to the standards. A superintendent who is responsible for a single large custom home may be evaluated at specific points during construction, with an overall appraisal at the end of the job. A superintendent for a production builder may be evaluated each quarter, with a comprehensive annual evaluation.

Techniques to evaluate performance measure traits, behaviors, or results. Trait methods, which often are criticized as subjective, measure the employee's characteristics, such as dependability, creativity, initiative, and leadership. Behavioral methods assess whether an employee exhibits specific behaviors appropriate to the job (visits each job daily, calls trade contractors one week in advance of a scheduled job). The results method assesses just that. It has gained popularity because it focuses on measurable contributions employees make to a company.

Provide feedback. Employees need feedback about their evaluations. A comprehensive appraisal process should include day-to-day interactions between managers and

Guidelines for Appraisal Interviews

- Conduct the appraisal privately.
- Allow sufficient time for a thorough discussion.
- Be direct and specific. Do not talk in generalities.
- Encourage the employee to participate and to initiate a dialogue.
- Focus on solving problems, not placing blame.
- Suggest possible means for the employee to improve his or her performance.
- Focus the discussion on relevant performance, behaviors, or outcomes.
- If poor performance is an issue, explain what your expectations for good performance are and the consequences for continued poor performance.

employees as well as formal appraisal interviews. In general, the interview should maximize the employee's acceptance of the feedback and intention to improve.

Compensation

Compensation provides employees with a tangible reward for their service, a source of recognition, and a livelihood. The compensation system sends a powerful message about what the builder values. Therefore, it must contribute to achieving a company's overall objectives. You promote the behaviors and outcomes you want by rewarding them, so ensure that what you reward is actually what you want. For example, if you base a superintendent's bonuses solely on the number of home completions, you may be encouraging him or her to focus on speed at the expense of quality and cost.

Employee compensation has three components: direct compensation, benefits, and nonfinancial compensation.

Direct compensation. Wages, salaries, incentives, bonuses, and commissions are examples of direct compensation. To maintain competitiveness in today's environment, managers are increasingly turning to pay-for-performance compensation including wage incentive plans, profit sharing, lump-sum bonuses, and stock plans.

Employee benefits. These benefits improve the quality of life and provide security for employees and their families. Once viewed as a gift from employers, benefits now are perceived as rights all employees are entitled to. Benefits can attract and keep employees, but they also make up one of the fastest growing areas of employment law and litigation. Typical fringe benefits include:

- Paid vacations, holidays, and personal days
- Paid leave for illness
- Pension or retirement plans
- Medical and life insurance

Certain benefits and payments are required by law. For many small-volume builders, required benefits comprise the majority of their benefit package. Employers must

- withhold a percentage of wages and salaries for Social Security, match that amount, and deposit the funds on a regular basis;
- contribute to state unemployment insurance funds and pay federal unemployment taxes; and
- in most states, carry workers' compensation insurance to cover employees for work-related accidents and illnesses.

Nonfinancial compensation. Rewards other than money can motivate employees. Some examples of nonfinancial compensation include the following:

- Career-related growth and development
- Opportunities to learn new skills
- Promotion opportunities
- Recognition from superiors and customers for doing a job well
- Autonomy
- Job security
- Respect from coworkers
- Responsibilty

Discipline

Occasionally, managers have to discipline employees to stop undesirable behavior such as absenteeism, poor work performance, or rule violations. Here are some guidelines for disciplining employees:

- Ensure all employees know the organization's rules and understand the consequences of violating them.
- Apply disciplinary actions fairly and consistently throughout the organization.
- Conduct disciplinary actions as soon as possible after investigating an infraction.

- Keep discipline impersonal. Focus on the behavior rather than the individual.
- Respect the employee's privacy throughout a disciplinary procedure.

Many organizations benefit by counseling errant employees. The employee and supervisor work together to prevent the problem from recurring. This approach entails a verbal warning, and then a written warning that the employee must sign. Continued violations may require either temporary suspension or termination.

Employment at Will

Employment at will, which applies in most states, enables an employer to legally discharge an employee at any time without stating a reason. Although federal laws prohibit employers from discharging employees because of their age, sex, religion, reporting of unsafe working conditions, or physical handicap, court decisions regarding at-will termination usually are rendered at the state level. Some states, including the District of Columbia, may have additional protections; consult with a local attorney on employment issues. Courts typically have restricted at-will termination for three reasons:

- The employee refused to commit an illegal act.
- An employment contract, either explicit or implied, existed between the employer and employee.
- The employer defamed the employee's character in the course of the termination.

Other Human Resources Issues

Whether a builder has 1 or 100 employees, he or she should be aware of the following human resources issues. If you don't manage these carefully, the work environment can become damaged and you may experience costly litigation.

Sexual harassment. Sexual harassment has become an important issue for all companies. Employees are increasingly likely to take legal action against the individuals they feel are guilty of harassment and the organizations that employ perpetrators of sexual harassment. Sexual harassment is illegal under Title VII of the Civil Rights Act. Federal guidelines define sexual harassment as unwelcome sexual advances, requests for sexual favors, and other verbal and physical conduct of a sexual nature that creates a hostile or offensive work environment.

Courts have held organizations liable for sexual harassment even if company policy prohibited the act and the organization did not know that the harassment occurred. In addition, organizations also can be held liable for conduct of visitors to the organization or trade contractors if their conduct falls within Title VII's prohibitions and is directed at the organization's employees. To minimize liability, management must establish a clear and strong policy against sexual harassment, communicate that policy to all employees, and conduct training for all employees on the employer's policies.

Family concerns. Employees sometimes have personal commitments that can detract from or conflict with their ability to perform assigned duties. A number of larger organizations have developed comprehensive programs to address issues such as child care, obligations to aging parents, and maternity leave. Although smaller companies usually do not have the resources to develop these programs, they still must recognize the impact of work-family issues on their businesses. Smaller organizations should become familiar with the requirements of the Family and Medical Leave Act (FMLA) and other employment-related statutes. You can work with an attorney specializing in employment law to identify areas that may affect your business, to define the scope of your obligations, and to establish consistent policies and procedures for employees.

An Ongoing Responsibility

Recruiting, hiring, training, and continuing to help employees develop their professional knowledge and skills are critical activities for ensuring the vitality and success of your company. Legal compliance, hiring, and firing are important core human resources functions, but so are knowing how and where to find the right employees and then managing them to succeed. Ongoing networking will help you find potential candidates. Professionalizing your hiring and training systems and practices will help you bring new employees on board with confidence and continue to build a functioning, productive, loyal team.

16

Working With a Construction Superintendent and Trade Contractors

Each home building company has a person responsible for managing construction activities. Most companies rely on trade contractors to perform many of these activities. In many small-volume builder companies, the owner manages construction, but most home builders employ a construction superintendent to do this. (Appendix C is a detailed job description for a superintendent.) Beyond the job description for your construction superintendent and scopes of work and quality checklists for work crews, you must understand how to work with people to ensure quality performance.

Superintendent Authority

Often, a superintendent acts as the builder's legal agent. This means he or she is authorized to enter into legally binding agreements with suppliers, trade contractors, and customers. If you choose to delegate authority this way, clearly indicate this in third-party contracts. If you revoke this authority, notify third parties accordingly.

Regardless of whether they personally assume the role of construction superintendent or delegate the responsibility to an employee, builders should understand the superintendent's role and how the position impacts profitability, quality, and reputation.

The Superintendent's Responsibilities

In the past, superintendents were limited to managing jobsite activities. They had relatively little contact with individuals other than suppliers, trade contractors, and employees. Today, superintendent responsibilities can be much broader. Many companies use titles such as "project manager" and "builder" to reflect these changes.

A superintendent's specific responsibilities depend on the builder's priorities. The following sections discuss various functions superintendents may perform before, during, and after construction.

Preconstruction

Superintendents often participate in estimating and planning. They may solicit bids from trade contractors and sign contracts with trade contractors on the builder's behalf. Superintendents also may meet and work with buyers to explain the construction process, schedule, and workmanship. Other areas of oversight for a typical construction superintendent include the following:

Reviewing estimates. The superintendent should review all estimates. In smaller companies, he or she may play a key role in developing them as well. Field experience helps a superintendent spot crucial errors or omissions.

Reviewing construction documents. The superintendent should understand the terms of the sales contract and his or her role in fulfilling the builder's contractual obligations. Before construction begins, the superintendent reviews plans and specifications for a list of materials and labor needed to finish a project. He or she also looks for conditions that might increase costs, compromise quality, or complicate the schedule, such as discrepancies among various drawings or between the drawings and specifications.

Inspecting and selecting lots. The superintendent often is responsible for ensuring the lot is suitable for the planned home. The superintendent then oversees site preparation, including tree or building removal, as needed; grading or filling; utility installation; and provisions for making the lot accessible.

Developing the construction schedule. The superintendent offers expertise to help develop the construction schedule, including the sequence and duration of construction activities and the relationships among them.

Meetings

A preconstruction meeting allows those who will be involved in the project, including the customer, an opportunity to get acquainted. The meeting agenda should include the following items:

Review of construction documents. Because these documents form the basis of the contract, everyone must agree the documents accurately represent all work to be done.

Discussion of responsibilities. Explain each party's responsibilities and how they interact to finish the job on time and within budget.

Management of customer expectations. Educate customers about what to expect during each stage of construction. For example, make sure they understand that even if their project appears to be inactive for a day or two, this does not mean their project is not progressing on schedule.

Explanation of policies and procedures. Use plain language to detail your practices for handling the following issues:

- Change orders
- Customer visits to the jobsite
- Orientations (walk-through)
- Payments
- Selections

During Construction

The superintendent generally coordinates materials, labor, equipment, and trade contractors, and schedules building inspections. He or she also may schedule lender's draw inspections and act as the customer's primary contact. Key responsibilities during construction are as follows:

Controlling costs. The superintendent assures that materials are used efficiently and construction costs are allocated correctly. Thus, the superintendent is central to controlling project costs.

Maintaining the schedule. The builder and superintendent work together to develop a realistic project schedule. The superintendent then ensures that activities conform to the schedule.

Providing customer contact. An increased role as the customer's key contact is the biggest change in the superintendent's job in recent years. Today, superintendents typically meet customers during the sales process or in preconstruction meetings to foster a working relationship from the beginning of the project.

Monitoring quality. The superintendent is responsible for meeting or exceeding standards for each construction activity. He or she works with the customer and with employees, suppliers, and trade contractors to meet this goal.

Ordering materials. The superintendent may have full responsibility for developing materials lists and ordering materials or only schedule delivery of previously ordered materials.

Ensuring jobsite safety. The superintendent must understand relevant Occupational Safety and Health Administration (OSHA) regulations and local health and safety requirements. He or she is responsible for ensuring that all construction activities comply with these regulations.

Managing the job. The superintendent generally manages all jobsite activities, whether for one custom home or 20 production homes. The number of jobs a superintendent can manage simultaneously varies from builder to builder. The degree of home customization, distances between jobs, job size, and how much contact the superintendent has with customers influence how much time each project takes.

Walk-through and inspection. The superintendent typically schedules the walk-through and inspections. Delayed or failed inspections can prompt construction delays, rework, and even fines or orders to cease work. A walk-through (or more than one walk-through) scheduled at various points during construction allows the superintendent to show customers the quality of the builder's work.

Warranty service. Superintendents in small-volume building companies often are responsible for warranty service. This service may include investigating customer requests for service and either performing warranty work or scheduling an employee or trade contractor to do it.

Skill Requirements

As managers, superintendents must have technical, interpersonal, and conceptual skills to perform their jobs effectively.

Technical skills. Superintendents who have been promoted through the ranks have a strong working knowledge of construction materials and practices. To be effective, however, they also must be computer literate and able perform at least some business functions.

Interpersonal skills. The superintendent often is the builder's point of contact with suppliers, trade contractors, inspectors, and buyers. As a manager, the superintendent must have excellent communication skills, which entail not only giving directions but also actively listening to others involved in the construction process. The superintendent must be able to negotiate prices, working conditions, and work duration. He or she also must be able to exercise leadership in resolving disputes to build a team of suppliers, employees, and trade contractors.

Conceptual skills. Superintendents must identify problems, investigate alternatives, and choose and implement solutions.

Recruiting

Finding and hiring a great superintendent entails much more than placing an ad on the Internet. Your best source of good superintendent candidates is probably within the ranks of employees, competitors' employees, lumber dealers, and others with whom you already have relationships. In addition, you may want to consider graduates of construction management programs at trade schools, community colleges, and universities.

When you drive past your competitors' jobsites, observe whether they are clean and well-organized. If they are, and if the superintendent responsible for them completes his or her jobs on time, he or she may be a good candidate for your company.

Because trade contractors typically work for a number of builders and see various superintendents in action, they are an excellent source of recommendations. Trades know which superintendents understand the construction process and can complete projects on time and within budget.

Hiring

Begin the superintendent hiring process by developing a written job description and job specification. Then interview people whose skills, behaviors, and attitudes best fit the job requirements and your company's culture. If one person stands out as a good fit but does not have all required skills, consider providing appropriate training.

How important is experience?

An experienced superintendent

- understands the construction process;
- often has established relationships with trade contractors;
- is familiar with essential trades to the home building industry;
- may need to "undo" habits that don't conform to the way you do business; and
- may need to update his or her skills.

Evaluating

In evaluating the superintendent, consider only the things they can control: time, quality, and cost.

Ask Customers for Feedback

On customer surveys, include items that will help you gather information about the superintendent's performance. Consider the following questions:

- Was the home in move-in condition at closing?
- Did the quality of workmanship meet your expectations?
- Did the superintendent keep you informed during construction?

Ask Suppliers and Trade Contractors

Suppliers and trade contractors also offer an important perspective. Ask them these questions:

- Are jobs ready when scheduled?
- Does the superintendent provide necessary information, plans, and specifications?
- Is the superintendent available to answer questions and solve problems as they arise?
- Were the builder's/superintendent's expectations communicated to trade contractors?

Use Variance Reports

Every builder should have a system to track construction cost by job category, compare actual costs to estimated costs, and identify what caused variances. If a variance was caused by something under the superintendent's control, it is an important measure of the superintendent's performance.

Consider, too, the impact of variances caused by others. Inaccurate estimates, for example, can cause scheduling delays, dissatisfied trade contractors, and project delays while the superintendent reorders materials. Repeating mistakes on estimates can constrain the superintendent's efficiency and effectiveness significantly. In evaluating a superintendent, consider whether factors beyond his or her control have hurt performance.

Working With Contractors

Home builders traditionally have relied on trade contractors for many construction activities for the following reasons:

- You can work on multiple projects simultaneously without significantly increasing overhead costs.
- Their specialized expertise allows trades to complete many construction activities with better quality, in less time, and at a lower cost than the builder's own crews can.
- They have their own tools and other equipment, which reduces a builder's capital investment.
- They allow a construction company to be nimble. As volume fluctuates seasonally or because of the housing cycle, using trade contractors reduces the need to hire or lay off employees.
- The trade contractor, rather than the builder handles responsibilities such as payroll, supervision, and reporting.
- You can make trade contractors responsible for warranty repairs (although the builder remains accountable to the home owner for repairs being correctly completed).

Still, there are some disadvantages to using trade contractors:

- Some locations, such as rural areas, may not have enough qualified trade contractors.
- You must compete with other builders for the services of qualified trade contractors.
- Because they are not your employees, trade contractors are not under your direct control.
- Trade contractors may be interested more in their own short-term well-being than in your company's long-term success.

Should I use contract workers?

Ask the following questions to determine whether to use trade contractors or hire your own work crews:

Do you already have employees with the skills to do high-quality work?

How does the cost of performing the work in-house compare with contracting it?

Do your crews have the time to perform the work?

Are special tools or equipment required?

Are qualified trade contractors available?

Does hiring trade contractors fit your business philosophy and management style?

Employee vs. Contractor

If the courts or the Internal Revenue Service (IRS) classify your contractors as employees, your general liability insurance, worker's compensation insurance, and unemployment insurance costs will increase. You also will have to withhold and pay employment taxes for the contractor and his or her employees. The IRS has established 20 criteria to determine whether workers are contractors or employees.

The courts and the IRS want evidence that a contractor's business is separate and distinct from a builder's. The following characteristics of a trade contractor's operation would suggest it is a separate business:

- Primary control over when and how work is done
- Performs similar work for other builders
- Licensed
- Paid by the job, not by the hour
- Has his or her own business name, letterhead, and phone number

You must understand the criteria used to distinguish contractors from employees and ensure that workers are classified correctly. A written contract that specifies the details of the builder-contractor relationship will minimize the risk of having the IRS reclassify your workers. If you have questions about classification, consult your attorney, accountant, or both. Also, be aware that lawmakers at both the federal and state levels have attempted to impose limits on independent contractor status. Builders should, therefore, be alert for possible changes that would make it more difficult to legally classify workers as independent contractors, and increase scrutiny when workers are classified as such.

Identifying Good Trade Contractors

You can use various methods to locate qualified trade contractors. One is to drive by local construction projects and observe which trade contractors you most often see on jobsites. You also can ask your existing contractors to recommend other trades. Trade contractors who perform quality work generally recommend other trade contractors who do likewise. For example, drywall hangers and interior trim contractors can identify high-quality framing trade contractors. Because a good framing job makes it easier for them to produce quality drywall and trim work, they want to follow good framers. You also can find trade contractors through lenders, suppliers, building inspectors, advertisements in local and regional newspapers, and membership directories published by local HBAs.

Developing Trade Contractors

If you cannot find qualified trade contractors, one alternative is to develop your own. Identify an individual (perhaps an employee or a competitor's employee) with potential and help him or her start a business. Provide information on identifying and getting required licenses and permits, developing a business plan, and hiring and managing employees.

Defining Quality

Choosing the right trade contractors helps ensure a builder's profitability and long-term success. Although price is important, it is only one of several criteria to consider. Establishing a set of criteria other than price helps identify quality trades. Before hiring a trade contractor, investigate whether they

- demonstrate financial stability (e.g., by their longevity in business, ability to obtain required bonding, and ability to provide favorable credit reports from suppliers and credit bureaus);
- provide workers' compensation insurance for their employees;
- carry enough general liability insurance;
- can provide both the required quantity and quality of work;
- demonstrate that they are reliable, will begin work when scheduled, and stay on the job until their work is completed;
- will stand by their work by assuming responsibility for repairs during the warranty period; and
- are available in an emergency, and on evenings and weekends.

Selecting Contractors

There are two basic philosophies for working with trade contractors.

Competitive bidding. One common approach is to obtain competitive bids for each house and use the lowest bid that satisfies the job's requirements. The primary advantage of competitive bidding is that it keeps trade contractor prices low. However, this approach does little to develop trade contractor loyalty or ensure high-quality work.

Negotiation. An alternative is to select a primary trade contractor and one or two secondary or backup contractors for each trade. The builder then works closely with the selected trades to negotiate scope of work, schedules, and prices. Many builders who use this approach report a higher quality of work, increased trade contractor loyalty and, often to their surprise, lower overall construction costs.

Enforcing Work Standards

One production builder forged common ground with trade contractors on acceptable performance. Following are some of the standards carpenters and other trade contractors must adhere to:

- **Timeliness**—Jobs must be started within 72 hours of notice and completed within an agreed-upon time frame.
- **Respect**—Other trades, employees, the customer, and the home buyer's property must be treated with care.
- **Cleanliness**—No smoking is permitted, no cigarette litter is permitted, and jobs must be left broom clean.
- **Safety**—Workers must wear boots and goggles and leave no hazardous materials on site.
- **Quality Assurance**—Contractors are expected to complete a checklist about their work before they are paid.
- **Follow Up**—Quality workmanship and service lead to customer satisfaction and referrals.

The builder developed this measurement system in partnership with trades, who understand the problems caused by sloppy work, tardiness, and lack of professionalism.

Encouraging "Ownership"

Because a builder's success relies on dependable, quality conscious trade contractors, you should treat them as part of the construction team. Here are some rules that will promote trade contractor loyalty:

Involve trade contractors early. Involving trade contractors in planning increases their ownership in a project. Because they have specialized knowledge, they can offer valuable suggestions during the design phase to improve quality, save time, prevent problems, and lower costs. Including them in other activities such as pre-construction meetings makes them part of the team and familiarizes them with the project and their role in making it successful.

Keep trade contractors informed. Provide trades with all the information they need, including detailed plans and specifications, schedules, and change orders. Provide sufficient advance notice when a job is almost ready for them and keep them abreast of schedule changes. Ensure trade contractors understand how your company operates and what you expect from them.

Tasks You Can Handle for Your Trade Partners

Managing the following areas for your trade contractors will help make you the premier builder to work with:

Estimating. Send out a generic bid package. Negotiate a best price over a one-year period for a standard item, such as a three-piece bath, and then offer regular jobs. This helps your trades with their work flow and cash flow.

Proposals. Provide detailed forms for price quotes, including all plans and specifications, so your trade partners only need to fill in the blanks.

Invoicing. Use purchase orders or work orders instead of invoices.

Scheduling. Send notice to trade contractors months, rather than days, in advance of when they will be needed on a jobsite.

Advertising. Keep the work flowing to trade partners who add value to your business, so they are happy to get their work from you. When you win an award for a project, recognize your trade contractors' contribution to a job well done.

Take-offs. You can have suppliers help you. Some will guarantee that their materials quantities are correct and will send more if they fall short.

Contracts. Provide your own standard agreement for trade contractors to sign.

Pay trade contractors fairly. Like builders, trade contractors must make a profit to stay in business. Builders who try to squeeze too much out of trade contractors' profits ensure that these contractors will not be around in the future to provide warranty service. You should work with your trade contractors to find a win-win pricing solution that fits your budget and allows the trade to make a fair profit. Preprint trade and supplier checks using the quotes or bids they provided in advance. Do not write additional checks for variances without a detailed and acceptable explanation for a change from what was bid or quoted.

Pay trade contractors regularly. Many trade contractors, particularly those small-volume builders hire, need regular payments to cover both business expenses and personal living expenses. Paying weekly for completed work will help you attract and retain good trade contractors.

Have the job ready. Builders expect their trade contractors to arrive at the jobsite ready to work as scheduled. In return, trade contractors expect the job to be ready for them when they arrive. That is, all preliminary work should be completed, materials should be ready, and the jobsite should be clean.

Having jobs ready when they are scheduled requires the builder to develop and maintain a realistic schedule. Scheduling projects too tightly can result in trip charges, alienated trade contractors, and work damage as various trades collide while trying to get their work done.

Develop standards. Trade contractors cannot meet your expectations unless they know your standards. Builders should have a quality standard for each work element and communicate it to the trade. Working together to set the standard draws on the trade's expertise and adds to a sense of ownership.

Provide feedback. Keep records about a trade contractor's punctuality, quality, efficiency, customer relations, neatness, relations with other trade contractors, and waste. Use the information to provide feedback on job performance.

Should You Back Charge?

Have a back-charge policy for trade contractors and suppliers. Trade contractors and suppliers sometimes damage others' work or their mistakes cost money in addition to repairing their work or replacing materials. However, back charging for these costs can create discord among trade contractors working on your jobsites. By keeping harmony on jobsites, trade contractors will help each other when problems arise, rather than fight each other.

Note problems in writing. Problems with trade contractors often stem from poor communication. Avoid many of these problems by putting trade contractor agreements in writing. If you change the agreement, make sure you put the change in writing.

Treat trade contractors fairly. Builders should keep all information trade contractors supply confidential. For example, don't "shop" a bid to get a better price from other trade contractors.

Get trade contractors' input. Periodically meet with all your trades to identify problems and opportunities. Meet with each trade individually or in small groups and solicit their input. Partnering is a two-way street. For a relationship to thrive in the long term, both the builder and the trade must gain something from it.

Reward outstanding work. When trades perform outstanding work, reward them accordingly: Pay a bonus, treat them to a party, give them a gift card. Acknowledge that their work is appreciated. Often, providing recognition rather than the material reward is most important to a worker. It also sends the message that you value punctuality, dependability, and quality work.

Critical Quality Control Checks

Your construction superintendent and trade contractors, when managed properly, will help you maintain and improve the quality of your housing product. A superintendent is much more than a jobsite supervisor. He or she is your agent, working with designers, estimators, trades, and customers before, during, and even after construction. Suppliers and trade contractors, likewise, must be managed well to perform well. Builders can employ proven strategies for using their knowledge and insight to improve quality and encourage a sense of ownership in projects and in the finished product.

17

Customer Service

Builders who understand the value of referrals to their business's success work to create comprehensive customer service programs that go far beyond correcting punch list items after a home owner moves in. A structured customer service program addresses all of your company's interactions with home buyers, not just policies and procedures for handling warranty claims.

Keys to Quality Customer Service

Your customer service policies and procedures will impact your competitive edge and the type of customers you attract. Therefore, before you develop comprehensive customer service policies and procedures, lay the groundwork by

- reviewing your current business practices;
- deciding what market segment you want to attract; and
- considering the customer service your competitors offer.

Then, develop policies that employees and trade contractors can understand and follow. This will help create an appealing atmosphere for customers.

Find your niche. No builder can provide products and services that satisfy all home buyers. Each builder has a unique array of resources, capabilities, strengths, and weaknesses that define the products and services they can offer. Focus on the products and services you are qualified to provide that will satisfy your customers beyond what your competitors can offer.

Know your customers. No two home buyers are exactly alike. Each brings his or her specific expectations about their new home and the builder. Builders must learn to identify these expectations early in the sales process. For example, a customer who talks about the poor drywall finish in her friends' homes and brings a flashlight to inspect the drywall finish in the model might expect a higher level of quality than you can or will provide. With experience, you will become better at noticing gaps between a customer's expectations and your capabilities.

Manage expectations. Customer expectations for product value are high not just for home construction but for consumer goods as a whole. For example, a 100,000-mile warranty is now the standard for the automobile industry. Moreover, consumers can study features, compare prices, and purchase nearly any product online. They will accept nothing less than the best price, on-schedule delivery, and long-term value.

However, you must help customers set reasonable expectations early in the home buying process. This lays the foundation for providing excellent service. You should "under promise and over deliver." Develop a system to satisfy the customer expectations you set. All of your efforts to manage expectations are fruitless if, ultimately, you don't meet them.

Customer Service as a Business Strategy

Increasingly, builders have incorporated comprehensive customer service programs into their overall business strategy. An effective customer service program can help builders achieve the following goals:

Alleviate customer fears. A new home is the most significant purchase most people will ever make. Customers generally come to the home-buying arena with a number of preconceived notions about home builders and the home-buying process. Friends and relatives are quick to share horror stories, striking fear in your customers. However, superior customer service can minimize these fears, transform negative customer attitudes into positive ones, and contribute to the development of long-term relationships with your home buyers.

Develop long-term relationships with customers. Hopefully, your relationship with buyers does not end when they close on, move into, or exceed the warranty period on their homes. Customer service can ensure that positive builder-customer relationships continue.

Increase referrals and repeat business. Research consistently shows that a referral from a satisfied friend or relative can draw prospects to your company. In addition to recommending you to others, satisfied customers are more likely to do business with you again.

Although most customers do not expect perfection in their new homes, they do expect you to correct problems efficiently and effectively. If you address problems satisfactorily, home buyers can become advocates and ambassadors for your company. They will see firsthand that you deliver what you promised.

Reduce negative customer comments. Satisfied customers tell an average of three people about their purchasing experience. Dissatisfied customers, on the other hand, tell an average of more than a dozen. With an array of new and resale homes available, many consumers will narrow the field by eliminating the least desirable alternatives before they enter the search phase. Any negative comment about your company provides a reason to eliminate you from their list of alternatives.

Boost employee morale. Employees want to be proud of their jobs and their companies. This becomes difficult if customers continuously complain, or negative comments about your company and its products are pervasive. Customer service can improve these situations so employees feel they are providing value to their customers.

Satisfying Customer Expectations

Customers evaluate service quality based on five key criteria: reliability, responsiveness, assurance, empathy, and tangibles. To consistently satisfy their customers, builders must address each of these.

Reliability. Deliver what you promise. Customers must feel confident that they can believe what their builder tells them.

Responsiveness. Listen to customers; keep them informed; provide timely responses to their questions and concerns.

Assurance. Instill confidence in customers. Make them feel they have made the right purchase decision. Employees should be professional, courteous, and well informed.

Empathy. Before you respond to a customer, ask yourself, "If I were the customer in this situation, how would I feel? What would I want?" You might not always be able to provide exactly what they want, but you can give them what they need and treat them as you would want to be treated.

Tangibles. Ensure the work environment is conducive to providing good service. Home buyers will notice clean vehicles; neat, professional looking employees; and tidy jobsites.

Providing Service before the Sale

Your quality standards, sales and marketing programs, warranties, and contracts are vital tools to maintain excellent customer service.

Standards. Builders should lay the foundation for their customer service programs by communicating their standards to the buyer in plain language. The standards are objective criteria to measure your performance.

Sales tools. All sales tools, including model homes, brochures, and completed projects, should reflect as closely as possible the features and workmanship the customer can expect in his or her new home. Clearly identify any product features or merchandising aids shown in model homes, but not included as standard.

Sales associates. Sales associates are a resource for information about the builder and the builder's products. They should be able to answer customers' questions promptly and accurately or know where to get the answer if they don't have it handy. If you rely on brokers for your sales, provide them with the information they need to communicate effectively about your product. For example, meet with them to discuss your products and services, and give them copies of warranties and owners' manuals. Builders who use multiple listing real estate agents should meet with buyers before contract signing to ensure consumers are fully informed before they sign a contract.

Marketing. When developing your marketing programs, consider these questions:

- Does my advertising accurately reflect my company and its products?
- Does my advertising provide relevant information that is easy to understand?
- Are my signs readable, informative, and in the right locations?
- Are my salespeople customer focused? Do customers trust them? Can they form long-term relationships with customers?
- Are my sales incentives aligned with my customer service goals?

Warranties. Provide clear, understandable warranties. Explain all warranty policies and procedures during the sales process. Home buyers need to know the length of the warranty period, service hours, procedures for emergency service, and who is responsible for maintenance and repair work.

Contracts. A thorough, well-written contract that both parties understand is a key customer service tool. The contract outlines each party's responsibilities and specifies, in clear and understandable language, the contract terms, conditions, and limitations. Any contract changes must be recorded in writing, and both parties must agree to them.

Customer Service During Construction

The home buying process extends through three phases: sales, construction, and warranty. You must decide who will be the key customer contact during each phase. In small custom-building companies, the builder often assumes this role for all three phases. In many larger companies, a sales associate is the contact before construction, the project manager or superintendent takes over during construction, and a customer service representative assumes responsibility during the warranty period.

Communication Opportunities

To provide continuity, more and more builders are assigning one person (typically the superintendent) to communicate with buyers from start to finish. The superintendent meets with the buyers during the sales process and becomes the primary contact point until the end of the warranty period.

No matter how you choose to do it, you must develop a system to ensure customers have access to timely, accurate information. This systematic approach to listening and responding to customers' needs fosters trust and reduces customer service problems.

Preconstruction meetings. The builder, the clients, the superintendent, and possibly the salesperson or broker, key suppliers, and trade contractors attend.

Jobsite access. Some builders require that all questions go through the buyers' contact and that jobsite visits are scheduled in advance. Others welcome impromptu customer visits to the jobsite. Clearly communicate your policy to customers. Most customers don't mind following the builder's procedures if they know them.

Schedules. Many builders wrestle with what information to provide to customers about the construction schedule. Some share detailed information about the flow and timing of construction activities. They believe this makes customers feel they are a part of the building process. If you do this, you must be able to develop a realistic schedule and adhere to it. The time and effort required to explain changes might negate the benefits of providing detailed schedule information.

Trade contractors. Set customer service standards as high for your trade contractors as you do or would do for your own work crews. Customers do not differentiate between employees and trade contractors.

Walk-Through

Although a walk-through can take place at any time, two types—the pre-drywall walk-through and the presettlement walk-through—have become a regular part of many builders' customer service regime.

Pre-drywall. Encouraging customers to tour their home before drywall installation allows them to see the quality of your workmanship from the inside out. You can demonstrate that framing has been completed according to accepted practices. The customer should note the placement of electrical outlets, light fixtures, and cable TV/telephone/Internet wiring. Changing their locations, if necessary, is easier and less costly before hanging drywall than after.

Preclosing. A preclosing walk-through generally has two related, but distinct, purposes. One is to conduct a final inspection of the home. The second is to provide an orientation for the new home owner. Orientation typically addresses the following issues:

- Procedures for requesting warranty service
- Phone numbers for emergency service requests
- Operation of appliances, HVAC equipment, and other systems
- Information on transferring utilities
- Home owner's responsibilities for maintenance and upkeep

Communicating at Critical Points

One builder developed a process to take customers through a series of meetings at critical points from purchase to closing, as part of its communication strategy:

- Home owner orientation—a class with other buyers
- Design sessions (four meetings)—to ensure buyers' decisions are not rushed
- Plan review and meeting the builder—in the field, to make customers real to the builder
- Pre-drywall meeting—to involve customers in their new home
- HomeLife orientation—an anti-stress intervention two weeks before closing
- Home presentation—with quality assurance workers and featuring slippers and snacks for the home buyers
- Closing—a celebration

After Move-In Follow-Up

Providing poor service after customers move in can undo months of superior customer service during sales and construction. On the other hand, providing fast, effective warranty service is another opportunity to make a good impression and reinforce a relationship with a satisfied customer. Taking the following steps will minimize problems during the warranty period:

Provide the warranty before contract signing. Your customer will need time—in fact, most states require a specific minimum amount of time—to review the warranty before they sign a contract. Ask your attorney for the requirements in the state(s) where you build and sell homes.

Inform customers of their responsibilities. Home buyers are responsible for routine maintenance (e.g., replacing furnace filters, touching up paint, recaulking) and for making the home accessible to your company or its representatives to make repairs during the warranty period. Make sure they also understand that nonemergency warranty service is provided during normal working hours.

Distinguish routine warranty service from emergencies. Establish separate procedures for routine warranty work and emergency work. Explain that nonemergency items are not fixed immediately, but are completed in a timely manner. Define what constitutes an emergency. Provide phone numbers for the company service representative, plumbers, electricians, and HVAC contractors to call in an emergency.

Establish a structure for warranty service. Many builders proactively contact buyers about required warranty work 1 to 2 months after closing, and again at 11 months—just before the one-year warranty expires. Make sure customers fully understand this process.

Standardize the warranty service request process. Establish specific procedures for customer service requests. Many builders require customers to submit nonemergency warranty service requests in writing. If you accept service requests by phone, whoever takes the call should create a permanent record by completing a warranty service request form. Many builders provide home owners with a multipart preprinted form that allows the home owner to keep a copy and send the remaining copies to the builder.

Warranty requests should include at least the following information:

- Customer name
- Customer address

- Customer phone numbers (home, work, and cell)
- Nature of problem
- Best time to call to schedule inspection or service
- Best time to perform inspection or service

Respond promptly. Establish policies that specify how much time the builder allows to respond to the customer's call, schedule an appointment to inspect, and if necessary, fix the problem. Educate trade contractors about your policies, and ensure they conform to the requirements.

Perform repairs as scheduled. After receiving a service request, your company must follow through to make necessary repairs in a timely manner. Having superintendents or construction crew members do the repairs often causes problems because they have not been trained properly in providing warranty service. Doing warranty work also takes them away from their primary responsibility—constructing new homes on schedule. Many builders address these problems by requiring trade contractors to perform warranty repairs that fall within their scope of work.

Follow up on each repair. Don't assume the customer is satisfied after someone is sent to their home to make a warranty repair. The party responsible for the repair should submit a repair form with the customer's signature indicating that the repair was made. Ideally, the builder should follow up with the customer to ask them questions about the quality, responsiveness, and courtesy associated with the service they received.

Provide owner's manuals. Provide each customer with an owner's manual. Most builders include product warranties, customer service policies and procedures, and operating instructions for items such as furnaces, water heaters, and kitchen appliances. Owner's manuals also may include information such as closing documents, local maps, or instructions on home maintenance.

Implementing a Customer Service Program

A customer service program involves employees and creates clear communication between the builder, trade contractors, and customers. Make sure customer service is foremost among employees and trade contractors. Develop and implement a customer service program. Put the company's customer service goals and procedures in writing. Make sure everyone reads the information. Incorporate language in trade contracts that requires all contractors on the jobsite to adhere to your customer service procedures.

Develop a climate for customer service. The builder in a small company, or the top management team in a larger one, plays a key role in providing customer service. Develop a climate that fosters customer satisfaction as a primary goal. Ensure that employees who handle customer service have both the technical skills to diagnose and correct warranty problems and the interpersonal skills to communicate effectively with the customer. Include customer service in your training programs.

Learn to say no. No matter how diligent you are in setting realistic expectations, you inevitably will have to deny some customer requests. You can say "no" politely but unambiguously. Here's how:

- Make sure you fully understand the request. Inspect the problem yourself or, if necessary, hire another professional, such as a structural engineer.
- Take sufficient time to evaluate a request before making a determination. Once you have decided to deny the request, promptly notify the customer. Delaying unpleasant news often exacerbates problems.
- When you must say "no" to a customer, do it in person or by phone—promptly, courteously, and with an explanation for your decision.
- Don't verbally slap the wrist of a customer who is giving you $1 million or more to build her dream home. One builder's three-page document on selections included the word "no" 18 times. So look at your paper work and practice rewriting your documents in a friendlier tone. "Instead of telling them what they can't do, tell them what they can do," says home builder customer service expert Carol Smith.
- Explain to customers in detail why you are denying their request.
- Offer suggestions to help customers correct the problem themselves. Customers sometimes ask builders for repairs simply because they don't know who to contact.

Separate warranty work from construction. Some builders allow customers to move in before all construction work is complete. Avoid this. Completing construction after the customer has moved in generally makes the remaining work more difficult, more time-consuming, and more costly. It increases the risk of damaging floor coverings, furniture, and other customer property. Workers must tiptoe around the customer's furniture and fixtures.

Provide training. Do not assume that your employees and trade contractors either understand what constitutes superior customer service or have the skills, abilities, attitude, or desire to provide it. Builders must develop training for their employees and trade contractors.

Use warranty service as a tool for continuous improvement. Builders often view the warranty period merely as a time when they have to deal with customer complaints. They also should view the warranty period as an opportunity to identify preventable problems to improve their company's performance in the future.

Tracking Warranty Requests

Tracking warranty requests using a computer program has a number of advantages. The computer can generate a list of outstanding service requests and can provide information efficiently on service requests by model, subdivision, trade contractor, or vendor. This information is invaluable for identifying and halting recurring problems.

Third-Party Warranties

In some states, builders may contract out warranty service. A small but growing number of companies provide services from performing specific warranty repairs and conducting customer orientations to managing a builder's entire warranty service program.

Measuring Customer Service

No matter what builders believe about the quality of their customer service, the only measure that matters is customer satisfaction. Therefore, you should measure customers' perceptions of service quality regularly. One of the most effective ways to do this is with questionnaires. Getting buyer feedback by sending questionnaires to them right after closing, after 30 days, and after one year can provide valuable information for targeted improvement.

18

Quality Management

The quality of a product or service is defined by how well it does what it is intended to do. A quality home matches the specifications to which it was built. Although the ultimate goal of quality is developing products, services, and processes that lead to customer satisfaction, quality is a process as well as an outcome. Therefore, quality requires participation by the entire organization—from top management through suppliers and trade contractors—to create value for customers. Quality-oriented businesses commit to continuous improvement company-wide. They focus on teamwork, increased customer satisfaction, and lowering costs.

Seven categories comprise the criteria for the most widely recognized quality award, The Malcolm Baldrige National Quality Award:[12]

- **Results**—Performance and improvement in the following crucial business areas:
  - Customer satisfaction
  - Financial and marketplace performance
  - Human resources
  - Supplier and partner performance
  - Operational performance
  - Governance and social responsibility.
  - How the organization performs relative to its competitors
- **Leadership**—How senior executives guide the organization, how the organization is responsible to the public, how it practices good citizenship
- **Strategic planning**—How the organization sets strategic directions and how it determines key action plans

---

[12] *Frequently Asked Questions about the Malcolm Baldrige National Quality Award*, NIST Public and Business Affairs (http://www.nist.gov/public_affairs/factsheet/baldfaqs.cfm), U.S. Department of Commerce, October 5, 2010.

- **Customer focus**—How the organization determines requirements and expectations of customers and markets; how it builds relationships with customers; and how it acquires, satisfies, and retains customers
- **Measurement, analysis, and knowledge management**—The management, effective use, analysis, and improvement of data and information to support key organization processes and the organization's performance management system
- **Workforce focus**—How the organization enables its workforce to develop its full potential and how the workforce is aligned with the organization's objectives
- **Process management**—Design, management, and improvement of key production/delivery and support processes

Each employee and activity related to the production of goods and services plays a role in establishing product quality. Management functions (planning, organizing, influencing, and controlling) inevitably influence the quality of goods and services.

The customer, rather than the salesperson, supplier, trade contractor, or builder, defines quality. Therefore, ask yourself these questions:

- Who are our customers?
- What do they need?
- What do they want?
- How do we develop products and processes that meet or exceed those needs or desires?

Being customer-focused does not require builders to try to meet unrealistic expectations or make undue sacrifices to please every customer. Instead, it requires that builders

- Actively recognize and manage customers' expectations
- Develop realistic standards for products and services
- Help customers understand and accept those standards

A Culture of Quality

A focus on quality is more than just a program or regimen. It is a culture that embodies the very values and behaviors of the organization and its employees. This quality culture provides the foundation on which the company operates, and institutionalizes how work is done.

Creating Value for the Customer

Anyone, at any point in the organization, can create value for the customer. Following are some practices that provide a foundation for a quality home builder.

- Assembling a creative, knowledgeable team
- Researching the market
- Offering products in a desirable location at a competitive price
- Hiring a superintendent or construction manager who communicates effectively with you, your trades, suppliers, and customers, to ensure timely, cost-efficient completion of each home
- Ensuring your sales associates and brokers thoroughly understand your products and services so they can help you match what the customers want with what you can provide
- Hiring a secretary, office manager, and/or bookkeeper to facilitate accurate, swift communication within the company and with external customers such as home buyers, suppliers, and trade contractors
- Using trade contractors and suppliers who keep abreast of new products and techniques and provide materials and workmanship that meet or exceed customer expectations

Effective leadership is the key to implementing a successful quality management program. Top management must support quality systems, processes, and behaviors. As a builder, you must continually communicate and reinforce your commitment to quality with consistent decisions and actions. Clear, consistent leadership will inspire employees, suppliers, and trade contractors, and recognize their best efforts.

A Sense of Ownership

In a culture of quality, employees, suppliers, and trade contractors develop a sense of ownership for the processes they contribute to or control. Each person understands he or she is the one who best understands and is responsible for the quality of his or her work. They know their workmanship impacts the company's success, and therefore, their own. They must control their own activities, be freed to make decisions, and be held accountable for the results. To support this feeling of ownership, builders who develop a quality culture work to ensure that employees receive adequate training.

When your team members feel empowered to do their best work, they are more likely to please the customer. In fact, some workers may be in a better position to know what customers want than you are, because they are on the front line working with the home buyers. Builders who empower employees to resolve or prevent problems don't have to intervene constantly to resolve crises.

A builder's customers are not just home buyers. The builder also has a number of internal customers. Virtually anyone connected with the builder's business or with a given project is a customer at some point. Employees and trade contractors should view those whose work follows theirs as internal customers. For example, an HVAC contractor who considers the needs of other trades, such as the electrician and the plumber, when designing and installing the duct system, is treating these trades as internal customers. Consider these questions:

- What do my trade contractors or suppliers need?
- What do they want?
- How can we develop products and processes that meet or exceed those needs or desires to help them work with us successfully?

Adjusting your business practices to help your internal and external customers succeed in their businesses increases the likelihood that you too will achieve success. Don't assume that you know best what your customers want or what you can do to help trade contractors improve their performance—ask.

Problem Solving and Reengineering

Quality improvement is a long-term goal. You cannot solve every problem simultaneously, but resolving one problem may naturally alleviate others. Solving small problems systematically will yield cumulative benefits over time.

"There isn't a quick simple solution. You have to go after the little pieces . . . to become more practical and efficient," says Joe Pfeiffer of Business ROI Inc.

Understand and monitor financial, operational, trade contractor, and supplier performance; know your cycle time; and then eliminate problems in these areas

Four Steps to Problem Solving

When you discover a problem, follow these steps and repeat them as necessary:

- Analyze information from sources relevant to the problem (i.e., customers, suppliers, trade contractors, competitors).
- Develop proposed solutions.
- Test the solutions.
- Measure whether or not you have solved the problem.

step-by-step. Adhering to quality principles requires you to evaluate each process to determine whether it is adding value to your product and customer satisfaction. You probably will need to reengineer at least some of your processes.

Averting quality problems using quality management will increase customer satisfaction and, all other things being equal, increase profits. Quality is free, said Philip Crosby in his landmark book.[13] That is, the return from putting quality processes in place exceeds the cost of having to redo work and make repairs. To build a home that satisfies buyers, examine every process in your company for the value it adds (or does not add) to your product. Ask yourself, "If I were performing this process for the first time, what methods and materials would I use?" Because reengineering requires you to question everything you do, it can change your operation for the better and ensure that you are continuously learning about and applying state-of-the-art approaches to home building and company management.

One builder documented 297 nonconstruction processes in its company and was able to eliminate more than half—155 to be exact—that were not adding value to the customer. Another builder was able to reduce 86 separate pieces of communication to 12. Other builders have committed to cutting cycle time to 30–45 days from 100–150 days to use scarce capital more efficiently, according to George Casey Jr. of Stockbridge Associates LLC.

Most National Housing Quality Award winners include these five features in their continuous improvement systems:[14]

1. **Note ideas and problems in writing.** One builder created a pocket-sized card that superintendents carry with them to jot down problems and ideas. They can be used at the jobsite, in discussions with trade contractors, or in production meetings.

2. **Prioritize improvements.** This can be accomplished in monthly team meetings. The team reviews ideas, selects monthly targets for improvement, and reviews progress.

3. **Define the problem.** Assign each targeted area for improvement to a team that includes the person who submitted the idea, and select a team leader. The team prepares a written statement of the problem.

4. **Determine causes and plan preventive actions.** With the problem clearly stated in writing, the team digs below the surface to identify causes and brainstorms possible preventive measures. After listing all ideas, the team

---

[13] Philip B. Crosby. *Quality Is Free: The Art of Making Quality Certain: How to Manage Quality— So That It Becomes A Source of Profit for Your Business*. New York: McGraw-Hill Companies, 1979.
[14] *Continuous Improvement for Small Volume Builders* (http://www.toolbase.org/Best-Practices/ Business-Management/Improvement-Small-Volume-Builders), NAHB Research Center, Upper Marlboro, Maryland, accessed December 29, 2010.

agrees to a sequence of preventive steps and writes a plan for management approval.

5. **Make improvements and measure success.** After each change has been in place for a predetermined time, the team reviews, evaluates, and records the results. If the proposed remedies did not achieve the goal, the team develops alternatives.

Benchmarking

Benchmarking can help you identify techniques and practices that have created superior performance in other organizations both inside and outside of the home building industry.

- Choose a process that is critical to customer service and the company's success to benchmark.
- Learn how the process is done currently.
- Identify a benchmarking partner—a company satisfies the same customer extremely well.
- Gather details about how the benchmarking partner performs the process.
- Adapt their process for your company.
- Monitor the results.

Quality Killers

Above all, avoid doing things in your business because "we've always done it this way." If that is the best answer you can provide when an employee, trade contractor, or customer asks "why?" then your processes are outdated and need a tune-up.

Monitoring Performance

A systematic quality management program monitors performance to see whether reengineering is working. Your quality toolbox should include instruments for measuring

- financial performance;
- customer satisfaction;
- employee satisfaction;
- warranty costs; and
- variances.

19
Diversification

Although you may start your business by focusing on one product or market, you eventually may want to expand into other product lines and markets. For example, you might purchase properties to renovate and rent them to earn passive income, or diversify into other areas of building, such as light commercial, to even out the ups and downs of the construction cycle. Diversification can add new profit centers that expand your company's growth potential.

You could explore the following areas for new businesses opportunities:

- Energy audits
- Warranty service
- Remodeling
- Consulting
- Property management
- Design/build
- Home inspection
- Insurance repair
- Light commercial construction
- Multifamily construction
- Land development
- Real estate brokerage

Each of these areas includes subcategories in which you might find a niche. For example, within multifamily, various options exist for mixed-use development, such as residential space built over office space or retail stores. You must consider vacancies and corresponding rent losses; lease-up time; and tenant credit, lease terms, renewals, and rent increases when considering a rental project's viability.

In the remodeling arena, consider working for suppliers that sell directly to consumers, such as the big-box stores. You do the work while they handle consumer credit and billing issues. You get a reliable source of income without administrative overhead. If you have cash or a source of financing, purchase vacant properties to update for sale or rent. You can find properties to purchase by maintaining relationships with banks and mortgage companies.

Within light commercial construction, you might consider the following clients:

- Utility companies
- School districts
- Medical facilities
- Government entities
- Churches
- National restaurant chain franchises

Land Development

Consider the following factors when assessing land value using a cost approach:

1. Comparative land values
2. Approval and permit costs
3. Site improvement costs
4. Building improvement costs
5. Remaining useful life of a building (if improving an existing structure)
6. Physical depreciation
7. Functional and/or location obsolescence

One experienced builder uses a 10-page checklist to gather objective data when evaluating properties for potential purchase. The checklist considers the following factors:

- **Location**—Property description, area, and shape; whether a survey exists; improvements, if any; easements; cemetery plots; historical structures and artifacts; encroachments
- **Neighborhood characteristics**—The surrounding area; type of buildings and their average age, new building activities, nuisance factors; access; FHA-VA properties; whether the approach to the property is "good," "fair," or "bad"

- **Site characteristics** (based on a visual inspection)—Terrain; presence of trees and creeks; soil characteristics; drainage; existing roads and road conditions

- **Community facilities and transportation**—Area schools and school capacity problems, if any; churches; amenities such as shopping centers; public transit; recreation facilities such as golf courses and playgrounds; businesses and employment centers

- **Title issues**—Easements, mineral rights, liens, and boundaries

- **Utilities and improvements**—Gas, electric, water, sewer, telephone, sidewalks, streetlights, curbs, gutters, fire hydrants

- **Local ordinances and zoning**—Whether there is any flexibility in current zoning; the comprehensive land use plan that encompasses the property; how future highway plans affect the property; lot size requirements; minimum setbacks; side yard requirements; how adjacent properties are zoned

- **Taxes**—Assessed valuation, tax rate, and total annual taxes

- **Technical considerations**—Sewer details, drainage details, soil, fill requirements, state and federal wetlands regulations, watershed regulations, and other environmental protection laws and regulations that might affect the property

Evaluating the Risk

Although some builders may view diversifying as a risk-reduction strategy, in reality, it carries its own risks. Concentrating on a single business helps maintain the focus of "who we are" and "what we do" that are important to maintaining quality. The company's energies and resources are directed down one business path. Focusing on one business increases the likelihood that company associates will know their business very well. Therefore, before you spend time and energy creating a new business, answer these fundamental questions:

- Will the new business divert resources from my current business?

- Does the company have personnel, equipment, or other resources that can be shared?

- Does the company have the required expertise to operate the business being considered?

- Will the capital investment produce a greater return than if resources were invested elsewhere?

- Is there a market for the new product or service?
- Does the company have a distinctive competency that applies to the new business?
- Will entering the new business increase or decrease the company's overall risk?

Trial and error is an expensive way to learn. You may want to dip your toe in before diving into another business area. You can test the waters by entering a joint venture with a more experienced partner. If you are considering commercial construction, for example, find a builder who already is doing commercial projects. How you split profits is negotiable, and he or she may be happy to have a backup partner who can step in on a project.

Loan Application Checklist

- [ ] Market study
- [ ] Property/project location
- [ ] Project description
- [ ] Survey
- [ ] Title report
- [ ] Pro forma budget
- [ ] Plans & specifications
- [ ] Regulatory approvals
- [ ] Impact fees paid
- [ ] Cost breakdown
  - ○ Excavation
  - ○ Slab/foundation
  - ○ Framing/rough carpentry
  - ○ Roof/mechanicals
  - ○ Exterior finishes
  - ○ Interior finishes
  - ○ Completion
- [ ] Signed sales contract (if presold home)
- [ ] Marketing plan (if speculative project)
- [ ] Company description and history
- [ ] Balance sheet
- [ ] Income statement
- [ ] Tax returns (two years)
- [ ] Professional references

Sample Job Descriptions

Senior Executives

CHIEF EXECUTIVE OFFICER

Reports to: Company owner

Objective: Ensure profitable growth and adequate financing of the company.

Responsibilities:

1. Take primary responsibility for establishing, assembling, and approving all business plans.

2. Conduct monthly corporate performance meetings. Work with president and vice presidents to generate action plans as needed.

3. Arrange for corporate financing to meet the needs set forth in the company's business plan. Investigate potential equity financing and debt financing sources. Assess the company's current financial structure and develop ideas for improvement.

4. Recruit, select and train president. Meet monthly with him or her to compare performance with objectives. Suggest solutions to problems, deal with current issues, and establish short-term objectives.

5. Develop a list of strategies for each department to improve its operations through benchmarking. Adapt strategies from other companies (not necessarily home builders) that have superior operating structures.

6. Approve all land acquisition decisions. Assist in planning and zoning of all new developments.

7. Review demographic and customer preference information studies to make sure product line reflects market research and suits customer preferences.

8. Work with president to monitor competition's product line, options, market share, financial status, etc.

9. Identify potential diversification opportunities and research their feasibility.

10. Visit one superior home builder/developer in other market during the first quarter of the year to observe how the company's management system works. Visit new home and development sites regularly and review findings with president.

REMINDER: Add skills, experience, and education requirements, and describe the work environment and physical demands for this position.

PRESIDENT

Reports to: Chief executive officer

Objectives: Ensure continuously profitable operations.

Responsibilities:

1. Develop company business plan with owner and vice presidents. Prepare annual operating budget.

2. Ensure implementation of business plan regarding land acquisition, profits, market share, construction quality, customer satisfaction, continuity, and growth.

3. Develop efficient organizational structure for company and staff.

4. Recruit, select, and train vice presidents as needed. Ensure proper recruitment, training, and selection for all company positions.

5. Set quarterly goals and evaluate performance of all vice presidents. Ensure proper goal setting and performance evaluation of all employees.

6. Set and approve compensation plans for vice presidents with assistance of chief executive officer. Approve all other employee compensation with vice presidents.

7. Maintain company in a sound financial condition with assistance of chief executive officer. Help chief executive officer and chief financial officer provide for adequate company financing.

8. Establish quality relationships with other home builders, developers, and industry consultants.

9. Represent firm in local civic, political, and industry activities and generate positive public relations opportunities.

REMINDER: Add skills, experience, and education requirements, and describe the work environment and physical demands for this position.

Operations

VICE PRESIDENT OF OPERATIONS

Reports to: President

Objectives: Oversee operations to produce high-quality, cost-effective homes that achieve a high level of customer satisfaction.

Responsibilities:

1. Coordinate home building operations with company's land development function.

2. Establish standard operating procedures and quality standards for new home construction. Establish and enforce warranty guidelines

3. Oversee the construction department's estimating, purchasing, contracting, and field operations functions.

4. Oversee cost reduction program through competitive bidding, contract negotiation, improved quantity take-offs, improved field control, and value engineering. Help maximize the perceived value/cost ratio.

5. Recruit and train managers who get things done through people.

6. Enhance contract flow efficiency from sales to closing.

7. Help prepare company business plan.

8. Establish quality relationships with other home builders, developers, and industry consultants.

REMINDER: Add skills, experience, and education requirements, and describe the work environment and physical demands for this position.

DIRECTOR OF PURCHASING, ESTIMATING, AND DESIGN

Reports to: Vice president of operations

Objectives: Oversee the production of take-offs, estimates, home designs, and construction drawings. Control and reduce costs.

Responsibilities:

1. Recruit, select, train, and manage personnel and establish standard operating procedures for purchasing, estimating, and design departments. Hold operating expenses to targeted ratio on sales.

2. Determine accurate standard specifications for each trade. Ensure that all trades are under trade contractor agreement. Develop relationships with trades committed to reducing costs and increasing quality.

3. Administer accurate quantity take-offs and estimates. Monitor competitive bidding, contract negotiation, and value engineering. Re-bid trades if cost increases occur.

4. Establish and maintain a trade contractor/supplier performance evaluation system and award program.

5. Analyze cost codes by phase for cost-saving measures and techniques. Communicate any substantial hard-cost changes to vice president of operations.

6. Maintain master price books for sales department price adjustment.

7. Conduct detailed lot programming analysis.

8. Research and approve invoices and variance purchase orders to meet accounting department deadlines.

9. Schedule starts to match monthly projections.

10. Stay current on innovative products, construction techniques, and trends affecting the home building industry.

REMINDER: Add skills, experience, and education requirements, and describe the work environment and physical demands for this position.

ESTIMATOR/PURCHASER

Reports to: Director of purchasing, estimating, and design

Objectives: Produce accurate, thorough take-offs and budgets. Purchase materials and hire trade contractors. Keep costs down while meeting quality standards.

Responsibilities:

1. Prepare detailed cost estimates for plans. Compile accurate quantity takeoffs. Establish and monitor budgets for all construction phases. Compute gross margin estimates. Help identify cost-saving techniques, materials, and procedures.

2. Research and eliminate all material, trade contractor, and back office-related variances. Monitor and communicate any hard-cost changes due to cost increases and quantity changes to director of purchasing, estimating, and design.

3. Interface with architect and engineering consultants on product development.

4. Establish and maintain a product database for the NAHB Chart of Accounts. Provide sales department with pricing and technical support.

5. Help prepare lot programming analysis reports for all current and future subdivisions.

6. Issue thorough, accurate purchase orders and work orders within allotted time frames.

7. Perform cost comparison and analysis as requested. Update cost information in price file.

8. Monitor plan changes. Estimate prices of all changes and provide written descriptions of change orders.

9. Recruit and maintain relationships with quality, reliable trade contractors, vendors, and suppliers. Supervise preparation of bid packages. Troubleshoot problems with trade contractors and suppliers.

10. Inspect homes under construction to ensure estimates are accurate.

REMINDER: Add skills, experience, and education requirements, and describe the work environment and physical demands for this position.

ESTIMATING/PURCHASING ASSISTANT

Reports to: Director of purchasing, estimating, and design

Objectives: Assist with the functions of the purchasing, estimating, and drafting departments.

Responsibilities:

1. Track new jobs from inception to field. Help prepare the quarterly gross margin summary sheet (at time of start package). Update and keep master price books current.

2. Provide backup support for entering job costs and preparing purchase orders. Distribute purchase orders, prints, and selection sheets to vendors, field personnel, construction office, and purchasing files.

3. Check estimates against budgets for proper coding after jobs have been sent to field.

4. Establish a policy for recording addenda related to budget changes. Issue and distribute addenda to builder, project manager, superintendent, and trade contractors.

5. Research and assist with problem billings, such as locating backup material and canceled checks.

6. Maintain certificate of insurance file for all vendors. On the 15th of each month, mail letters to insurance agents requesting current certificates for the vendors whose certificates will expire the next month. Keep monthly file current.

7. Develop a computerized mailing list for all trade contractors, suppliers, and vendors.

8. Perform clerical tasks for purchasing, estimating, and design departments.

REMINDER: Add skills, experience, and education requirements, and describe the work environment and physical demands for this position.

ARCHITECT/DESIGNER

Reports to: Director of purchasing, estimating, and design

Objectives: Oversee the architectural and structural design aspects of the home building process. Strive for zero-defect construction documents.

Responsibilities:

1. Design plans for new models. Interpret and implement building code changes.

2. Oversee production of start packages (blueprints, plot plans, permits, etc.).

3. Update existing plans to reflect feature and specification changes, with an emphasis on value engineering and office-related cost variance reduction.

4. Communicate any substantial plan changes to director of purchasing, estimating, and design.

5. Specify materials, trims, fixtures, and construction assemblies (floor joist, floor sheathing, roof deck layouts, etc). Prepare inked floor plans for sales brochures.

6. Oversee the production of construction drawings. Make sure they are fully coordinated with structural calculations, and that structural drawings are sealed and signed.

7. Solicit trade contractor input to enhance value engineering of floor plans and construction drawings. See if homes' energy-efficiency, cost-effectiveness, construction methods, quality, etc., can be improved.

REMINDER: Add skills, experience, and education requirements, and describe the work environment and physical demands for this position.

SELECTIONS COORDINATOR

Reports to: Architect/designer, project manager

Objectives: Educate customers about products and options. Ensure they make selections by established deadlines.

Responsibilities:

1. Evaluate market and recommend options to architect/designer to suit the needs of targeted buyers.

2. Review construction cutoff dates as they pertain to options and selections. Schedule customer appointments accordingly.

3. Conduct design meetings with customers to review option selections. Provide professional advice on the types of materials and/or upgrades that are most appropriate for customers.

4. Display samples and educate customers about natural characteristics and maintenance of the products offered.

5. Review any custom options with customers. Obtain pricing and evaluate feasibility and cost breakdowns with estimator/purchaser and project manager.

6. Communicate customers' selections to sales, estimating, and construction departments.

7. Attend meetings with superintendent, customer service manager, and sales personnel to review status of construction and cutoff dates, and to troubleshoot issues pertaining to product selections.

8. Review new products with industry representatives.

9. Attend industry trade shows, sales training, and product knowledge seminars to maintain knowledge of building products and keep current on industry trends.

REMINDER: Add skills, experience, and education requirements, and describe the work environment and physical demands for this position.

HUMAN RESOURCES MANAGER

Reports to: Vice president of operations

Objectives: Oversee all functions related to employee recruitment and retention.

Responsibilities:

1. Develop benefit programs and payroll procedures. Oversee their administration.

2. Help the president and vice president of operations establish company policies and procedures. Compile and distribute employee handbook.

3. Advertise open positions, interview candidates, and participate in employee selection. Coordinate the hiring process with all managers. Check references and conduct personal profile testing. Consult with legal counsel on all employment-related issues.

4. Process all paperwork for new hires as well as for status changes, terminations, vacation/sick forms, time cards for hourly employees, overtime forms, insurance/401(k) enrollment forms, etc.

5. Conduct new-hire orientations and exit interviews.

6. Help managers and other personnel write job descriptions for all positions in the company. See to it that job descriptions meet ADA requirements.

7. Coordinate employee training workshops and/or seminars.

8. Facilitate team building to increase employees' productivity and maintain high morale.

9. Create effective employee relation strategies that increase and improve communication.

10. Assist, counsel, and coach other managers experiencing performance issues with their staff. Counsel employees as needed on performance- and work-related issues.

REMINDER: Add skills, experience, and education requirements, and describe the work environment and physical demands for this position.

OFFICE MANAGER

Reports to: Vice president of operations, human resources manager

Objectives: Maintain professional appearance and operation of company office.

Responsibilities:

1. Help establish general office procedures.

2. Purchase all office supplies, food, and beverages. Order and distribute parking/security cards and office keys.

3. Purchase office equipment and arrange for maintenance when needed. Work with information technology manager to purchase computer equipment, software, telephones, and cell phones. Negotiate cell phone plan with provider.

4. Monitor G&A-related expenses and invoices to make sure they stay within the budget.

5. Organize company outings, dinners, meetings, trips, award programs, etc.

6. Maintain company bulletin board. Post current events, flyers of items for sale, fun facts, employee and company news, and other items.

7. Give all new hires a tour of the office on their first day and introduce them to all office employees.

8. Bring incoming courier packages and other deliveries to employees if they don't pick them up from the receptionist's desk.

9. Make sure incoming mail is opened (except items marked "personal" or "confidential"), sorted, and distributed by the end of the business day. Make sure outgoing mail is stamped and sent downstairs for pick up by 4:30 p.m.

10. Tidy the kitchen and copy room periodically throughout the day. Encourage employees to keep their work areas neat to maintain the office's professional appearance.

REMINDER: Add skills, experience, and education requirements, and describe the work environment and physical demands for this position.

INFORMATION TECHNOLOGY MANAGER

Reports to: Vice president of operations

Objectives: Coordinate the company's technology and computer needs.

Responsibilities:

1. With executives and other managers, assess company's existing manual systems and procedures to see which should be computerized.

2. Research available technological options to serve company's current and future needs.

3. Select, install, and oversee the maintenance of hardware, peripherals, software, and phone system. Set up firewalls as necessary.

4. Train personnel on equipment and software as needed.

5. Maintain company's server, including virtual private network and other connection devices.

6. Regularly back up all company databases and electronic information. Archive data and electronic information off-site.

7. Establish procedures for employees to report malfunctioning equipment. Troubleshoot and solve technological problems, including malfunctioning computer equipment, software, phones, etc.

8. Oversee the development and maintenance of the company's website.

9. Develop programs to extract electronic data into reports.

10. Stay abreast of current and future technological equipment, software, resources, etc.

REMINDER: Add skills, experience, and education requirements, and describe the work environment and physical demands for this position.

INFORMATION TECHNOLOGY ASSISTANT

Reports to: Information technology manager

Objectives: Assist with the coordination of the company's technology and computer needs.

Responsibilities:

1. Install, maintain, and support hardware, peripherals, software, and phone system.

2. Respond to employee requests for help with equipment and software.

3. Help train personnel on equipment and software. Perform data backups.

4. Develop and maintain company website. Gather information from other departments to keep content fresh.

5. Help develop programs to extract electronic data into reports.

6. Assist with various spreadsheet applications.

7. Stay abreast of current and future technological equipment, software, resources, etc.

8. Assist information technology manager with special projects.

REMINDER: Add skills, experience, and education requirements, and describe the work environment and physical demands for this position.

Accounting and Finance

CHIEF FINANCIAL OFFICER

Reports to: President

Objective: Obtain financing commitments and manage the company's financing and accounting operations.

Responsibilities:

1. Acquire necessary debt and equity financing for residential construction, land development activities, and general operations.

2. Develop new lender relations and financial sources.

3. Select title company and negotiate charges for services.

4. Acquire mortgage commitments and coordinate with marketing department.

5. Review and interpret financial statements and operations to facilitate better upper management decision making and to enhance profitability.

6. Develop an administrative, accounting, and finance budget in response to the company's business plan. Monitor company's and departments' performance against the budget. Identify significant variances that require corrective action.

7. Prepare and maintain project pro forma.

8. Manage the overall operations of the corporate office. Administer company's insurance plans and overall risk management program.

9. Analyze the nature of the company's equity, the associated risk exposure of each component over time, and the corresponding return on each component.

REMINDER: Add skills, experience, and education requirements, and describe the work environment and physical demands for this position.

VICE PRESIDENT OF FINANCE

Reports to: Chief financial officer

Objective: Perform overall financial management.

Responsibilities:

1. Manage long- and short-term cash functions and cash flow projections. Establish and maintain all banking relationships. Review monthly financial statements. Direct year-end annual audits.

2. Assist with ongoing project-by-project financing needs. Provide ongoing project-by-project cash flow projections and communicate with bankers, equity partners, and others.

3. With the assistant controller, develop and implement systems and procedures to monitor and analyze the progress of homes under construction to evaluate estimating, purchasing, variance, and cost-to-complete functions.

4. Review the compilation of information required to prepare annual tax returns.

5. Prepare annual G&A operating budget. Review other departments' operating budgets; modify as operating performance and assumptions dictate.

6. Prepare annual pro forma operating statements.

7. Oversee and review all corporate data processing and information technology functions.

8. Supervise financial department staff. Manage the division of responsibilities, staff needs, and coordination with other personnel.

9. Complete property management functions (budgets, capital expenditures, repairs, rents, etc.). Maintain any required communication with HUD, limited partners, syndicator, etc.

10. Conduct periodic inventory verification via physical inventory count/verification. Transmit receivable and inventory support documentation to bank officers per loan covenants.

REMINDER: Add skills, experience, and education requirements, and describe the work environment and physical demands for this position.

CONTROLLER

Reports to: Vice president of finance

Objectives: Oversee the company's overall accounting operations.

Responsibilities:

1. Hire and train accounting personnel. Manage department functions.

2. Implement and maintain accounting software system.

3. Prepare timely, accurate financial statements.

4. Supervise the preparation, accuracy, and timeliness of draws. Implement and supervise daily and weekly cash reporting systems.

5. Control cost center expenditures. Monitor compliance with budget. Accumulate construction cost data.

6. Monitor and control trade contractor insurance and lien waivers.

7. Manage human resources, information technology, and insurance functions where volume doesn't dictate separate positions.

8. Help the president prepare the annual operating budget.

> **REMINDER:** Add skills, experience, and education requirements, and describe the work environment and physical demands for this position.

ASSISTANT CONTROLLER

Reports to: Chief financial officer, vice president of finance

Objectives: Manage day-to-day accounting functions and cycles to produce timely, accurate financial information.

Responsibilities:

1. Supervise and manage the accounting staff and daily accounting department operations.

2. Help the controller prepare monthly financial statements. Review financial statements prepared by the staff accountant.

3. Prepare and maintain appropriate subsidiary schedules for various financial statements.

4. Review all job cost-related payables for accurate cost coding and adherence to appropriate payment terms.

5. Help the vice president of finance develop systems and procedures to monitor and analyze the progress of homes under construction.

6. Help compile information for preparing the annual corporate tax return. Help the staff accountant with annual audit and tax return.

7. Oversee payroll function administration. Compile and file all quarterly and annual tax returns, W2s, 1000s, etc.

8. Administer and reconcile the 401(k) profit sharing plan. Communicate and coordinate with the plan sponsor as necessary.

REMINDER: Add skills, experience, and education requirements, and describe the work environment and physical demands for this position.

STAFF ACCOUNTANT

Reports to: Assistant controller

Objectives: Perform daily accounting tasks.

Responsibilities:

1. Process accounts receivable. Prepare monthly detailed A/R aging schedules and submit to the bank.

2. Incorporate accounts payable and A/R functions into cash management/planning system.

3. Prepare monthly financial statements and subsidiary schedules to be reviewed by the assistant controller and vice president of finance. Submit monthly financial statements to the bank along with the A/R aging.

4. Prepare monthly bank reconciliations for all checking accounts.

5. Monitor and take periodic inventory.

6. Prepare and file quarterly and annual payroll tax returns.

7. Assemble backup material for audits as directed by the outside auditing firm and the assistant controller.

8. Establish and maintain appropriate record keeping for various home owners associations. Transfer records to residents at appropriate time.

REMINDER: Add skills, experience, and education requirements, and describe the work environment and physical demands for this position.

GENERAL LEDGER ACCOUNTANT

Reports to: Vice president of finance

Objectives: Assemble, analyze, and coordinate accounting data to prepare monthly financial statements.

Responsibilities:

1. Record month-end journal entries.

2. Update and maintain fixed asset schedules.

3. Collect and monitor accounting data. Report data trends and patterns to vice president of finance.

4. Prepare (or assist with the preparation of) monthly financial statements.

5. Produce other financial reports as needed.

6. Help assemble backup material for audits.

REMINDER: Add skills, experience, and education requirements, and describe the work environment and physical demands for this position.

ACCOUNTING CLERK

Reports to: Controller

Objectives: Perform accounts payable, data entry, and other accounting functions.

Responsibilities:

1. Audit invoices; review approvals, back up, general ledger allocations, and amounts to be paid. Code and classify all invoices.

2. Batch and enter invoices into accounting database. Assign vendor numbers for inputting manual checks. Run and review edit and post to general ledger.

3. Review invoices for manual payments and forward to controller for approval.

4. Obtain signatures for accounts payable checks and disburse checks.

5. Review cleared checks. Supply copies of cancelled checks, if requested. Maintain file of daily cleared checks. Maintain disk copies of cancelled check images.

6. Reconcile vendor statements. Mail W-9 tax forms to vendors and enter information in accounting database.

7. Perform variance analysis of job costs.

8. Run general ledger information as requested by general ledger accountant.

9. Help assemble backup material for audits.

10. Gather info for quarterly and annual payroll tax returns.

REMINDER: Add skills, experience, and education requirements, and describe the work environment and physical demands for this position.

Land Acquisition

VICE PRESIDENT OF LAND ACQUISITION

Reports to: President

Objectives: Locate and acquire land for residential construction or for sale to other building and development companies.

Responsibilities:

1. Collect data on available residential land. Provide for sufficient land to meet strategic plan. Profitably sell land when and where necessary.

2. Option economically feasible properties.

3. Explore vehicles to acquire and hold land. Pursue financial contracts.

4. Conduct timely feasibility studies to assess land's physical, political, and financial aspects, as well as market potential. Provide continuous economic feasibility projections from feasibility pro forma to preliminary pro forma.

5. Select consultants and coordinate land use design and approval process.

6. After final plat, deliver to appropriate parties all terms/conditions of approval for site development.

7. Develop and administer a master planning, scheduling, and tracking system to account for all land acquisition activities.

8. Keep president and director of planning and site development informed about land acquisition status.

REMINDER: Add skills, experience, and education requirements, and describe the work environment and physical demands for this position.

DIRECTOR OF PLANNING AND SITE DEVELOPMENT

Reports to: Vice president of land acquisition

Objectives: Manage site investigation and evaluation, site plan preparation and approval process, and site engineering.

Responsibilities:

1. Research community ordinances, maps, topographical data, soil information, community review procedures, political considerations, availability and capacity of utilities, and other information.

2. Research special easement conditions in title work or surveys for each parcel.

3. Prepare summary of research findings on each parcel under review as part of a purchase agreement. Provide recommendations about proposed costs, feasibility, time frame for proposed development, special conditions, etc.

4. Prepare a chart of potential planning and development costs through the permit approval stages. Review and approve all billing invoices related to the site investigation and evaluation process.

5. Select professional contractors. Develop schedule and budget for site plan development and engineering. Deliver site plan within those predetermined guidelines.

6. File site engineering plans with the utilities, complete applications, and provide necessary documentation as required. Serve as liaison between utility companies, community departments, and the company. Schedule pre-engineering meetings and special meetings as needed during overall review and preparation of service plan process.

7. Obtain storm, sewer, and water approvals from municipality during site engineering approval and follow their submission through county, city, and state approval and permit issuance. Obtain permits for installation of sales trailer, construction trailer, equipment yard, etc.

8. Attend pre-construction meetings for site development and underground construction.

9. Spot-check site development throughout construction to make sure it addresses community concerns and meets special site plan conditions.

REMINDER: Add skills, experience, and education requirements, and describe the work environment and physical demands for this position.

LAND ACQUISITION/SITE DEVELOPMENT ASSISTANT

Reports to: Vice president of land acquisition, director of planning and site development

Objectives: Assist with the acquisition, identification, and processing of land for development or sale.

Responsibilities:

1. Identify potential acquisitions and inform vice president of land acquisition about them.

2. Conduct market research or work with market researcher to evaluate prospects' and buyers' interest in potential home sites.

3. Establish a database of land development information, including contract information, geographic, topographical data, etc.

4. Coordinate and assist with feasibility studies.

5. Coordinate and assist with site plan approval process.

6. Coordinate and communicate development stages and schedules to vice president of land acquisition and director of site planning and development.

7. Distribute information and documents to government agencies, utilities, development contractors, and others outside the company.

8. Maintain current records of all site plan approvals, approved graphics, and engineering plans, permits, etc., per project.

REMINDER: Add skills, experience, and education requirements, and describe the work environment and physical demands for this position.

Construction

VICE PRESIDENT OF CONSTRUCTION

Reports to: President

Objectives: Oversee business aspects of construction activities. Assist with management of land development functions as they relate to construction.

Responsibilities:

1. Work with director of site planning and development on land development for residential construction.

2. Establish quality standards. Ensure that homes meet those standards, are on budget, and are delivered on schedule.

3. Establish systems to measure and track performance of land development and home construction divisions.

4. Establish and enforce warranty guidelines.

5. Help the director of purchasing and estimating oversee the construction department's estimating, purchasing, and contracting operations.

6. Oversee value engineering of construction plans to maximize the perceived value/cost ratio.

7. For each house, perform postconstruction analysis of all costs and problems encountered during production.

8. Develop trend analysis methods and monitor trends in performance benchmarks.

9. Produce weekly and monthly performance reports for upper management.

REMINDER: Add skills, experience, and education requirements, and describe the work environment and physical demands for this position.

BUILDER/GENERAL CONTRACTOR

Reports to: Vice president of construction

Objectives: Manage the overall construction operation.

Responsibilities:

1. Work with sales and construction personnel to schedule starts. Develop production schedule for each home.

2. Approve all final estimates before submission to buyers/owners or lending institutions. Sign contracts and coordinate all legal aspects of construction.

3. Hire, train, and manage construction department staff. Approve trade contractor selection.

4. Maintain thorough knowledge of construction practices, materials, and procedures for all trade contractors.

5. Consult with superintendent and others to establish standard construction methods as well as operating procedures for managing cost control, change orders, trade contractors, quality control, etc.

6. Establish and conduct a construction safety program that meets OSHA standards and assures safety of employees, trade contractors, and others.

7. Stay current on industry trends by reading publications, talking with material suppliers, staying involved with NAHB and state and local associations, etc.

8. Maintain ultimate responsibility for all material, fixture, appliance, and product selections. Work with selections coordinator and customer service manager to ensure that home owners' selections occur within established timeframes.

9. Maintain knowledge of applicable building codes, zoning ordinances, and other legal regulations.

REMINDER: Add skills, experience, and education requirements, and describe the work environment and physical demands for this position.

PROJECT MANAGER

Reports to: Builder/general contractor, vice president of construction

Objectives: Schedule and coordinate all new-home construction phases.

Responsibilities:

1. Ensure that homes are built to requirements and specifications established by construction drawings, building codes, and clients.

2. Monitor production schedules, critical paths for projects, trade contractor schedules, and cost control to ensure that homes are completed on time and meet expected quality and profit levels.

3. Develop and maintain strong, productive supplier and trade contractor relationships. Communicate company's quality and performance standards to each trade contractor and supplier. Conduct periodic work inspections to ensure that those standards are met.

4. Monitor project quality and cost control.

5. Work with the selections coordinator to ensure that clients make selections on time.

6. Keep builder and vice president of construction informed of each project's progress.

7. Design and implement checklists for inspections, quality control, and standard operating procedures.

REMINDER: Add skills, experience, and education requirements, and describe the work environment and physical demands for this position.

SUPERINTENDENT

Reports to: Builder, project manager

Objectives: Manage daily construction activities.

Responsibilities:

1. Consult with architect, engineer, builder, selections coordinator, trade contractors, and clients on plan revisions and change orders.

2. Walk through homes daily. Take overall responsibility for keeping sites tidy during construction. Schedule municipal inspections.

3. Explain safety program to field employees and trade contractors, and make sure they follow it.

4. Guide and direct field employees, trade contractors, and suppliers. Assist trade contractors with tasks, when necessary.

5. Explain quality control standards and supervise their implementation. Make sure homes are built to quality standards. Strive for no-defect construction.

6. Keep builder and project manager informed of each home's production status. Update schedule as necessary and produce weekly production reports.

7. Order materials and supplies and schedule deliveries. Receive, inspect, and verify all deliveries. Check vendors' and trade contractors' invoices. Authorize payment.

8. Notify trade contractors and material suppliers far enough in advance to assure materials are delivered and trade contractors arrive on schedule.

9. Communicate with customers on jobsites. Answer their questions and ensure that construction meets their expectations.

10. Conduct preclosing walk-throughs with customers and customer service/warranty coordinator. Coordinate punch list work.

REMINDER: Add skills, experience, and education requirements, and describe the work environment and physical demands for this position.

LABORER

Reports to: Superintendent

Objectives: Prepare sites for various construction tasks and assist with those in progress. Keep jobsites safe and clean.

Responsibilities:

1. Perform tasks as assigned by superintendent. May include excavation, demolition, carrying supplies and materials, setting up and breaking down workstations and scaffolding, minor carpentry, tool maintenance, punch list tasks, assisting trade contractors, etc.

2. Report any problems, damage, hazardous conditions, and oversights to superintendent.

3. Keep jobsites clean. Make sure debris is contained in proper Dumpsters. Do exterior pick-up and interior sweeping/tidying once a day (or more often, as directed by superintendent).

4. Help superintendent receive material deliveries. Unload trucks and stack and store materials. Protect lumber and other large materials from exposure to weather.

5. De-ice, shovel snow, and supply heat to homes under construction in winter.

6. Install and remove temporary sidewalks and stairwell railings.

7. Make sure excavated areas, trenches, and holes are marked for safety.

8. Keep model homes tidy. Make repairs as necessary.

REMINDER: Add skills, experience, and education requirements, and describe the work environment and physical demands for this position.

CUSTOMER SERVICE MANAGER

Reports to: Vice president of construction

Objectives: Ensure that customers' expectations are met during each phase of the sales, construction, and warranty service processes.

Responsibilities:

1. Participate in all conferences with customers.

2. Coordinate all color, finish, and product selections with customers and selections coordinator.

3. Track change orders.

4. Work with the salesperson to coordinate with the client before closing on the home; verify that all documents are complete, financing is in place, and ensure there are no surprises at closing.

5. Monitor customer requests for warranty service.

6. Ensure that warranty service work is completed on time and meets the customer's and the company's standards.

7. Resolve all claims and disputes about warranty issues.

8. Develop and administer customer satisfaction survey. Monitor customer satisfaction rates and produce reports.

9. Identify parts of the homebuilding process that need improvement to improve customer satisfaction. Develop action plans with appropriate departments and personnel.

10. Work with marketing manager to develop referral programs: forms, letters, giveaways, or other devices to solicit referrals, plus gifts or other incentives to thank customers for providing referrals.

REMINDER: Add skills, experience, and education requirements, and describe the work environment and physical demands for this position.

WARRANTY COORDINATOR

Reports to: Customer service manager

Objectives: Maintain quality assurance and provide warranty service to home owners after closing.

Responsibilities:

1. Train home owners to use and operate their homes' mechanical and electronic equipment.

2. Conduct periodic home inspections before closing, at closing, 60 days after closing, and at the one-year warranty walk-through.

3. Document items needing repair during inspections and walk-throughs. Schedule repair work. After repairs are complete, conduct another inspection to make sure the repairs meet the company's quality standards and the home owner is satisfied.

4. Receive home owner calls and e-mails for warranty service. Gather warranty service request information. Keep a detailed log of all warranty service requests. File daily summaries.

5. Review service requests against closing dates and the warranty manual. If any items are not warranted, send a letter to the customer stating which items are not warranted and why.

6. Schedule warranty service work with home owners, field personnel, and trade contractors. After repairs are complete, conduct another inspection to make sure the repairs meet the company's quality standards and the home owner is satisfied.

7. Complete all warranty service requests within ten (10) working days.

8. Consult with builder, project manager, and vice president of construction to update warranty book.

REMINDER: Add skills, experience, and education requirements, and describe the work environment and physical demands for this position.

CUSTOMER SERVICE ASSISTANT

Reports to: Customer service manager

Objectives: Coordinate warranty service requests. Make sure customers' expectations are met during each phase of the sales, production, and warranty service processes.

Responsibilities:

1. Answer customers' questions and help guide them through each stage of the home buying, construction, and warranty service processes.

2. Assist customers with color, finish, and product selection.

3. Participate in orientation tour with customers to deliver the home. Beforehand, collect all appliance manuals, security system instructions, community information sheets, and other documents and place them in the home (preferably in an envelope or a binder in a kitchen drawer).

4. Ensure that home owners get copies of the warranty manual during the orientation tour. Explain the manual to them.

5. Ensure that warranty service work is completed on time and meets the customer's and the company's standards. Make sure all paperwork is complete.

6. Help customer service manager resolve all claims and disputes about warranty issues.

7. Administer customer satisfaction survey. Tabulate results.

8. Administer referral programs: Distribute referral forms and gifts to customers.

REMINDER: Add skills, experience, and education requirements, and describe the work environment and physical demands for this position.

CONSTRUCTION ASSISTANT

Reports to: Project manager, superintendent

Objectives: Perform construction-related administrative and clerical duties.

Responsibilities:

1. Maintain database of trade contractor, supplier, and vendor contact information. Maintain files of proposed and approved bid solicitations and options.

2. Distribute plans, specs, production schedules, and related documents and correspondence to field personnel, trade contractors, suppliers, and others.

3. Distribute change orders to suppliers and trade contractors. Follow up to make sure they have received the proper information.

4. Communicate with vendors, trades, and superintendent about scheduled deliveries, confirmations, and follow-up calls.

5. Compare invoices against quotes, budgets, or cost sheets.

6. Compile job costs related to base cost, options, and extras for budget preparation.

7. Coordinate the scheduling of routine inspections with municipalities and utilities.

8. Prepare and distribute permit applications to municipal building departments. Track the documents' status with the building department.

9. Prepare waiver packages and other documents for home closings. Complete necessary follow-up after closings.

10. Maintain stock material and equipment inventory records.

REMINDER: Add skills, experience, and education requirements, and describe the work environment and physical demands for this position.

Sales and Marketing

VICE PRESIDENT OF SALES AND MARKETING

Reports to: President

Objectives: Develop strategies to successfully promote company and product. Meet or exceed sales and profit goals.

Responsibilities:

1. Conduct market research to define market segments and identify potential buyers' needs and desires. Monitor industry trends and competitors' activities in current and future market(s).

2. Calculate and project absorption rates within each defined market segment by area. Plan and forecast demand by price segment and location for future land acquisitions and holdings for market development.

3. Work with the estimating department to develop products and specs that appeal to the targeted market. Establish standard and optional features for each project.

4. Work with president to develop company's sales and marketing plans and budget for the next fiscal year. Work with director of sales to forecast sales.

5. With president, review sales and marketing plan and compare to company performance each quarter. Adjust plan as necessary.

6. Oversee market research to identify current customer trends, profiles, and developments.

7. Prepare spec lists for Realtors. Ensure home pricing is on collateral and website.

8. Collect relevant and useful information on competing companies. Conduct market share analysis.

9. Work with director of marketing to establish an effective marketing program suited to the company's target market.

10. Oversee Realtor and customer referral programs.

11. Manage processing of purchase agreements and oversee mortgage applications.

12. Stay up-to-date on industry trends by attending educational seminars, visiting other builders, reading industry periodicals, talking with consultants, staying involved with NAHB and state and local associations, etc.

13. Oversee online initiatives, including website, blog, and social media sites, as well as search engine optimization (SEO).

14. Develop company processes and training for marketing and sales personnel.

REMINDER: Add skills, experience, and education requirements, and describe the work environment and physical demands for this position.

DIRECTOR OF MARKETING

Reports to: Vice president of sales and marketing

Objectives: Generate traffic through effective marketing programs.

Responsibilities:

1. Manage marketing budget. Develop and supervise marketing, including website advertising and public relations, and social media programs. Market should establish a positive, professional company image (branding) and create interest in its homes.

2. Select vendors and media outlets. Negotiate media and vendor contracts.

3. Merchandise sales office, models, and model lots. Order signs and update signage as needed.

4. Coordinate and develop comprehensive community outreach plan.

5. Oversee production of company newsletter, e-mails and other ongoing communications to agents, buyers, and home owners. Work with information technology assistant to develop and maintain information on company website.

6. Develop materials for sales presentation books.

7. Develop and maintain company presence on World Wide Web.

8. Develop customer satisfaction program and survey materials.

REMINDER: Add skills, experience, and education requirements, and describe the work environment and physical demands for this position.

DIRECTOR OF SALES*

Reports to: Vice president of sales and marketing

Objectives: Develop and implement strategies to meet or exceed sales goals.

Responsibilities:

1. Help recruit, select, and train sales personnel.

2. Work with Vice President of Sales and Marketing to set sales goals for department. Monitor sales activity. Produce weekly, monthly, quarterly, and annual sales reports. Keep president and vice president of sales and marketing informed of sales activity.

3. Understand the requirements for mortgage financing.

4. Implement and monitor Realtor and customer referral programs and customer traffic evaluation system.

5. Implement lead tracking and analysis systems. Review leads weekly.

6. Work with purchasing and design departments on any project or contract changes related to sales.

7. Oversee Realtor interactions on social media and listing sites.

*Director of Sales duties can be merged with Sales Manager duties to create one position.

REMINDER: Add skills, experience, and education requirements, and describe the work environment and physical demands for this position.

SALES MANAGER

Reports to: Director of sales

Objectives: Help the company meet or exceed its sales and profit goals by managing the sales functions and sales personnel.

Responsibilities:

1. Recruit, select, and train sales personnel. Help them develop strategies to increase sales. Teach them how to set and manage customer expectations.

2. Establish procedures for doing sales presentations and qualifying prospects.

3. Keep sales book updated with current pricing, floor plans, specs, and memos.

4. Monitor sales activity. Help compile sales reports. Analyze prospect traffic and generate reports.

5. Mystery shop all sales people each quarter. Report results to sales management.

6. Establish relationships with prospects and follow up with them. Monitor lead tracking to develop sources for most productive leads.

7. Maintain knowledge of financing options and lenders.

8. Stay current on the competition's prices, floor plans, special discounts, and advertising.

9. Maintain relationships with customers from sales process through production and closing.

10. Ensure that model homes are staffed and are open on time.

REMINDER: Add skills, experience, and education requirements, and describe the work environment and physical demands for this position.

SALESPERSON

Reports to: Sales manager

Objective: Meet sales quotas as specified in business plan or determined by sales executives.

Responsibilities:

1. Set and manage customer expectations throughout sales, production, and warranty phases.

2. Make initial contact with prospects through referrals, demonstrated interest, or show home visits. Qualify prospects' interest and ability to purchase homes.

3. Conduct sales presentation for prospective customers. Follow up with phone calls, e-mails, and other communications per company procedures. Prepare home purchase agreements and construction contracts. Assist and monitor financing process.

4. Maintain consistent contact with clients during home construction to make sure their expectations are met.

5. Track loans with mortgage companies and troubleshoot problems. Act as liaison between mortgage company and purchaser to prevent miscommunication and expedite the process.

6. Work with the customer service manager to coordinate with the client before closing on the home; verify that all documents are complete, financing is in place, and there are no surprises at closing.

7. Participate in the final house walk-through with the client.

8. After closing, present the new home owners with a house-warming present from the company. After 60 days, meet with the home owners to give them the client satisfaction survey.

9. Maintain knowledge of community demographics and amenities: schools, local businesses, employers, parks, recreation facilities, etc.

10. Oversee maintenance of models and spec homes.

11. Maintain relationship with Realtor community by actively seeking new business. This may include delivering gifts to offices, connecting via social networks, or dropping off flyers.

12. Develop leads by actively participating in community activities, networking groups, and social media.

REMINDER: Add skills, experience, and education requirements, and describe the work environment and physical demands for this position.

MARKETING/SALES ASSISTANT

Reports to: Director of sales, director of marketing, sales manager

Objectives: Provide support for marketing and sales functions.

Responsibilities:

1. Work with public relations, advertising, marketing, website and interactive firms on marketing initiatives. Proof all materials for content, brand and message.

2. Record date and placement location of all print and media ads. Keep copies of all ads.

3. Distribute weekly, monthly, and quarterly sales reports.

4. Help with market research and market analysis activities.

5. Gather historical and current market information for sales forecasting.

6. Track cycle time from receipt of deposit to home delivery.

7. Monitor use of various mortgage lenders.

8. Monitor, update, and manage multiple listing services and Realtor licenses.

9. Help monitor customer satisfaction throughout sales, production, and warranty processes.

10. Keep customer information files up to date. Manage data entry for prospect file.

11. Manage website updates.

REMINDER: Add skills, experience, and education requirements, and describe the work environment and physical demands for this position.

INTERNET SALES CONSULTANT

Reports to: Sales Manager

Objectives: Respond promptly to inquiries from Internet and telephone, answer questions, set appointments, and develop a strategic follow-up program.

Responsibilities:

1. Utilize and maintain a customer relationship management (CRM) system.

2. If maintenance of the website is not a primary duty, actively ensure accuracy of all information on site(s).

3. During regular business hours, ensure responses to all contacts and leads within 30 minutes.

4. Ensure responses as soon as possible the next business day for all contacts and leads received after regular business hours.

5. Comply with CAN-SPAM Act, including maintaining a compliant database under both state and federal laws and regulations.

6. Follow best practices for e-mail and maintain e-mail templates.

7. Staff live chat to interact with buyers and set appointments.

8. Where applicable, maintain social media sites, as applicable, to interact with buyers.

REMINDER: Add skills, experience, and education requirements, and describe the work environment and physical demands for this position.

SALES HOST/HOSTESS

Reports to: Sales manager, salesperson

Objectives: Demonstrate model homes and communicate with prospective buyers.

Responsibilities:

1. Make sure model home signage is installed properly and is in good repair. Examine signs daily when traveling to and from models.

2. Arrive at model home(s) 15 minutes before opening time to disarm the security system, fluff the pillows, and check the lightbulbs.

3. Maintain inventory of price list and brochure packets. Notify salesperson or sales manager when supplies get low.

4. Greet prospects, give them tours of the model(s) if they want them (ask first), and answer their questions about the product and community. Point out standard and special features of the home and mention options during the tour.

5. Distribute price list and brochure packets. Show plot plans to prospects.

6. Register interested prospects. Input contact information in computer database. Notify salesperson and sales manager of interested prospects.

7. Encourage interested prospects to select a lot, leave a security deposit, and set an appointment with the salesperson to write a contract.

8. Answer phone calls promptly. Be sure computer equipment and fax machine in sales office is up and running.

9. Make sure models are tidy, are locked up properly, and the security system is set before leaving the premises.

10. Notify the sales manager or salesperson of any needed repairs or missing items.

REMINDER: Add skills, experience, and education requirements, and describe the work environment and physical demands for this position.

Administrative/Clerical

EXECUTIVE ASSISTANT

Reports to: Chief executive officer, president

Objectives: Provide administrative and clerical support to company executives.

Responsibilities:

1. Maintain all files (including product library). Help produce business correspondence.

2. Screen incoming calls. Help place calls and send e-mails for executives.

3. Maintain executives' weekly schedules. Notify CEO and president of meetings, appointments, and other activities.

4. Process and pay bills and maintain tax records for executives as needed.

5. Prepare reports, charts, graphs, etc, for meetings. Record minutes.

6. Help train all incoming clerical personnel.

7. Keep executive offices clean and orderly.

REMINDER: Add skills, experience, and education requirements, and describe the work environment and physical demands for this position.

RECEPTIONIST/ADMINISTRATIVE ASSISTANT

Reports to: Office manager

Objectives: Receive and route incoming calls and communications. Perform administrative and clerical duties.

Responsibilities:

1. Receive all incoming phone calls. Provide callers with information and/or route calls to appropriate personnel.

2. Receive general e-mails (those not sent to a specific employee). Reply with information, and/or route e-mails to appropriate personnel.

3. Receive deliveries and incoming mail. Sort for distribution to appropriate personnel. Route purchase orders, delivery slips, and invoices to accounting department.

4. Type correspondence, envelopes, and memos.

5. Enter data as directed by executive secretary.

6. Maintain the professional appearance of reception area. Greet customers and other visitors. Offer coffee and other refreshments to guests.

7. Maintain management databases and binder of all master forms.

8. Maintain filing systems. File copies of all correspondence and documents in proper binders and files.

9. Complete other duties as requested.

REMINDER: Add skills, experience, and education requirements, and describe the work environment and physical demands for this position.

Sample Superintendent Job Description

Sample Job Description

Reports to: Production Manager

Objectives: The superintendent oversees construction of individual homes to ensure high-quality work that is produced under budget, on schedule, and to the home owners' satisfaction. The superintendent takes full responsibility for producing homes in an efficient and safe manner through effective management of trade contractors, material suppliers, inspectors, and others on all homes under his or her direction. The superintendent is the primary representative of the company on construction matters. He or she orchestrates the work, coordinates the various complex aspects of the construction process, and trains trade contractors as needed in the performance of their work.

Responsibilities:

The superintendent must

- maintain a high degree of integrity and honesty in all business dealings
- be self-motivated and solve problems effectively
- get along well with others and lead by example
- communicate well; know how to listen
- be well organized and thorough
- solve problems within his or her authority
- be emotionally stable and able to work through difficult situations calmly and professionally
- be professional in dress, manner, and conduct; represent the company at all times and everywhere, and maintain a high degree of integrity and company loyalty

In addition, the superintendent must be able to

- read, understand, and resolve inconsistencies and problems in plans and specifications
- understand basic surveying principles and practices and interpret site-specific topography
- understand appropriate scheduling methods
- understand safety practices and procedures and conduct an effective job-site safety program
- instruct, train, and work with trade contractors and others to ensure compliance with proper material usage, approved construction methods, and operating procedures
- delegate responsibilities to subordinates while remaining accountable for their performance
- make quick, accurate decisions when necessary and take responsibility for those decisions
- use established supervisory and motivational techniques to elicit peak performance from all employees, suppliers, and trade contractors in regard to both quantity and quality
- use a computer, including word processing, spreadsheet, database, and applicable scheduling programs
- plan, organize, and conduct ongoing training sessions for construction personnel and others related to the trades
- situate a home on the lot, establish elevations and depth of excavation, and adjust plans to accommodate specific site and code requirements
- conduct site and preconstruction meetings with home owners
- communicate site changes to drafting and estimating personnel accurately so that the plans and estimate can be revised to reflect accurate quantities of materials for homes under the superintendent's direct control
- maintain effective, cooperative, working relationships with architects, engineers, trade contractors, employees, material suppliers, home owners, public officials, and the general public
- use diplomacy to mitigate negative situations and address home owners' concerns professionally while maintaining excellent relations with them
- integrate all tasks into an organized, controlled, and smooth-flowing system
- coordinate the work of all trade contractors on the jobsite to avoid conflicts and dry runs

The superintendent should also know and understand

- applicable building codes, zoning ordinances, OSHA requirements, and other laws and regulations
- current accounting and other business practices
- performance criteria and construction standards of each trade contractor
- the latest construction industry trends by keeping abreast of professional publications, talking with material suppliers, and through other channels
- how and when to say "no" to home owners without being offensive

The superintendent will

- maintain a current record of all code interpretations and local ordinances for each jurisdiction in which he or she works
- maintain a list of available local qualified trade contractors that strikes the company's desired balance of pricing and quality
- establish and enforce safety measures; ensure that trade contractors perform their work safely, according to OSHA guidelines; and that trade contractors have an effective safety program
- not tolerate unsafe work practices and will take appropriate but firm action to promptly remedy safety violations
- review business forms, checklists, and reports that aid in controlling aspects of the construction process under his or her responsibility
- complete and submit all necessary production reports and information in a readable, accurate, and timely manner
- work with the appropriate manager to establish pricing for custom options
- maintain uniform construction methods within the company
- support company policies and construction standards, suggest improvements within the system, and execute policies to ensure compliance with company quality standards
- attend production meetings, seminars, and training sessions on production-related subjects
- review each job file in advance to make the transition from sales to production a pleasant experience for the home owner(s)
- review estimates of necessary materials and labor for the construction process
- build high-quality homes and achieve high-quality work and home owner satisfaction by effectively managing resources and the construction process
- update construction schedules daily to ensure their accuracy

- use two-week interval schedules to monitor and manage home construction
- review project status reports weekly or as required by company policy
- work with peers to coordinate trade contractor scheduling
- monitor construction times and focus attention of all construction personnel to ensure a smooth, efficient, and continuous flow of work on each individual home
- walk through homes under construction daily
- conduct detailed inspections of each construction phase before authorizing any work for payment, using quality checklists for inspections, quality control, and to ensure adherence to standard operating procedures
- review quality checklists with all trade contractors at appropriate times
- conduct a detailed framing inspection with the framer before framing is completed
- conduct pre-drywall inspection with the home owner(s) and ensure that all structural, mechanical, and electrical components are appropriately completed
- coordinate utility installation and connections with home owner(s), local and code officials, and utility companies
- ensure that home owners approve and sign completed change orders before changes are made
- review purchase orders and authorize payments to trade contractors and material suppliers by the accounting department, and ensure trade contractors' work is 100% complete before authorizing payment
- write variance purchase orders (VPOs) daily for all items that were not included in the original purchase order and accurately justify the reason for each variance
- coordinate the return of all excess or inferior material and ensure that the company receives credits for these
- maintain a clean, safe jobsite during construction, including on surrounding streets; ensure that neighborhood streets and yards are clean and free of trash and construction debris; and ensure that silt-control fences are in place and functioning properly
- determine alternative work assignments for inclement weather or schedule changes
- work to develop and continuously improve the relationship with local building inspectors, city and county agencies, and other members of the building team

- develop positive customer relations with each home owner based on timely performance; ensure complete customer satisfaction by meeting regularly with home owner(s) and maintaining effective two-way communication with them
- communicate with each home owner at least once a week, or more often as necessary
- keep a communications log with the home owner(s), answer their questions, and address their concerns before, during, and after construction
- keep home owner(s) informed of the status of all allowances
- walk through each completed home before the home owner walk-through to make sure that the home is complete and clean and that it reflects the company's quality standards
- make sure all punch-list items are completed quickly and professionally, and make necessary repairs properly, avoiding quick fixes or cover-ups
- ensure that each home is 100% complete, with no punch-list items remaining before closing, and make sure home owners sign off on the completed repairs
- participate in home owner walk-throughs as necessary to ensure smooth hand-offs of homes to the customer service (warranty) personnel and to ensure that the home owner is happy with the transition
- make sure all final bills have been paid
- work with the accounting department to perform an analysis of each house after all bills have been paid
- assist the customer service (warranty) personnel and trade contractors with warranty service and home owner complaints
- help maintain the construction office, keeping it clean and organized
- drive courteously, conscientiously, and safely, to maintain a good driving record
- accomplish other tasks as required by the position or the production manager

Glossary

2/10 net 30. A payment term, often noted on an invoice, that indicates the payer either may pay the bill in 10 days and take a 2% discount off the invoice price or pay the full amount due within 30 days.

achievement. In terms of testing for employment, a measurable quality of what a person knows and can do.

account. The basic unit of an accounting system

accounting. Systematically collecting, analyzing, and reporting financial information.

accounting cycle. The transformation of raw financial data into financial statements that typically is accomplished in five steps

accounting equation. A statement that forms the basis for the accounting process. It shows the relationship between the firm's assets, liabilities, and owner's equity

accounts payable. Liabilities in the accounting equation that must be paid in cash

accounts receivable. Assets that the business collects from selling products or performing services for customers; what customers owe the business.

accrual. An accounting method that recognizes revenues when they are earned, regardless of when the company actually receives a cash payment.

accumulated depreciation. The value of an asset that has been used up or the total decline in its value since it was acquired

additional insured. A person or entity covered under an insurance policy in addition to the policy's owner.

adjustable rate mortgage (ARM). A mortgage with an interest rate that varies according to the prevailing interest rates noted in various indexes, such as the U.S. Treasury Average Index.

AIDA. An acronym used to define effective advertising or advertising that captures attention, maintains interest, fosters desire, and spurs action.

Americans with Disabilities Act (ADA). A federal statute that protects the civil rights of people with disabilities, including physical conditions that affect their mobility, stamina, sight, hearing, and speech.

aptitude. In the realm of employment testing, a measurable ability to learn or acquire skills.

assembly. A component of house construction that sometimes is used as the basis for estimating or trade contractor bid solicitation.

asset. Something of value a business owns; a resource a builder can use or exchange to produce products or services.

balance sheet. A statement of financial position; a snapshot of the dollar value of a company's assets, liabilities, and owner's equity at a designated time, typically the end of an accounting period.

benchmarking. Comparing a company's financial performance with that of other builders and with recommendations from industry experts

benefit. In new home sales, the tangible advantage to the homeowner of a particular home feature.

bilateral contract. A contract in which one party extends an offer and another party accepts the offer and promises something in return

break-even analysis. An assessment, using mathematical equations, to determine the sales volume needed to cover all of the company's costs and expenses.

cash flow statement. A financial document that shows the source and destination of cash in a business. It classifies cash receipts and payments by operating, investing, and financing activities.

cash planning. Identifying funding sources and uses of cash, and ensuring that the company always has sufficient operating funds.

chart of accounts. A list of all accounts in a business's accounting system

closely held corporation. A company with one or a small tight-knit group of stockholders. The company's stock is not traded publicly on a stock exchange.

cognitive ability test. A test that measures mental capabilities such as general intelligence, verbal fluency, numerical ability, and reasoning ability.

coinsurance clause. A property insurance company's requirement that the policyholder purchase coverage at least equal to some specified percentage (typically 80%) of the property value

commercial general liability insurance. Insurance against bodily injury and property damage that occurs in and from the builder's operations

common size income statement. A financial statement that shows a company's costs, expenses, and profits as a percentage of sales.

comparative balance sheet. A balance sheet that includes information for two consecutive accounting periods

completed contract. The most commonly used accounting method for home builders, which recognizes revenues and corresponding construction costs when the work is completed and the sales contract is fully executed.

construction-to-permanent loan. A construction loan that converts to a permanent mortgage when the home is completed

contribution margin. The percentage of each sales dollar left after deducting variable costs

conversion ratio. Percentage of prospects' inquiries converted to sales.

corporate veil. A legal concept that separates a corporation from its shareholders

corporation. A legal entity that is separate from the individuals who own and manage it

cost code. A numerical code assigned to each category of a construction project for estimating, purchasing, and accounting purposes. For example, a builder might use a single cost code to track all plumbing costs.

cost-plus contract. A contract in which a builder or remodeler agrees to perform work for a client in exchange for the costs associated with the project plus a markup, typically specified as a percentage in the contract

critical path. A logical, orderly approach to a new home sales presentation originated by the Greenman Group Inc. in the 1970s. The path follows a buyer's thought process, from the general to the specific, achieving confirmation of each step. The steps are: greet, qualify, area orientation, community orientation, product demonstration, summary/reduction to writing, and close.

critical task. A task that must be completed on schedule in order for a project to finish on time.

current assets. What a business has available to pay current liabilities—typically cash, accounts receivable, inventories, and short-term investments.

current liabilities. Accounts payable, short-term notes payable, portions of long-term debt that will become payable within one year; accrued income taxes; and other accrued expenses (principally wages).

debt financing. A business investment strategy that uses borrowed money from a lender such as a bank.

default. Fail to meet loan payment or other obligations

direct construction costs. *See* direct costs

direct costs. Materials and labor easily identifiable with a specific unit of production, such as framing materials, roofing labor, and HVAC trade contractors.

double-entry bookkeeping. An accounting method that tracks where money comes from and where it goes. Therefore, each financial transaction changes at least two accounts.

double taxation. Imposing two taxes on the same income as with corporate income and distributions to shareholders from that income

draw. A portion of a construction loan used to finance a project. Typically, draws are made according to a schedule based on phases or percentages of completion.

equity financing. A way to raise capital by selling ownership interest in your company. Stocks are ownership interest.

expenses. The costs incurred to produce revenues; the assets you must give up or consume to produce goods for sale or to serve customers. Expenses decrease the owner's equity in a business.

express contract. A contract in which the terms are specified, usually in writing, in contrast to an implied contract.

extended price. The total number of units multiplied by the unit price of an item to be used in construction.

Fannie Mae. The Federal National Mortgage Association, a government-sponsored enterprise (GSE) that helps ensure the availability of credit for home purchases.

Freddie Mac. A government-sponsored enterprises (GSE) that helps ensure the availability of credit for home purchases

feature. In home sales, an attribute of a particular home, such as having a bonus room or Thermopane® windows.

financial analysis. Comparing actual performance with expected and past performance, with the performance of other builders, and with industry norms.

financial ratios. Instruments of analysis businesses can use as indicators of their financial performance

financing expenses. Interest charges and other costs associated with borrowing money

fixed assets. Assets that are expected to be held or used for a period longer than one year

general and administrative expenses. The daily costs for operating a business, including expenses like office supplies, payments for telephone service, and legal and accounting fees.

general journal. A comprehensive chronological record of business transactions

general ledger. An accounting document that shows the increases, decreases, and current balance of a company's accounts.

graduated payment mortgage. A mortgage that allows the borrower to make lower monthly payments during the early years of the loan and higher payments for the remainder of the loan term

gross profit. The amount of cash that remains after deducting the cost of sales from the selling price

gross profit margin. The percentage of each sales dollar that remains after deducting the cost of sales

HVAC. Heating, ventilation, and air conditioning.

implied contract. A contract defined by the parties' actions, rather than their words

income statement. A summary of a company's revenues and expenses during a specific period, generally one year.

indirect construction costs. Sometimes called "soft costs," these are costs not attributable to a specific project, including superintendent salaries and construction vehicle expenses.

indirect costs. Sometimes called soft costs, the costs not attributable to a specific construction project. They include superintendent salaries, construction vehicle expenses, and jobsite offices.

interview selling. An aspect of relationship selling wherein you obtain specific information from the customers so you can satisfy their needs.

inventory. Assets that comprise, or will comprise, the products the company will sell to customers. For builders, typical inventory includes land slated for development, development costs, direct construction costs, and construction materials inventory.

job variance report. A document that lists budgeted costs, actual costs, and variances for each cost center within a specific job.

journal. A chronological record of business transactions. It may be comprehensive (general) or category specific (specialized).

liability. Responsibility. A business owner's liability encompasses financial risks, worker safety risks, and other areas of risk that may be limited through various strategies including company organization, process controls, and insurance policies.

lien. A legal claim on property for the payment of a debt or obligation

limited liability company (LLC). A business structure provided for in state laws that has the benefit of pass-through (to the individual partners) taxation, rather than corporate, but which limits the LLC participants' personal liability for debts and obligations.

line of credit. The amount of money a lender, usually a bank, will make available to the borrower to use on an as-needed basis.

liquidity. Ability to meet short-term financial obligations

liquidated damages. Damages, or money, the parties to a contract specify will have to be paid for breach.

loan origination fee. A cost of credit, usually equal to 1%–2% of the value of the loan.

loan-to-value ratio. The percentage of a loan amount to the value of the property securing it, such as land or a construction project.

long-term liability. A debt, such as a mortgage or bond, that is not due for at least one year.

macro. A saved recording of keystrokes or mouse actions assigned to a specific key on a keyboard or to a clickable icon in a computer program to perform multiple actions with one click or keystroke

marketable securities. Stocks, bonds, and other liquid investments that could be converted quickly to cash.

marketing mix. Product, promotion, price, and place—four essential elements of a marketing strategy.

NAHB Chart of Accounts. An accounting system framework specific to residential building and remodeling companies found at www.nahb.org/chart

net loss. On an income statement, the change in owner's equity for the applicable period when total revenue is less than the cost of sales plus operating expenses.

net profit. On an income statement, the change in owner's equity for the applicable period when total revenue is greater than the cost of sales plus operating expenses.

net profit margin. The percentage of each dollar from sales revenue that remains after all costs, expenses, and taxes are deducted from sales.

nonconforming use. Existing improvements that no longer meet zoning requirements after a land parcel's zoning classification changes

notes payable. Obligations secured with promissory notes

notes receivable. Promissory notes (promises to pay) that customers or others have given the company

option contract. A contract that gives one of the contracting parties the right to enter into another contract at a later date, such as for a land purchase.

originate. In residential lending, to be the first holder of a lien in a loan transaction.

other expenses. On an income statement, costs that cannot be classified as operating, financing, sales and marketing, or general and administrative expenses.

overhead. Fixed costs not attributable to a specific home, such as salaries and other expenses of running an office, insurance, vehicles, and marketing and sales.

owner's equity. Profit kept in a company, the owner's financial stake in his or her business.

parol evidence rule. A legal rule that states that when parties reduce their agreement to a detailed, complete writing, that writing is recognized as the complete agreement.

partnership. A business ownership arrangement in which two or more parties agree to come together to own a business

percent of sales. A method of estimating the cost of sales that assumes the relationship between revenue and construction costs and between revenue and expenses generally remains constant over time.

percentage of completion. A standard accounting method generally used for large custom homes or commercial projects that span a number of accounting periods that recognizes revenues and construction costs as a project progresses toward completion.

personal guaranty. A promise to use your personal assets to make principal or interest payments if your company cannot make the payments

personality test. A test that assesses personal characteristics that tend to be consistent and enduring such as extroversion, conscientiousness, emotional stability, agreeableness, and openness to experience.

physical ability test. A test that measures attributes such as strength, body coordination, and stamina.

predecessor activities. In scheduling, the activities that must be completed before another specific activity can begin.

prepaid expenses–assets. Assets that have been paid for but not used, such as an insurance premium on a policy that eventually will expire

primary mortgage market. The market for lenders who originate real estate loans

profit planning. Examining expected revenues, costs, and expenses associated with planned activities.

profitability. The goal of all business ventures, a company's ability to generate income.

pro forma financial statement. A financial statement used for planning purposes that relies on assumptions to forecast future results of actions, such as business expansion or a new product launch.

promotional mix. A combination of advertising, sales promotion, and personal selling.

qualify. To determine the readiness, willingness, and ability of a prospect to purchase a home.

ratio analysis. The use of financial ratios to evaluate a company's performance

real property. Interests in land and anything firmly attached to it

receivables. Amounts owed to the business including promissory notes

recording fee. The fee a government agency charges to enter a real estate transaction in the public record

relationship selling. Also known as consultative selling, the process by which a friendship or relationship is created with the prospect by listening and responding to their needs. Building a relationship demonstrates that you care and helps you earn the customer's trust. People tend to do business with those they like and trust.

reliability. In hiring, the degree to which interviews, tests, and other selection procedures consistently assess what they are intended to.

restrictive covenant. A deed restriction, a limitation on how a property may be used.

retained earnings. Accumulated profits that have not been distributed as dividends

return on assets. A financial ratio based on the amount of income returned on investment in assets

return on equity. A financial ratio that reflects the dollars of net profit earned for each dollar of owner's capital (both invested and earned capital)

revenues. Assets (such as cash or accounts receivable) that a business collects in selling products or performing services for customers

risk management. Evaluating risks and seeking ways to minimize the total costs associated with them

sales and marketing expenses. Advertising, sales commissions, model homes, and the costs of running a sales office.

S corporation. A legally recognized type of corporation that is taxed as a sole proprietorship or partnership

secondary mortgage market. The group of institutions that purchase mortgages and resell them to investors, who purchase the right to receive all future payments associated with the mortgage.

sole proprietorship. A company owned by a single individual, without partners, directors, or shareholders.

solvency. A business's ability to pay debts as they become due

specialized journal. In accounting, a chronological record of specific types of transactions that occur frequently, such as payroll, sales, cash disbursements or receipts, and purchases.

statute of frauds. A law requiring contracts to be written, rather than oral, and signed by all parties to be binding. The types of contracts the law applies to vary by state and jurisdiction.

straight mortgage. A loan that becomes due and payable at the end of its term. Popular for second mortgages and home improvement loans, straight mortgages usually have a short maturity (three to five years) and require periodic payments during the loan term.

subsidiary ledger. In accounting, a more detailed ledger than a general ledger, such as a job cost subsidiary ledger with unit-by-unit costs.

summary variance report. A document that lists the total budgeted costs, actual costs to date, and variances for each job.

take-off. A construction document that identifies the types and quantities of all materials, labor, and trade contractor activities for a project.

temporary account. An account that contains the revenue and expense information that will transfer to owner's equity at the end of the accounting period

unearned revenues. Advance payments, such as customer deposits, made for goods or services. They are a liability on your balance sheet.

unilateral contract. A contract that contains only one promise, such as a real estate contract promising to pay a commission to a real estate agent only if the property is sold while the listing agreement is effective.

unique selling proposition (USP). The attribute(s) that distinguish your company's product(s) from those of competitors

utility easement. A strip of land used by utility companies to construct and maintain overhead and underground lines.

validity. In employment testing, the accuracy of a selection device in predicting job performance

variance. A discrepancy between the estimated and actual costs

variance purchase order. A purchase order for materials or labor not included in the original estimate or purchase

work package. A well-defined piece of a project that can be managed, measured, and budgeted.

work sample test. A performance-based evaluation of employment candidates that requires them to do a task or tasks that will be required on the job

Resources

Construction Management

Rogers, Leon. *Basic Construction Management: The Superintendent's Job*. Washington, DC: BuilderBooks.com, 2009.

Contracts and Law

Home Builder Contracts & Construction Management Forms, compiled by NAHB Business Management and Information Technology Committee. Washington, DC: BuilderBooks.com, 2006.

Jaffe, David S., David Crump, and Felicia Watson. *Warranties for Builders and Remodelers, Second Edition*. Washington, DC: BuilderBooks.com, 2007.

Estimating

Christofferson, Jay P. *Estimating with Microsoft® Excel, Third Edition*. Washington, DC: BuilderBooks.com, 2010.

Financial Management

Cost of Doing Business Study, 2012 Edition, by NAHB Business Management & Information Technology Committee. Washington, DC: BuilderBooks.com, 2012.

Shinn, Emma. *Accounting and Financial Management for Residential Construction, 5th Edition*. Washington, DC: BuilderBooks.com, 2008.

Land Development

Green Models for Site Development: Applying the National Green Building Standard™ to Land and Lots, by NAHB Land Development. Washington, DC: BuilderBooks.com, 2011.

Kone, Daisy Linda. *Land Development, 10th Edition.* Washington, DC: Builder-Books.com, 2006.

Marketing and Sales

Flammer, Carol M. *Social Media for Home Builders 2.0: It's Easier Than You Think.* Washington, DC: BuilderBooks.com, 2011.

Gullo, Gina and Angela Rinaldi. *Option Selling for Profit: The Builder's Guide to Generating Design Center Revenue & Profit.* Washington, DC: BuilderBooks.com, 2008.

Lynch, Tammy. *Think Sold! Creating Home Sales in Any Market.* Washington, DC: BuilderBooks.com, 2009.

Nowell, William J., *ValueMatch™ Selling for Home Builders: How to Sell What Matters Most.* Washington, DC: BuilderBooks.com, 2009.

Smith, Carol. *Beyond Warranty: Building Your Referral Business.* Washington, DC: BuilderBooks.com, 2008.

Webb, Bill. *Sweet Success in New Home Sales: Selling Strong in Changing Markets.* Washington, DC: BuilderBooks.com, 2006.

Scheduling

Marchman, David and Tulio Sulbaran. *Scheduling for Home Builders with Microsoft Project.* Washington, DC: BuilderBooks.com, 2012.

Warranty

Residential Construction Performance Guidelines, 4th Edition, Contractor Reference by National Association of Home Builders. Washington, DC: BuilderBooks.com, 2011.

Residential Construction Performance Guidelines, 4th Edition, Consumer Reference by National Association of Home Builders. Washington, DC: BuilderBooks.com, 2011.

Smith, Carol. *Homeowner Manual: A Template for Home Builders, Second Edition*. Washington, DC: Builderbooks.com, 2000.

Your New Green Home and How to Take Care of It: Homeowner Education Manual Template, by National Association of Home Builders. Washington, DC: BuilderBooks.com, 2011.

Your New Home & How to Take Care of It. Washington, DC: BuilderBooks.com, 2006.

Index